THE LEADER'S WINDOW

Mastering the Four Styles of Leadership to Build High-Performing Teams

JOHN D. W. BECK

NEIL M. YEAGER

JOHN WILEY & SONS, INC.

New York • Chichester • Brisbane • Toronto • Singapore

Library of Congress Cataloging-in-Publication Data:

Beck, John D. W.
   The leader's window: mastering the four styles of leadership to build high-performing teams / John D.W. Beck & Neil M. Yeager.
      p.   cm.
   ISBN 0-471-58525-4 (cloth).—ISBN 0-471-02554-2 (paper):
   1. Leadership I. Yeager, Neil. II. Title.
HD57.7.B428   1994
658.4'092—dc20   93-41890

Printed in the United States of America

10 9 8 7 6 5 4 3

Acknowledgments

The Leader's Window is based on The L4 System for High-Performing Teams which was designed and developed by co-author John Beck, one of the founders of the Charter Oak Consulting Group of Berlin, Connecticut. Charter Oak is a team of consultants who specialize in helping organizations strengthen their performance capability through leadership development, teambuilding, experiential learning, and organization development. Over the years, significant input to The L4 System has been provided by the members of the Charter Oak team. L4 was initially developed with substantial support from Elizabeth Beck, Jonathan Spiegel, and Tony Daloisio. Additions were then made by Roberta McLaughlin, Diane Flaherty, Barry Carden, and Jim Hassinger. Most recently, significant transformations to the system have been provided by co-author Neil Yeager. As a team effort, The L4 System is based on over 100 years of collective experience working with Fortune 500 companies, as well as small and medium-sized businesses, government agencies, universities, and not-for-profit organizations.

Special acknowledgment needs to be given to Ken Blanchard and Paul Hersey (1982), co-authors of Situational Leadership Theory which was the forerunner of The L4 System, and without which L4 would not exist.

When Ken was a professor at the University of Massachusetts, both of us had the honor of learning about leadership at the feet of one of the masters. Feedback from our clients and input from our colleagues has made L4 significantly different from Situational Leadership, but without Ken's guidance and the knowledge base of Situational Leadership, we would never have started down the L4 path.

The Hersey-Blanchard Situational Leadership Theory defined the four leadership styles in terms of task behavior and relationships behavior; and Blanchard's Situational Leadership II described the same styles in terms of directive behavior and

iii

supportive behavior. In addition, the designations of S1-S2-S3-S4 were first used by Hersey and Blanchard (1982) as a shorthand way to refer to the four leadership styles in a sequence that progresses from most control to least control. Their theory is the foundation of what we call the development cycle.

The L4 System also has some roots in the earlier leadership models on which Situational Leadership was based. In fact, the four basic leadership styles are based on a long history of leadership theories which we would like to acknowledge. Lewin, Lippitt, and White (1960) used the terms authoritarian and democratic to define leadership styles; Tannenbaum and Schmidt (1958) defined a continuum of boss-centered versus subordinate-centered leadership styles; Stogdill and Coons (1959) used the terms initiating structure and consideration to define the four leadership styles in the Ohio State University Leadership Studies (which laid the ground work for all situational leadership approaches). Rensis Likert (1961) studied the differences between production-centered and employee-centered leaders; Blake and Mouton's (1964) Managerial Grid defined leadership styles in terms of concern for production versus concern for people; Fred E. Fiedler's (1967) Contingency Theory examined the situations that were best suited for task-directed versus human relations leaders; William J. Reddin's (1967) 3-D Model defined the four styles in terms of task-oriented versus maintenance-oriented leaders, effective versus ineffective; R.F. Bales (1958) used the terms task-oriented versus maintenance-oriented in his research on leadership in groups.

We would also like to acknowledge Victor Vroom for his work on decision making, Joe Litterer and Al Ivey for their thoughts on managerial communication, and B. F. Skinner for his ideas on behavioral reinforcement theory.

In the area of group development, we want to acknowledge the work of many theorists including Will Schutz, Jack and Lorraine Gibb, Warren Bennis and Herb Shepard, Bruce Tuckman, and Don Carew and Eunice Parisi-Carew.

We also want to thank Jack Orsburn for his insights on self-directed teams and the ways that L4 helps them work.

We greatly appreciate the support of our colleague, Judy Wardlaw, whose research, editorial assistance, and indexing made our task easier; our agent, Elizabeth Knappman, whose advice and unfailing confidence helped make this book a reality; our editor, John Mahaney, whose insightful comments and suggestions helped strengthen the final product; and the Charter Oak team of Chris Galske and Lisa Hague for their constant support and assistance.

We also want to say thank you to our clients—the companies who have hired us and the thousands of participants who have attended our seminars and workshops. Without them, our ideas would not have been given a true trial by fire. Their compliments have encouraged our belief that we are onto something new and very valuable. Their criticisms have helped us refine our thinking and make it highly practical. And their war stories from the front lines of management experience have given us the understanding to bring our ideas to life.

Finally, on a more personal note, we are deeply appreciative of our spouses, Elizabeth Beck and Cletha Roney, for their encouragement and support. We also want to thank our children, Laura and Andrew Beck and Ben Roney-Yeager, for sharing us with our computers, modems, and fax machines throughout this endeavor.

REFERENCES

Bales, R. F. "Task Roles and Social Roles in Problem-Solving Groups." In *Readings in Social Psychology*. 3rd ed., edited by N. Maccoby et al. New York: Holt, Rinehart, & Winston, Inc., 1958.

Blake, Robert R., and Mouton, Jane S. *The Managerial Grid.* Houston, Tex.: Gulf Publishing, 1964.

Fiedler, Fred E., *A Theory of Leadership Effectiveness*, New York: McGraw Hill, 1967.

Hersey, Paul, and Blanchard, Kenneth. *Management of Organizational Behavior: Utilizing Human Resources.* 4th ed. New Jersey: Prentice Hall, 1982.

Lewin, K., Lippett, R. and White, R. "Leader Behavior and Member Reaction in Three Social Climates. In *Group Dynamics: Research and Theory*. 2nd ed. edited by D. Cartwright and A. Zader. Evanston, Ill: Row, Peterson & Company, 1960.

Likert, Rensis. *New Patterns of Management.* New York: McGraw Hill, 1961.

Reddin, William J. "The 3-D Management Style Theory." *Training and Development Journal* (April 1967): 8–17.

Stogdill, R. M., and Coons, Alvin E. eds. *Leader Behavior: Its Descrip-*

tion and Measurement. Research Monograph No. 88. Columbus: Bureau of Business Research, The Ohio State University, 1957.

Tannenbaum, Robert, and Schmidt, Warren H. "How to Choose a Leadership Pattern." *Harvard Business Review* (March–April 1958): 95–102.

Preface

If you are part of any business, at any level, in almost any part of the world, you probably know by now that leadership and teamwork are two key characteristics of successful organizations of the 1990s. You may also be aware that leaders find themselves continually challenged by the constant change, flux, instability, and uncertainty of the contemporary workplace.

The global economy is putting unprecedented pressure on every organization to give their customers what they want in the most cost-effective ways. The organizations—and the people—that will survive and thrive amidst this competition will be the ones that can focus the brainpower of their organizations—and their people—on these overarching goals.

Are you one of those people who finds themselves constantly challenged by the odds confronting you as a leader or potential leader in your organization?

Do you find yourself continually thwarted by the inability to harness the energy of all the potentially high-performing individuals in your organization and transform them into a high-performing team?

Do you wish you knew what kind of leadership would work in whatever situation you found yourself in and how you could be sure you were using the right leadership approach with the right person at the right time?

Do you wish you knew how to turn nonmotivated people into highly effective workers?

Do you feel as though the demands placed on you make it increasingly challenging for you to get those around you to do what needs to be done to meet organizational goals?

If these are the kinds of questions that hound you and prevent you from being effective in harnessing the power of the people in your organization, then we'd like to introduce you to a proven, sure-fire formula for success that we call The Leader's Window.

What exactly is The Leader's Window? Simply stated, it's a structure with four small windows of leadership that show you four different styles for leading people. None of these styles is better than the others. Each one has its place and this book will give you many examples of leaders who use each style with great success.

The challenge is to know where and when to use each one. That's what The Leader's Window is all about.

In this book, we are going to show you a new paradigm for leading individuals. The best leaders in every organization have been using this paradigm for years. Once you understand it, you will know what to do to help your people perform to the best of their potential.

We will also show you a new paradigm for orchestrating group dynamics in a way that gets every player contributing to a well-oiled machine. The best leaders know how to inspire groups to great accomplishments. Once you know what they do, you will know how to take advantage of the power of group interactions.

Finally, we will show you how to put these two paradigms together: four simple secrets for building and maintaining the high performance teamwork that is necessary for guaranteeing your organization's long-term success.

"Isn't being a leader more about using good instincts than using elaborate techniques?" you may ask. While it's true that using your sense of intuition to help you be effective as a leader can prove very valuable, there is a complexity in today's workplace that requires more than just good instincts.

"Aren't real leaders born?" you might ask. We believe that leading is more than a birthright reserved for the lucky few. We know from our work in many organizations for the last 20 years that most people can learn how to lead. We also know that learning to lead in today's complex world is a lot more complicated than relying on common sense.

Most of the leaders and aspiring leaders we know talk about feeling boxed-in by conflicting demands—one message from the people above them who pressure them to lead proactively, and a different message from the people below who expect them to lead empathically. Do you feel trapped in this kind of box? The Leader's Window will show you the way out of this trap with a solution that meets the needs of both superiors and subordinates.

By following the secrets of The Leader's Window, you'll learn a step-by-step approach to maximizing the full potential of everyone around you and you'll learn how to adapt and change your approach as situations change and circumstances shift.

These are demanding times in an increasingly competitive world. The organizations that will endure are those that are able to make the most of their human resource—their people. We know from our experience that The Leader's Window can help you be one of those people who gives your organization the competitive edge—and we welcome the opportunity to help you develop that edge.

JOHN BECK
NEIL YEAGER

Contents

Introduction

Welcome to the World of Leadership

THE LEADER'S DILEMMA: THE PROBLEM

It's easy to be confused about leadership.

First you heard that being a leader means having a vision, pursuing it with passion and doing whatever it takes to get your people to bring that vision to life. So you got busy driving your people, challenging them to do the right things, pushing them to do everything the right way.

Then you heard a speaker who seemed to make a lot of sense. She said that you won't get the most out of your people over the long run if you keep pushing them relentlessly. You have to support their efforts, this speaker said, help your employees grow and develop, encourage them, motivate them. So you sat down and talked with the people who work for you, listened to their concerns and tried coaching them as well as you could.

Then, just when you thought things were moving in the right direction, you read an article claiming that the answer lies in empowerment. Make people feel powerful, it said, and you will be enhancing your own power. Give your people lots of responsibility, and they will learn how to do whatever needs to be done. So you backed off, left your people alone, and waited for them to start feeling empowered. And you really hoped they would because, after the recent downsizing, you didn't have time to spend with them anyway.

The bad news was that your empowered workforce quickly became stretched-thin and stressed-out from all those responsibilities. The good news was that you had just read a new book that assured you that good leadership is decisive leadership. Take people's suggestions, this author said, but keep hold of the reins. That is the best way to get your employees' buy-in and commitment while ensuring that things get done right. So now you have started spending more time with your people, listening to their ideas and redirecting them whenever they seem to be having problems.

The next wave of inspiration will probably send you back to cracking the whip again like you used to do in the first place. If this merry-go-round sounds familiar to you, welcome to the Leader's Dilemma.

The Leader's Dilemma is a concern for anyone faced with managerial responsibilities as we head into the twenty-first century. For years, those attempting to explain good leadership have suggested that leadership is a science. From the mechanistic influence of Frederick Taylor's (1911) *The Principles of Scientific Management* to the "humanistic, behavioral science" approaches of the 1960s, to the search for excellence and one-minute solutions of the 1980s, people have been trying to pinpoint the answer to the leadership question.

While *In Search of Excellence* (Peters and Waterman, 1982) helped a lot of executives recognize the need to build a strong organizational culture, and *The One-Minute Manager* (Blanchard and Spencer, 1981) reminded all managers to set goals and give praise, most managers are still looking for more complete explanations about how to lead. Unfortunately what has emerged are more philosophical explanations for leadership. Leaders need to take control, said Warren Bennis and Burt Nanus (1985) in their book *Leaders: The Strategies for Taking Charge*. There is an art to leadership, proclaimed Max Depree (1990), chairman of the Herman Miller Furniture Company, in his inspirational book *The Art of Leadership*. Having effective habits and the right principles are the keys, suggested Stephen Covey (1990) in his recent book, *Principle-Centered Leadership*. Why not look back to the *Leadership Secrets of Attila the Hun?* asked Wess Roberts (1985).

Yet most people who have tried to lead—successfully or otherwise—know that taking charge is easier said than done, that inspiration, good habits, and right principles are absolutely critical but aren't always enough, and that Attila's reputation is not exactly the one they were after. While taking charge can give you credibility, and inspiration may be the catalyst for getting others to take action, and principles are most likely the right foundation for aligning yourself and your organization, and even Atilla may have a few saving graces, the bottom line is that performance that leads to the desired results must be orchestrated carefully if you are going to succeed as a leader.

So what's the answer? Every client we work with is trying to increase their competitiveness by driving down costs, listening to their customers, empowering their employees, and creating a team-based culture committed to continuous improvement. Some days they find themselves going crazy because they aren't sure if they should be driving or listening, empowering or improving. What they want to know is how to do all of these things at once.

THE LEADER'S WINDOW: THE SOLUTION

We believe that there is a solution to this complex question of leadership. It does not come from a debate about art versus science, inspiration versus perspiration, character versus competence, or principles versus power. It comes from understanding the essential behaviors for simultaneously challenging a team of people to reach for a vision while empowering each individual team member to take the actions that are needed to achieve that vision. High performance leadership exists when everyone, leaders and followers, are performing at their highest levels—whether alone or in teams—all of the time.

The guide we use for ensuring that your approach to leadership works all the time, every time, is called The Leader's Window. The Leader's Window will not give you a quick fix because leading people requries a concerted effort and needs to be sustained over time. What The Leader's Window will give you is a methodology for using your actions as a leader in a focused and purposeful way. It is a guide for promoting teamwork that maximizes the potential of every individual while fully utilizing the power that can come from getting a group of people to work together to achieve a shared mission.

To understand the secrets of The Leader's Window, you will need to learn the art and the science of what we call The Leadership 4 System. Sometimes we just refer to the system as Leadership 4. And sometimes we simply call it L4. Whatever you decide to call it, Leadership 4 is a highly refined approach to understanding the needs of both individuals and groups in a way that leads to high performance teamwork—people doing their best because they're skilled, knowledgeable, empowered, interested, confident, willing, and aligned with the goals of your organization.

Using prior research on leadership, communication, decision making, reward systems, individual motivation and group development, by expanding on those ideas, making them more precise and user friendly, The L4 System will teach you how to lead others in a way that maximizes results for them, for you, for your team, and for the organization you are a part of.

From your journey through The L4 System and mastery of its simple yet proven techniques, you will discover the secrets of The Leader's Window and unravel the mysteries of high performance leadership. As you read through this book, you will receive practical as well as inspirational advice that will make you a more effective leader.

Here's an overview of what you will find:

• Chapter 1 sets the stage for thinking about leadership by emphasizing that teamwork requires getting each individual team member to perform to the best of his/her potential plus creating group dynamics that foster synergy among those individuals. It also includes a short questionnaire which invites you to say what you would do if you were the leader in 10 common cases.

• Chapter 2 defines the four leadership styles of The L4 System in terms of decision making, communication, and recognition strategies and illustrates each style with well-known TV characters.

• Chapters 3 through 6 bring each leadership style to life with profiles of political and business leaders plus real case studies that show the value of each style.

• Chapter 7 shows you your personal Window of Leadership including the main, back-up, and limited styles that you selected on the questionnaire in Chapter 1. You will also get feedback about the strengths and weaknesses of your leadership profile.

• Chapter 8 explains how to match all four styles to a follower's task-specifc potential by using a simple method for diagnosing ability and motivation. This chapter also gives you additional feedback about your responses to the 10 cases in Chapter 1. You will see whether or not you are using the styles with the right people at the right times.

• Chapter 9 introduces a new paradigm for leading individuals which is based on our research about what best leaders really do. This paradigm totally revamps the way most managers have been taught to work with people and it is extremely simple to use.

• Chapter 10 invites you to try out this new paradigm and shows you how to bring it to life with real cases and a question & answer format that guides you to create your own applications.

• Chapter 11 shifts away from leading individuals to the question of creating effective group dynamics. It also introduces a new paradigm for understanding and leading groups and includes cases to illustrate this way of thinking.

• Chapter 12 puts The Leader's Window together by showing you how to integrate the individual paradigm with the group paradigm. The four secrets in this chapter explain how to use all four leadership styles in a clear sequence that builds and maintains high-performing teams. Cases illustrating this sequence show you clear examples of how it is done and the consequences of ignoring the secrets.

Whether you are the CEO of a company, an upper-level manager, a front line supervisor, or the informal leader of the XYZ task force, The Leader's Window will provide you with insights, information, and practical tools for harnessing the potential of each individual and transforming that potential into high-performing teams.

REFERENCES

Bennis, Warren, and Nanus, Burt. *Leaders: The Strategies for Taking Charge.* New York, Harper & Row, 1985.

Blanchard, Kenneth, and Johnson, Spender. *The One-Minute Manager.* New York: William Morrow, 1981.

Covey, Stephen R. *Principle-Centered Leadership.* New York: Summit Books, 1990.

Depree, Max. *Leadership is an Art.* New York: Dell, 1989.

Peters, Thomas J., and Waterman, Robert H. *In Search of Excellence: Lessons from America's Best-Run Companies.* New York: Harper & Row, 1982.

Roberts, Wess. *Leadership Secrets of Attila the Hun.* New York: Warner Books, 1985.

Taylor, Frederick Winslow. *The Principles of Scientific Management.* New York: W.W. Norton, 1911.

Chapter 1

Windows on the World of Leadership

SHIFTING PERSPECTIVES FOR THE VOLATILE ORGANIZATION OF THE 1990s

When corporate giants like IBM and General Motors announced massive white-collar layoffs in 1991, 1992, and again in 1993, it became clear that the corporate landscape was changing forever. If you had been hoping that job security in America was going to make a comeback, or that lifelong employment would be adopted as the way to compete with the Japanese, you knew that hope was gone and started digging in for the long fight.

The truth is that the implicit pact between worker and leader has been banished forever. The idea of motivating good performance with job security may have helped the leaders of the industrial age or even the intrapreneurs of the first leg of the information age, but it is not enough for the leaders of the emerging age of uncertainty.

Successful leaders of the twenty-first century will be those who give followers what they need, when they need it, in a form in which they can use it. The new leaders will be those who provide followers with what they need to perform to the best of their potential. This approach is a far cry from either the authoritarian or gentle helper approaches espoused in earlier leadership theories. It is an approach based on the belief that volatile organizations require adaptable leaders—people who understand the dynamics of life in the contemporary organization and who are experts at matching their leadership actions to employees' performance needs.

As the business world continues to reinvent and restructure itself, one of the most significant changes is the demise of the professional manager. Since the onset of the industrial revolution, those at the top have depended on these "middle managers" to make sure that those at the bottom do what needs to be done. The wholesale elimination of layers of middle managers whose role was to orchestrate the activities of others means that everyone in an organization is now a potential manager. What these new managers—including everyone from the CEO to the lowest person in the shrunken hierarchy—need most is to learn how to lead.

Working with other people to do more with less resources is the biggest challenge facing organizations as we approach the twenty-first century. Not just big corporations. Small and medium-sized businesses are struggling just to stay alive, and as big corporations continue to reorganize and downsize, more small businesses are cropping up on the horizon. Not-for-profits are also squeezed tighter than ever. And government agencies are under incredible scrutiny, not to mention that whole governments themselves are being toppled all over the world.

Leadership is in the headlines every day. Bill Clinton versus George Bush in 1992. Hillary Clinton versus the AMA in 1994. Boris Yeltsin versus the Soviet hardliners. Assassinated leaders in India. Zealous leaders perpetuating conflict between Israel and the Palestinians. The clerical leadership of the Mullahs in Iran. The military leadership of Saddam Hussein in Iraq. Tribal leadership in Bosnia and in Somalia.

Leadership is what makes business news as well. Upheaval at the top of General Motors. Lee Iacocca's last at bat at Chrysler. Sam Walton's legacy at Wal-Mart. Jack Welch's tough-minded but people-involving success at General Electric. Roy Vagelos' most admired culture at Merck. Stanley Gault's amazing turnaround at Rubbermaid. Andy Grove's ongoing success at Intel. Bill Gates' intellectually confrontational software mecca at Microsoft. T.J. Rodgers' No-Excuses management at Cypress Semiconductor. Bill McGowan's stir-up-the-pot battlefront at MCI. Warren Buffet's quiet and consistent stewardship of conglomerate Berkshire Hathaway. The transition from Steve Jobs' technowizardry to John Sculley's marketing acumen at Apple. The rise and fall of Donald Trump. Greenmailer Carl Icahn's attempts to manage survival at TWA. Profits and greed on Wall

Street. The internationalization of entire industries. Searching for the right partnership between business and government in order to compete in the worldwide marketplace.

Leadership is everywhere—not just at the top like the world leaders and business leaders above. Whether you are a CEO or a front-line supervisor, knowing how to lead people is the hardest part of the job. And the underlying questions behind every discussion about leadership are: How do you succeed and how do you avoid failure? How do you breed winners instead of losers? How do you build competetive spirit and avoid complacency? What do you say and do to deliver top-quality results and enhance your reputation as a leader?

Leadership is no picnic. If you are going to learn how to be a good leader, you are going to have to open your mind to new ideas without discarding all of your old ideas. Moving into the future does not mean letting go of everything you have done in the past. It means getting perpetually smarter about how you integrate the old and the new. It means taking what you know about the science of leadership and blending that with the finesse that comes from the art of leadership.

Learning to lead also means not getting caught up in the unrealistic search for quick-fix solutions to complex problems. If we have learned anything in our years of working with thousands of managers from all kinds of organizations, it is that leadership is one very big challenge. If leadership were easy, a lot more people would be good at it.

Finally, becoming a good leader also means taking a good hard look at yourself, because what you think you do may not be what you really do. To help you look at yourself, before you read too far, we want to invite you to play the leadership game with us. This will give you a chance to think about yourself as a leader while you read the book.

WHAT KIND OF LEADER ARE YOU?

On the following pages, you will find 10 short cases that will help you think about the ways that you lead people. Each case describes a common work situation that is typical of the problems that confront most managers. After each case, you will find four possible actions, each of which is used frequently by a large number of leaders.

As you read each case, don't try to guess the "right" answer, because what is right for you may not be right for someone else. Just choose the actions that are typical of you and the ways that you interact with people when you are the leader. Here's what to do:

1. Read each case and imagine yourself as the leader in that situation.
2. Read the actions and think about what you typically do in that type of situation.
3. If one action stands out as describing you, give 5 points to that action by writing the number 5 in the space beside it.
4. If no single action describes how you would handle the situation, you can divide the 5 points in any combination that adds up to 5: (4 + 1), (3 + 2), (2 + 2 + 1).
5. Be sure that your responses for every case add up to exactly 5 points, no more and no less. For example:

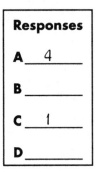

So, read these cases and have some fun thinking about what you would do in each one. Remember that what you really say and what you really do is where the rubber meets the road in the game of leadership. Later on, in chapters 7, 8, and 10, we will show you how to interpret your responses to these cases so that you can see what your own leadership profile looks like.

CASE 1

Tom has recently joined your department and seems nervous about his new work. He is reluctant to take on much responsibility because he is not sure his skills are right for the job. You are confident that he will be fine as soon as he learns the job.

Actions

Responses

A. Ask him to identify the skills he brings into the job, then tell him how to use them in productive ways.

A _____

B. Give him a full orientation to his new job and tell him what he needs to do to get started.

B _____

C. Keep an eye on him from a distance to see what he can figure out on his own.

C _____

D. Ask him to identify the skills he brings to the job and help him discover his own ways to apply them.

D _____

CASE 2

Susan was assigned to you after a rocky experience in another region. She is talented and confident, but she resists learning the job requirements and wants to work with customers entirely in her own way.

Actions

Responses

A. Ask her about her past experience, then tell her how her work here should be done.

A _____

B. Ask her about her past experience, then help her think through a plan for getting started.

B _____

C. Review the customer list with her and tell her what to do to get started.

C _____

D. Give her a chance on her own before saying anything.

D _____

CASE 3

Joe has joined your department with great enthusiasm and confidence. He has a proven track record and is in tune with your goals. Mostly, he needs to get oriented to the specifics of his new responsibilities and the ins and outs of how this company works.

Actions

Responses

A. Help him to think through the new assignment and develop his own training plan.

A_____

B. Let him know that you are confident that he can learn the job on his own.

B_____

C. Explain the job requirements, then tell him what he should do and why.

C_____

D. Explain the job requirements, then seek his input as you develop a training plan for him.

D_____

CASE 4

Jane is a great saleswoman who consistently makes you and the company look good. Usually, you just stay out of her way, but lately you have thought that you should let her know that you are still the manager.

Actions

Responses

A. Give her recognition for doing so well and remind her that you're there if she needs anything.

A_____

B. Ask her to update you on her activities, then tell her which ones you think she should pursue.

B_____

C. Ask her what seems to be working best for her and listen to her plans for the near future.

C_____

D. Review her customer list and tell her what she should be doing with each one.

D_____

CASE 5

Ted has worked in your department for the last five years. He is technically sound but does not understand the big picture. He has also turned off several people with his aggressive enthusiasm. Since his last performance appraisal, in which you gave him some honest feedback, his confidence seems to be shaken.

Actions

A. Redirect him so that he understands exactly what he needs to do differently.

B. Listen to his concerns, then help him think through the steps he wants to take.

C. Be patient and wait for him to come around on his own.

D. Listen to his concerns, then redirect him so that he understands exactly what he needs to do differently.

Responses

A _____

B _____

C _____

D _____

CASE 6

You have assigned Martha, one of your best employees, to collect consumer data that will be needed for your department's upcoming strategy meeting. She has been working diligently to get the assignment done on time. Your boss has just requested the data a week early, and you know she will be really upset.

Actions

A. Let her know the boss is looking for the data.

B. Give her a deadline and outline the steps for her to complete the assignment.

C. Ask her what has been done on the assignment, then outline the steps for her to complete it.

D. Ask her what has been done on the assignment and help her create a plan for finishing it.

Responses

A _____

B _____

C _____

D _____

CASE 7

Barry has been in your area for many years. He is normally a self-starter, and you have always been able to rely on him to get the toughest of jobs done. He has deadlines for several major assignments approaching rapidly.

Actions

A. Ask him about his assignments and give him your support on them.

B. Anticipate that he may need support but wait for him to approach you first.

C. Ask him about his assignments, then lay out clear expectations for each one.

D. Lay out clear expectations for each of his assignments and be explicit about what he should be doing.

Responses

A _____

B _____

C _____

D _____

CASE 8

Jenny is frustrated with her job and actively looking for a transfer. She knows all the required tasks well, but has a tendency to be careless even under normal circumstances.

Actions

A. Stay close to the situation and be sure that standards are maintained.

B. Ask her about her concerns, then give her a plan for maintaining standards during the interim.

C. Ask her about her concerns and help her develop her own plan for the interim.

D. Let her know that she is needed to handle the work.

Responses

A _____

B _____

C _____

D _____

CASE 9

Your organization has embarked on a Quality initiative and you have been assigned to lead a Continuous Improvement Team. The team members represent all of the departments that have a direct interface with yours. The first meeting is today.

Actions

A. Lead group discussions that help the members define the team's mission and their roles.

B. Let the members outline the improvements they are planning to make in their own departments.

C. Clarify the team's mission and explain members' roles and responsibilities.

D. Incorporate members' suggestions as you determine operating principles and procedures.

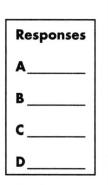

Responses

A_____

B_____

C_____

D_____

CASE 10

You are leading a team that has performed well in the past. The team members are experienced and have always handled responsibilities well. Recently, they have seemed burned out and you are afraid their interest will drop off completely.

Actions

A. Leave them on their own for a while before you take any formal action.

B. Redefine their responsibilities clearly and work closely with them until the group is back on track.

C. Ask the group for ideas about changes that are needed and use their input to make improvements.

D. Lead discussions about the current situation and help the group decide what changes are needed.

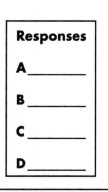

Responses

A_____

B_____

C_____

D_____

WHY WERE SOME CASES ABOUT INDIVIDUALS AND OTHERS ABOUT GROUPS?

The cases you just read focused on eight problems about individuals and two that involved group efforts. That is because we believe that to have a high-performing team, you need to lead the individuals on the team in unique ways according to who they are and what they have been asked to do. In addition, you need to lead the group dynamics that emerge as the individual contributors interact with each other and with you. This applies to teams in functional units, departments, and divisions. It also applies to cross-functional teams, project teams, committees, task forces, joint-venture teams, special teams, super teams, etc.

WHAT IS A HIGH-PERFORMING TEAM?

In our teambuilding practice, we work with leaders and their team members to help them develop productive working relationships and overcome self-imposed constraints. We help them clarify where they are going and how they are getting there. We help them eliminate ways in which they are tripping over each other's feet while discovering better ways to take advantage of the full resources available to the group.

This teambuilding work has given us a unique vantage point for understanding teams. In essence, it has taught us that high-performing teams have:

- A clear and unambiguous *mission*
- Clear *goals* with measurable targets for the team as well as the individuals on the team
- People who have the *skills* necessary to accomplish the mission
- Clear *roles* and responsibilities for each member of the team
- Well-defined *leadership* responsibilities that are shared among team members in ways that maximize openness without sacrificing control
- Clear, timely, and open *communication* down, up, and all the way around, within the team as well as with suppliers and customers
- Effective *decision-making* structures that enable the team

to tackle tough problems in a systematic way without getting bogged down in trivia

- Efficient *systems/procedures* that help people get their work done
- Formal or informal *rewards* that value people for their contributions as well as the team's successes
- An overall *climate* that encourages people to push the edge of the envelope and creates a positive team spirit.

Creating and sustaining a high-performing team is no small task. According to Tony Daloisio, the leader of our Charter Oak team that compiled these findings, "Each of these factors represents a key ingredient of a high-performing team. We find that teams can get stuck on any of these issues. What's interesting is that the solutions always come back to the issue of leadership. An ambiguous mission, unclear goals, poor communication, inefficient decision-making procedures, or a lackadaisical climate can all be corrected if the leader is commited to working on the problem. If not, it is not likely to get resolved."

So it comes down to you, the leader. You are the driving force. What you say and what you do will determine the success of your team. And what all the leaders throughout your organization say and do will determine the success of your entire organization.

WHY IS TEAMWORK SO IMPORTANT?

Teamwork is essential to the culture of most successful organizations. In our *organization alignment* practice, we have learned that an organization's culture can make or break any change initiative aimed at improvement. All too often, a leader will declare a new vision, develop a new strategy, announce a reorganization, or invest millions of dollars in new systems only to find that a few years later, there is not much different about the way the company is doing business. That is because the leader has not paid enough attention to the organization's culture. Without confronting old habits and established ways of working together, any major change is likely to fall flat on its face.

Basically, the concept of organization alignment can be likened to the alignment of an automobile or the human skeletal system. When a car is out of alignment it does not function optimally—the tires wear unevenly and more quickly, the gas mileage decreases, and the ride is far more bumpy than it would be with an aligned vehicle.

Likewise, when a person's body is out of alignment the person is likely to experience back pain, be less flexible, and move far less efficiently and effectively than when the body is aligned. Just as a good mechanic can bring a car back into alignment and a good chiropractor can adjust the body to bring it back into alignment, organizational leaders can do things to bring an organization—or part of an organization—into alignment.

In order to align an organization, there are five dimensions to consider. First, you need to look outside the organization at the *environment* that surrounds it. Who are your customers? Who are your main competitors? What are the technological, economic, or demographic developments that might have a major impact on your organization's future?

Second, you need to identify the core *values* that will align your organization with your environment and simultaneously align your workforce in pursuit of a shared *vision*. Values are at the center of an aligned organization. They are the core of the vision that drives it forward into the future.

Third, the vision needs to be translated into specific strategies which must be articulated as departmental missions with measurable goals. The *strategy* makes the vision more concrete by turning the core values into an achievable set of targets.

Fourth, the strategy has to be implemented by a *structure* that outlines the roles and responsibilities needed to make the strategy succeed. To bring the structure to life, you also need *systems* in place that can put the strategies into motion.

Finally, the *culture* of the organization must motivate people to act in ways that are consistent with customers' expectations and the core values that drive the organization.

We don't want to minimize any aspect of what it takes to lead a high-performing organization. For an organization to be effective, its leaders have to consider each of the elements of alignment. They need to be aware of the environment, able to articulate a vision that is shared by followers, know how to focus on the right strategic initiatives, design efficient structures, and put productive systems in place. They also need to create a culture where purposeful, focused teams work smarter and learn faster than the competition.

As Jonathan Spiegel, the head of Charter Oak's alignment practice, says, "Leaders need to recognize that they must create a culture that enables people to achieve their vision. Without integration of individual efforts into productive teamwork, no customer-oriented vision has a chance of succeeding."

Our emphasis in this book is on working with individuals and groups in ways that create the high-performing teams that will give your organization a culture capable of achieving greatness. Whether you are a CEO or a first-line supervisor, The Leader's Window can help you create an organizational culture that supports long-term success. This new paradigm for leadership can also enable managers at all levels of your organization to build an organizational culture in which everyone is inspired to perform to the best of his/her potential.

Management by Buzzword

One of the biggest impediments to organizational success is the abundance of buzzwords that wash through corporate hallways in successive waves. While many of these catch phrases reflect worthwhile ideas that have stood the test of time, they cannot, in and of themselves, offer complete solutions. The key is to get beneath the slogans and understand what to do with the meaning they reflect.

Ideas don't become buzzwords unless there is some truth beneath the surface. The problem is that often a leader will latch on to a buzzword and try to align his or her organization behind the particular philosophy that a buzzword implies.

Here are some of the buzzwords we hear most frequently. We suspect that they will sound familiar to you too. We have grouped them into four small windows held together by a window frame to give you a sneak preview of The 4 Windows of Leadership (See Figure 1.1). You will see later that each set of these buzzwords has its place in a good leader's tool kit.

Window 1 focuses on words like *vision, passion, drive, results*. Window 2 includes words like *participation, involvement, synergy,* and *quality*. Window 3 emphasizes words like *listening, coaching, development,* and *support*. And Window 4 focuses on terms like *empowerment, delegation, trust,* and *letting go*.

Throughout this book we will try to build on these familiar buzzwords. As we've suggested, behind every buzzword there lies some truth. Our goal is to help you understand what to do with the wisdom of each small window and how to blend all of these truths together into a complete paradigm for effective leadership.

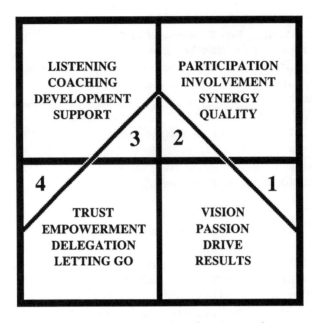

Figure 1.1 Management by Buzzword.

Each of these windows can be a powerful force in a leadership relationship when used appropriately. Each can also be a misguided attempt to jump on a buzzword bandwagon.

One of the reasons we suspect "management by buzzword" happens so often is that people are seeking simple answers to complex problems. The truth is that effective leaders do a lot of different things under different circumstances—and that all the things they do make sense some of the time. The problem is that the same actions don't make sense at other times.

Articulating a vision for your organization and being impassioned about that vision can be a wonderful thing. Driving those who report to you to achieve results can prove worthwhile. However, forcing your vision on those who have a vested stake in their own vision of their work and are self-motivated may result in diminished returns.

Preaching the virtues of participation, involvement, team synergy, and the importance of quality can lead to cutting-edge problem solving if you're serious about using people's input. It can also wreak havoc with your credibility if you're not prepared to follow through.

Using a nurturing approach to managing people by listening

to them, coaching, developing, and supporting them can lead to high performance; but you'd better be sure those you're developing are ready, willing, and able to take on the responsibility that comes with this approach or you're likely to find yourself doing a lot of unnecessary damage control.

Finally, finding ways to truly empower people by delegating to them, trusting them, and letting go of control can prove to be beneficial to everyone involved provided you are all positioned to take advantage of this high level of autonomy.

Within each window, there is a set of buzzwords that offers a potential blessing and a possible curse. The blessing emerges when the particular philosophy matches the conditions. The curse rears its ugly head when there is a mismatch between the methodology employed and the leadership needs of the situation. The biggest problems occur when a leader embraces one window for all circumstances and ends up trying to force every situation to fit the strategy instead of the other way around.

Throughout the book, our mission is to help you develop the tools to use the right leadership styles at the right times. We will help you learn to open each window when its messages are needed. Ultimately, that ability will determine whether you are viewed as a fad-following sloganeer or a savvy master of leadership.

USE ALL YOUR GOLF CLUBS

Whether you are supervising an individual, spearheading a team effort, or captaining an entire organization, one point we want to drive home at the outset is that you need to be open-minded about using a variety of approaches. Every situation will confront you with a new set of circumstances, and each window will give you a set of options. The challenge is to match the right response to each situation.

Instead of thinking of yourself as a professional manager with a set of leadership tools, think of yourself as a professional golfer with a set of very valuable golf clubs.

In golf, there is a reason that you have woods, long irons, short irons, and a putter in the golf bag. You need the woods on the tee and the fairway, the long irons in the rough, the short irons for the sand traps and approach shots, and the putter on the greens.

Imagine how ineffective you would be if you tried playing

golf with only one club. If all you had was a putter you'd be terrible off the tee and in the traps. If you had only woods, you'd be awful in the rough and on the greens. And if all you had was a short iron, you wouldn't get very far off the tee, and you'd tear the greens to shreds. Not only would you be ineffective, you would look ridiculous.

Many managers try the equivalent at work. They walk around with one approach and try to use it in every situation. They often take pride in being consistent when they are actually being ineffective in most situations—and they often do look ridiculous.

The point is that if you want to be effective as a leader you have to be prepared to use all your clubs. You don't want to use them all at once, but you do want to use each one of them as the circumstances demand.

This may sound easier than it actually is. When you play golf it's easy to know which club to use. On the golf course there is a nice flat spot with little markers to let you know that you are at the tee. The fairway is clearly distinguished from the rough. You definitely know when your ball is in a sand trap. And the well-groomed grass and the flag give you clear indicators that you're on the green.

At work it's a lot harder because the clues are never marked that clearly. That's what The Leader's Window is for, to help you see the clues that are there and figure out which clubs to use and when to use them.

Chapter 2

The 4 Windows
of Leadership

When you responded to the ten cases in the last chapter, you had four actions from which to choose. Each of those actions is associated with one of the leadership styles of The Leader's Window. In this chapter, we will give you a deeper understanding of these four different approaches to leadership so that you will have a clear picture of what each style looks like.

This is the first step toward mastering the four leadership styles. If you are going to open and close all four windows at the right times and apply the wisdom behind the buzzwords in value-added ways, you need to know the words and actions that bring each of these leadership styles to life.

You can't play golf with the pros until you know how to hold each golf club.

THE FOUR LEADERSHIP STYLES

The most common way to think about the four leadership styles is in terms of two general types of leader behavior, direction and support.

Being directive means telling people what to do, when to do it, how to do it, and why it should be done. It involves explaining assignments, providing information, and giving people instructions. Direction is typified by downward communication and influence from above. It usually results in close supervision and frequent feedback.

Being supportive is quite different. It is typified by encouraging upward communication, seeking people's ideas, and listening carefully to their responses. Support means respecting people's knowledge and involving them in decision making. It involves building people's confidence, helping them accomplish assignments, and encouraging them to assume responsibility.

Actually, you should think of each type of behavior as a continuum. With direction, you might range from a limited direction, laissez-faire approach to a high-direction, very controlling approach. With support, you might range from a limited support, minimal interaction approach to a high-support, active communication approach. Between these extremes, there are many points on each continuum.

Figure 2.1 shows what the four styles look like in terms of Direction and Support.

These are the basic tools that a leader uses when interacting with other people. Style 1 (S1) is the High Direction style. Style 2 (S2) is the High Direction, High Support style. Style 3 (S3) is the High Support style. And Style 4 (S4) the Low Direction, Low Support style.

S1, the High Direction Style

This style is typified by taking action without seeking input from others. Leaders who use Style 1 are good at giving out assign-

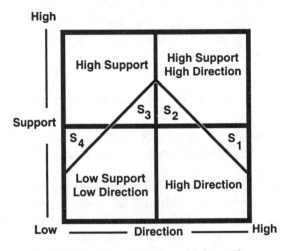

Figure 2.1 The 4 Basic Leadership Styles.

ments and informing team members of the actions they need to take. Their tendency is to tell people what, when, why, and how to proceed while providing close supervision.

S2, the High Direction and High Support Style

This style is typified by direction from the top based on ideas that are actively solicited from members of the group. Leaders who use Style 2 are good at seeking information from key people and asking their opinions on issues. They like to share problems, listen to other people's points of view, then set a course of action and make assignments.

S3, the High Support Style

This style is typified by assisting others in areas where they have responsibility. Leaders who use Style 3 are comfortable listening as people discuss problem situations. They ask many questions and provide some input to other people's decisions. They act as a guide and a resource but leave the responsibility with those who are closest to the problem.

S4, the Low Direction and Low Support Style

This style is typified by leaving people on their own. Leaders who use Style 4 are good at getting out of the way and letting team members make decisions on their own. They don't overwhelm followers with information in order to let them work out the details of assignments. They also don't require reams of information about problems or actions that followers have taken.

This is just the beginning. To fully understand these four leadership styles, you have to know more about the key behaviors that put direction and support into action. This means looking at the ways that you go about making decisions, your preferred modes of communication, and the types of behavior that you tend to recognize and reward in the people you surround yourself with.

WHAT KIND OF DECISION MAKER ARE YOU?

One of the most important aspects of your job as a leader is making timely, high-quality decisions that other people are committed to implementing. This can be done in four different ways. In part it depends on the amount of responsibility you like to retain or are willing to give up. It also depends on your preference for interactive participation in the decision-making process.

Responsibility for decision making is a source of tremendous conflict and frustration in most organizations. Too often, several people believe that they have the right to make certain decisions. In other cases, no one wants to or is permitted to make decisions.

Consequently, you have to be clear about who has the final word about any key decision. As the leader, do you need to make the decision? Do you simply *want* to make the decision? Or should a member of your team be empowered to make the decision? Who makes the call? You or someone who reports to you?

Participation is the other important element of decision making. If people with critical information are not involved, it is unlikely that a high-quality decision will be made. If people who have to live with the consequences of a decision are not involved, it is unlikely that they will be committed to implementing it. On the other hand, if people are asked to participate when they are not affected by the decision or they have nothing meaningful to contribute, they usually resent the unnecessary demand on their time.

So it is equally important for you to understand when participation is needed and be clear about people's roles as participants in the decision-making process.

Figure 2.2 depicts the four leadership styles in terms of responsibility and participation.

On the right, with Styles 1 and 2, the leader is responsible for making the decisions. On the left, with Styles 3 and 4, a member of the team is responsible for making the decisions.

On the top, with Styles 2 and 3, both the leader and team members are involved in the decision-making process. On the bottom, with Styles 1 and 4, only one party is involved, either the leader or the team member but not both.

So, if you are the type of leader who prefers to retain responsibility and doesn't tend to invite other people to participate in

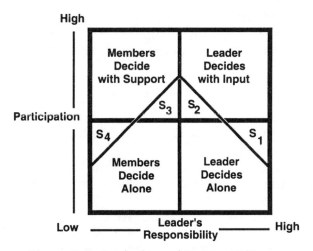

Figure 2.2 Leadership and Decision-Making.

the process, then your preference is for making decisions on your own and you probably come across as a Style 1 leader.

On the other hand, if you are the type of leader who encourages people to bring problems to your attention and asks for their recommendations, but still likes to be the one who is in charge, then you tend to make decisions based on followers' input and you probably come across as a Style 2 leader.

However, if you like the members of the team to have the responsibility for making decisions, but still like being an active participant in the process, then you tend to support others as they make decisions with your input and you most likely come across as a Style 3 leader.

Finally, if you let the members of the team have the responsibility without your being involved in the decision-making process, then you prefer to let others make decisions on their own and probably come across as a Style 4 leader.

HOW ARE YOU AS A COMMUNICATOR?

What you say and how you say it can be as important as anything else you do as a leader. When you think of your leadership in terms of communication, the question is, what happens when you open your mouth? To answer that question, try thinking of your communications in two broad categories, *giving information* and *seeking information*.

Giving information requires the use of *influencing skills*. These communication tools include providing directions, giving advice, giving explanations, pointing out consequences, and giving feedback.

At the beginning of a project, people need clear directions that include complete information about what is to be accomplished and when it needs to be done. They also need complete explanations about why actions are needed, including background information and interpretation of key events. People are also prompted to action if they understand the consequences at stake, including the potential payoffs or pitfalls for them, the organization, or the customer.

As work progresses, people also function better if they have access to timely advice or constructive suggestions. They also benefit from ongoing feedback about their performance and their progress toward the intended objectives.

If you tend to use these influencing skills frequently, then you are probably good at giving others the information they need to perform successfully and influencing them to take action.

Listening skills are the communication tools for seeking information. Listening is not a passive act. It means actively seeking information from people, then using their thoughts and feelings to identify problems and resolve them. Listening skills include paying attention, encouraging openness, asking probing questions, paraphrasing ideas, empathizing with feelings, and summarizing key points.

Paying attention to other people's concerns, listening to the problems they are facing, and hearing their recommendations for corrective action are critical skills for any leader. Whenever people have ideas to share, it is important to give them verbal and nonverbal messages that encourage them to be as open as possible.

Non-verbally, that means using an inviting, non-judgmental tone of voice that encourages people to speak candidly. It also means avoiding body language that says, "Go away, don't bother me," or makes people feel intimidated.

Verbally, that means asking relevant and thoughtful questions that help everyone fully understand the situation. It also means valuing others' point of view by empathizing with their feelings and paraphrasing their thoughts. In addition, whenever problems are complex or many people are involved in discussing them, it is essential for the leader to keep everyone on track by summarizing the key points of a conversation.

If you tend to use these listening skills frequently, then you are probably good at encouraging people to be open with you and making them feel like valued contributors.

Figure 2.3 shows the four leadership styles in terms of influencing and listening.

On the right, Styles 1 and 2 are Active Influencing styles. On the left, Styles 3 and 4 are Active Listening styles. At the top, Styles 2 and 3 involve a lot of interaction between the team leader and team members. At the bottom, Styles 1 and 4 require less two-way communication.

Think about yourself again as a leader.

Focusing on the lower right-hand window, if you are the type of leader who tends to tell people what to do, when to do it, how to do it, and why, or if you provide close supervision and frequent feedback, then you are an active influencer and will be perceived as using Style 1.

Focusing on the upper left-hand window, if you like to be a sounding board to help followers think through their decisions, if you ask good questions, pay careful attention, reflect back their ideas, and empathize with their feelings, then you are more of an active listener and will be perceived as using Style 3.

Focusing on the upper right-hand window, if you tend to listen to people's problems, then tell them how to fix them, or if

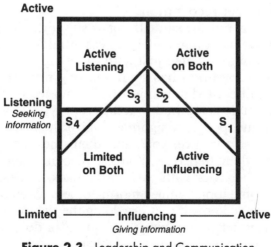

Figure 2.3 Leadership and Communication.

you explain problems to others so that you can get their input before you make your decision, then you use a balance of influencing skills and listening skills and will be perceived as a Style 2 leader.

Finally, in the lower left-hand window, if you tend to leave followers on their own without giving them lots of information or spending a lot of time keeping yourself informed about what they are doing, you will probably be perceived as using Style 4.

WHAT DO YOU GIVE PEOPLE RECOGNITION FOR?

Recognition is another factor that influences the way you are perceived as a leader. Recognition refers to a variety of ways that you might let followers know that they are doing what you want them to do. Sometimes this means giving people tangible rewards like a raise, bonus, promotion, good performance review, interesting assignments, or even pleasant working conditions. But sometimes it just means giving them some appreciation or any form of praise that makes them feel their efforts have been noticed.

Everyone wants recognition. When they get it, they and the people around them are more likely to continue behaving in the ways that led to recognition. Conversely, if they are reprimanded, they and the people around them are more likely to avoid doing the things that led to criticism. In addition, if people are used to receiving some form of recognition, and it stops coming, they are likely to stop acting as they did in the past and start looking for new ways to get recognition.

Recognition is not the same thing as support. Unlike participation and active listening, which are essential to Styles 2 and 3, recognition is not associated just with these high support styles. Instead, since recognition has such a strong impact on followers, it is a significant dimension of all four leadership styles. However, each style is typified by a different type of recognition.

When you give people assignments, give them feedback, and evaluate their performance, you send them messages about the ways you expect them to behave. You also recognize and encourage certain types of behavior with pats on the back, smiles, or simply picking up on some topics while ignoring others. Even these subtle messages let people know if they are doing the right things and are appreciated. As much as anything that you say or do, the behaviors that you reward or pay attention to establish the way that you come across as a leader.

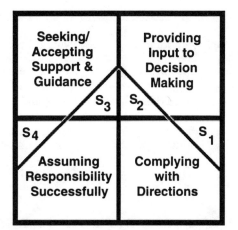

Figure 2.4 Leadership and Recognition.

Figure 2.4 shows the four leadership styles in terms of recognition.

If you tend to value people who like you to call the shots, praise followers for asking what to do, when to do it, and how to do it, and reward people who follow directions and do what they are told, then you are sending out Style 1 messages.

If you like followers who bring problems to your attention so you can resolve them, appreciate people for making recommendations, and encourage people to provide input into your decision making, then you are giving off Style 2 messages.

If you are available and willing to help people when they get stuck, encourage followers to ask for your support and use you as a resource, respond positively when others need help, and reward people who ask for your advice before making tough decisions, then you are broadcasting Style 3 messages.

If you surround yourself with people who are willing to assume responsibility and make their own decisions, encourage followers to be creative and take risks, and reward people for solving problems on their own, then you are giving team members Style 4 messages.

WHICH LEADERSHIP STYLES DO YOU USE?

Now that you understand what behaviors are associated with each style, here are the four styles of The Leader's Window (Figure 2.5). Each style window contains a summary of the

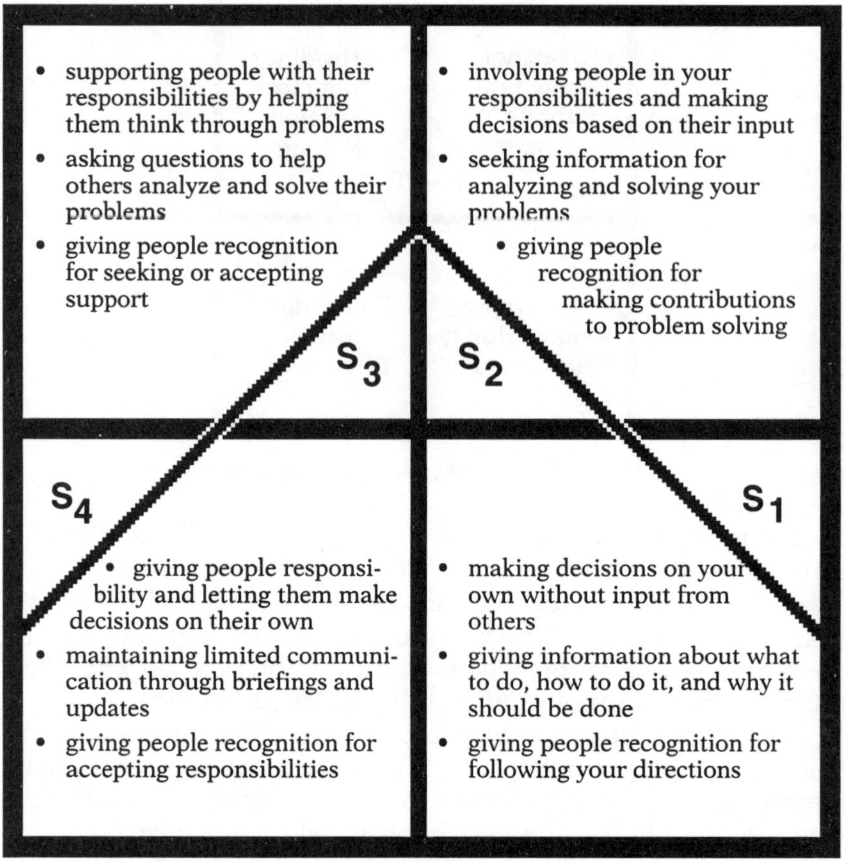
• supporting people with their responsibilities by helping them think through problems
• asking questions to help others analyze and solve their problems
• giving people recognition for seeking or accepting support
• involving people in your responsibilities and making decisions based on their input
• seeking information for analyzing and solving your problems
• giving people recognition for making contributions to problem solving
S3
S2
S4
S1
• giving people responsibility and letting them make decisions on their own
• maintaining limited communication through briefings and updates
• giving people recognition for accepting responsibilities
• making decisions on your own without input from others
• giving information about what to do, how to do it, and why it should be done
• giving people recognition for following your directions

Figure 2.5 The Four Styles of The Leader's Window.

decision-making, communication, and recognition strategies for that style. As you look at these summaries, ask yourself which behaviors you tend to use with the people who work with you. What do you typically do? How do you think you come across to the people around you? Are you a Style 1, Style 2, Style 3, or Style 4 leader?

NOT SURE WHICH ONE IS YOURS? TRY THESE LABELS ON FOR SIZE!

Look at the labels below and you will see that each style can be effective or ineffective. People will speak of you admiringly with the effective labels if you use the right styles at the right times.

But they will use the ineffective labels to complain about you if you use the exact same behaviors at the wrong times. Look at the labels in Figure 2.6 and the descriptions that follow and maybe they will help you discover the type of leader you are.

Style 1: Directing

A leader using S1 effectively gives people clear directions when they are inexperienced or new to their responsibilities. These leaders also provide complete explanations and honest appraisals of consequences. They give people the information they need to do their jobs and structure work carefully when team members are not sure how to get started. They offer advice when it is requested and help people avoid negative consequences with frequent feedback. In these situations, *directing* is appreciated.

Style 1: Dominating

A leader who is highly directive will be ineffective if team members have more information than the leader, already understand the situation clearly, know what needs to be done and have already been taking appropriate actions. In these situations, the leader is *dominating*, taking control when it is unnecessary, interrupting the efforts of followers, and overriding their initiatives.

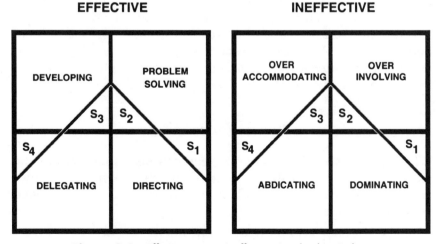

Figure 2.6 Effective versus Ineffective Leadership Styles.

Style 2: Problem Solving

Most leaders who use S2 effectively have a systematic approach for:

- Identifying problems
- Clarifying goals
- Generating alternatives
- Choosing the best solution
- Building an action plan
- Monitoring implementation

The leader listens to people's concerns, making them feel like important identifiers of organizational problems and necessary participants in finding solutions. The leader seeks input from those people who have to live with the consequences of decisions, meets only with those people who need to be involved, runs effective meetings when they are needed, and makes assignments that speed up the decision-making process.

Style 2: Overinvolving

When S2 is used ineffectively, including people in decision making is perceived as *overinvolving*. Team members feel frustrated with the amount of time they spend in meetings. Committees and task forces slow down the organization's responsiveness to problems and issues are discussed at too many levels. The important problems never get heard or are ignored while attention gets diverted to forms and charts and new names for old ways of doing business. Leaders who seem to meet for the sake of meeting, discuss issues but do not listen, involve people but produce no action, are *overinvolving*.

Style 3: Developing

When S3 is used effectively, the leader assists members of the team when they need support with decision making. The leader asks open questions that guide followers to focus on overlooked steps of problem solving:

- How have you defined the problem?
- What is the goal in this situation?

- What alternatives are you considering?
- Which alternative is the best for achieving the goal?
- What is your plan for implementing the solution?
- How will you monitor the implemenation?

The leader listens to the responses, paraphrasing key points, paying attention to nonverbal cues, and summarizing the issues. The leader may provide information or opinions but stresses that responsibility for decision making is still with the team member. By encouraging people to discuss problems openly, the leader is *developing* them to assume responsibility. People feel supported and gain confidence in their own problem-solving skills. Conversations focus on organizational problems. They occur when people want support and need help managing their responsibilities.

Style 3: Overaccommodating

Listening to people's problems and giving them support can also be perceived as an *overaccommodating* style. Often leaders are too focused on relationships for their own sake. They try to be liked by everybody and keep everyone happy. They come across as friendly but are not well-respected. They listen but don't let people know if they're on the right track. They agree with anything, bending over backwards to be supportive even when requests are inappropriate or recommendations don't make sense. Their need to help can also be distracting to people who work better on their own. Having to check in with the leader and seek guidance takes such people away from productive activities.

Style 4: Delegating

When S4 is used effectively, the *delegating* of responsibility and authority empowers members of the team to make decisions and take action in areas where they have expertise and are motivated to follow through. Communication is limited to receiving periodic progress reports and providing renewed confidence in followers' work. Team members feel trusted, believe that the organization's success depends on them, and know that they are responsible for their area as well as coordination with related areas. These people respond enthusiastically to the opportunity to use their knowledge and skills, be involved in challenging work, and achieve results. These intrinsic motivators satisfy them and, consequently, the only encouragement they need is recognition for their performance.

Style 4: Abdicating

When S4 is used ineffectively, the same act of giving responsibility and authority takes place. However, the leader is also perceived as losing accountability. If team members lack the ability to identify problems or the confidence to take necessary actions, they feel like they are out on a limb or in over their heads. As frustrations mount, the leader is blamed for dumping responsibilities onto followers. People complain about lack of support, ambiguous authority, and absentee management. In time, this *abdicating* becomes the focus of people's attention, distracting them from the organization's business problems. Members of the team may try to provide substitute leadership, often resulting in factions or strife.

COMPARE YOURSELF TO THESE LEADERS!

If you're not sure how you come across as a leader, one way to clarify what each of the styles looks like is to identify familiar people who use each style. A fun way to do this is to think about some well-known TV characters whose two-dimensional personalities make them dramatic examples of each style. Understanding the labels that describe these leaders should help you be objective about your own tendencies as a leader. Some of our favorite examples follow. If these examples aren't enough, then think of your own favorite TV or movie characters to see if you can identify their main styles and analyze their effectiveness.

"M*A*S*H" MEMORIES

Those of you old enough to remember, or who watch reruns of the hit comedy series "M*A*S*H," will find a rich array of leadership styles exhibited. Here's a quick rundown of what we see when we look at that venerable M*A*S*H unit.

Henry Blake, the original M*A*S*H commander, is a classic

example of an ineffective Style 4 leader, *abdicating* at every turn. Henry is usually distracted from his work, off on a fishing expedition, or hung over. He is best known for asking Radar to make most of his decisions for him. Had he not been so ineffective in performing his own duties, he might be seen—as evidenced by Radar's flawless completion of his duties—as a masterful delegator.

When Henry Blake is away, Frank Burns sometimes becomes acting commander. He does all he can to be the antithesis of Henry and becomes a classic Style 1 leader. Since no one takes Frank seriously or feels that they need his guidance, Frank is quite ineffective and *dominating* as a leader. The only person in the 4077 camp who is more dominating than Frank is Margaret (Hot Lips) Houlihan, who is an expert at dominating him!

Occasionally Hawkeye Pierce is left in charge of the camp. As a leader Hawkeye is a good example of Style 3, *over-accommodating*. The problem is that he spends most of his time indulging the troop's (and his own) social needs by throwing parties, running his still, and chasing nurses. Most of the time he is an ineffective socializer. Sometimes he rises to the occasion and uses his Style 3 skills for *developing* some fledgling recruit or listening to a needy patient and giving them the support they need to survive.

Radar O'Reilly is another example of Style 3, *over-accommodating*. As a follower, Radar's accommodating nature is an asset. Whatever he is asked to do he will pursue diligently. But there are a few occasions when he is left in charge of a project that involves several of his superiors. Then Radar is seen spinning around like a top saying, "Yes, sir. Yes, sir. Yes, sir. Yes, all of you sirs!" Finally he gives up in exasperation.

LEADERSHIP AND THE LAW

The popular television series "L.A. Law" offers several examples of leadership styles. Consider the three characters who have shared senior partner responsibilities at various times: Leland McKenzie, Douglas Brackman, and Rosalind Shays.

Leland McKenzie seems to spend most of his time using Style 4, effectively *delegating* the office administration to Brackman, and letting the lawyers run their own practices. At times, however, his Style 4 results in ineffective *abdicating*, like during a controversial period when he declared he was stepping down temporarily and giving responsibility for decision making to Brackman. Most of the lawyers felt that he was shirking his responsibilities.

At times he also operates as a Style 2 leader, hearing people out and then making decisions based on their analysis of the situation. He can at times overuse this style, too, for example, when he asked firm partner Ann Kelsey whether or not he should marry Rosalind Shays. She didn't want to give her input, and he eventually ignored it when it wasn't what he wanted to hear. He managed to *overinvolve* himself and her at the same time.

Douglas Brackman is the quintessential Style 1, and while his style would seem to be protective of the bottom line, his constant interrogation, attempts at control, and nitpicking about keeping costs down discredit him in the eyes of most of the attorneys. He is rarely taken seriously and is seen as unnecessarily *dominating*.

While Rosalind Shays was the senior partner she also functioned as a Style 1 leader; however. her approach was considerably different from Brackman's. She was very *directing* about broader issues like the types of clients who were most profitable and who had the right to make decisions about the firm's direction. While her directive style boded well for the bottom line, she frequently crossed over into *dominating*. Not only did she constantly fight with the other lawyers, she took steps to undercut them behind their backs. The result was that in the end her power and its potential positive impact were undermined by the lack of trust her actions generated, and she was eventually forced to resign.

ENTERPRISE LEADERSHIP

Perhaps the best models for effective leadership are the two starfleet commanders, Captain James T. Kirk from "Star Trek" and Captain Jean Luc Picard from "Star Trek: The Next Generation." Both Kirk and Picard demonstrate the uncanny ability to use the right styles with the right people at the right time. A quick look at these two characters provides a broad-stroked view of effective leadership in action. Both Kirk and Picard spend a good deal of time operating in Style 2 and Style 3. When there is a problem that requires their attention, they summon their experts and engage in intensive *problem solving* to find a resolution. If the problem is of a highly technical nature regarding an aspect of the ship they know little about, they form a team of experts and *support* their efforts in solving the problem. When faced with a crisis requiring action away from the ship, they employ their Style 4 skills by *delegating* a landing party, or if leading the landing party, *delegating* control of the ship to their trusted first officer. On occasion they will demonstrate their ability to use Style 1 when time or circumstances make it necessary for a single person to make a decision. And their use of Style 1 always comes across as *directing* since neither has failed to make the right decision or issue the proper order when faced with imminent annihilation from a Klingon or Romulan vessel!

KEEP READING TO GET MORE VIEWS OF EACH WINDOW

In each of the next four chapters, you will read about well-known public figures who typify each leadership style. The profiles of these real leaders should leave no doubt in your mind as to what each window of leadership looks like.

Chapter **3**

Window 1: The Leader as Director

Chapters 3 through 6 will help you understand what The 4 Windows of Leadership look like in real life. Each chapter is filled with profiles of real leaders in many different settings. As you read these profiles, you can clearly envision the range of leadership behaviors that are associated with each leadership style.

In each window, the profiles will highlight the way leaders make decisions, the way they communicate, and the recognition they give to followers because, as mentioned earlier, these are the essential behaviors that determine how a leader comes across to the rest of the world.

Each chapter will show you the effective use of that leadership style as well as the result of the right style being used with the right people at the right times. It will also show you the ineffective use of that leadership style and the result of that same style being overused with the wrong people at the wrong times.

As you read this chapter and the ones that follow, think about the choices you made on the cases in chapter 1. Which window were you looking through when you responded to those cases? Which one is your favorite view?

Let's start with Window 1. Taking charge, being in control, steering the ship, being at the helm, commanding the troops, and giving people their marching orders are all images that most people associate with strong leaders. The view through Window 1 will show you a number of effective leaders who come across as *directing*, decisive people who are good at getting things done.

Window 1 will also show you some leaders who are so good at directing that they overdo it and therefore are perceived as *dominating*, squelching other people's attempts to take initiative.

UNIFORM RESULTS

Ray Kroc, the founder of McDonalds, was the quintessential Window 1 leader. He had a vision that the key to his success would be to create a uniform product—the hamburger—that could be replicated and accessible at a reasonable price anywhere in the country. "Ray Kroc pictured his empire long before it existed, and he saw how to get there. He invented the company motto—'Quality, service, cleanliness, and value'—and kept repeating it to employees for the rest of his life" (Labich 1988). The key to his success was establishing a standard and adhering strictly to that standard. Kroc's *directing* leadership style was (and is) echoed throughout his organization. When you put on a McDonald's uniform to work as a cook they don't ask you what you think the best way is to make a hamburger—they tell you in no uncertain terms precisely how you will make it. "Kroc left nothing to chance. He wrote manuals specifying exact grill heats, cooking times, amounts of ketchup and mustard. Score marks on every burger were to be precisely the same distance apart" (Ola and D'Aulaire 1987).

While some may argue that the Kroc approach breeds conformity and stifles creativity, it would be difficult to argue with the success of his venture. Further, while this type of management approach might not be attractive to some, it is well-suited to the frontline workers at McDonald's, most of whom work part-time. High school kids, at-home parents, and moonlighters can walk in, put on an apron, and turn out perfect quality with little difficulty.

One way Kroc was able to create and sustain such consistent conformity was by creating a corporate culture that reinforced his personal approach to hamburger production and sales. The creation of Hamburger University is a vivid example of Kroc's legacy of control. "Franchisees, accountants, lawyers, managers, and executives—everyone in the decision-making process—are required to attend Hamburger University in Oak Brook, Illinois. During 12-day courses, 28 'professors'—actually ex-restaurant operatives—lecture to thousands of students a year. Here they learn the essentials of restaurant management, human relations and grill skills." (Ola and D'Aulaire 1987). Essentially, they learn the gospel according to Kroc.

An even more vivid manifestation of Kroc's legacy of control is Kroc's "presence" years after his death, at corporate headquarters in Oak Brook. "Ray is not only quoted, he is, uh, sort of there in Oak Brook today. In a headquarters exhibit called 'Talk to Ray,' a visitor can phone up Ray, as it were, on a videoscreen, and with a keyboard ask him questions. Over several years he recorded his thoughts for the company archives, and his appearances on talk shows were taped as well, so those left to carry on can find out about nearly everything they might need to know" (Moser 1988, p. 113).

Perhaps the greatest testament to Kroc's ability to use his *directing* approach to sustain his vision for his organization comes from CEO Mike Quinlan. "If there's one reason for our success, it's that Ray Kroc instilled in the company basic principles. Standards of excellence" (Moser 1988, p. 113).

Finally, what makes Kroc's Style 1 approach so successful is that, as with most successful visionaries, he has given the public what it wants. People go to McDonald's because they know exactly what they are going to get—and they are rarely surprised. Consider these reflections by journalist Penny Moser (Moser 1988, p. 114): "Rather than being bored with McDonald's sameness, we learned to appreciate it. In a world where one of my ancestral homes became an on-ramp for the Illinois tollway and another was claimed for an atomic accelerator site, McDonald's became a symbol of stability. A McDonald's meal tastes pretty much the same everywhere. It can cure homesickness and make strange places less strange. I brightened up considerably when, after a long day on Guam earlier this year, the golden arches greeted me around a bend."

FUN FOR THE ENTIRE FAMILY—ON DEMAND

Another extraordinarily successful Window 1 leader was Walt Disney. Examination of Disney's leadership style throughout his career paints the picture of a relentless Style 1 leader, committed to realizing his vision of his organization through a carefully controlled orchestration of every detail. Disney used to walk into the theme parks and pick up errant cigarette butts, sending a clear message to each "cast member" working on the street-cleaning crew. In every aspect of Disneyland and Disney World, Walt demanded that things be picture perfect. Every detail was important, to ensure that each guest would experience the total illusion. In fact, the entire Disney dynasty was built on the premise that success would be predicated on the theme parks' ability to practically guarantee perfect vacations—and this goal was accomplished through a very directive mode of leadership.

As with Kroc and the McDonald's approach, the organization was driven by the leader's vision and a *directing* leadership style down to the last detail. Every employee has a specific role in Disney's plays and every play is scripted. Whether an employee is leading an adventure cruise down a jungle river or directing guests to their desired destination, there are scripts or, as everyone at Disney calls them, spiels for what to say and what to do to ensure that the desired effect is created and conveyed. This prescriptive control gets played out in every aspect of the organization. Whether an employee is walking the streets of the Magic Kingdom as Goofy or behind the scenes in the accounting department, there are instructions as to what to wear, how to behave, and the role to play in the organization.

Disney's approach to managing his dream was with him throughout his career, and continues to drive the Disney organization even after his death. Even early on as a fledgling animation editor, Disney would take control of ideas developed by other studio employees and create the finished product himself. In fact, he was the first in his business to utilize the storyboard approach for animation, which involves taking general ideas and plotting them out meticulously, step-by-step, to create a cohesive, integrated result.

Perhaps the most vivid view of what drove Disney to maintain his high-control approach to his business can be seen through his own eyes. "In a story typical of his tendency to portray his actions in mythic terms, Disney was fond of telling how he first got the idea for his Disneyland. He was sitting at a park bench with his daughter at a traditional amusement park, when, in looking around, he angrily mused to himself that there ought to be fun-oriented parks which are clean and wholesome enough for the whole family. In planning his park, Walt Disney created a relentlessly clean environment through an almost compulsive passion for order and control" (Croce 1991, p. 94).

Disney's need for control was driven by his desire to create an experience that was reliable and dependable in providing entertainment, but his style was driven by more than just his entrepreneurial interests. "Walt Disney did not develop his cheerful creatures all alone, yet his organization was also, to a great extent, an extension of himself. . . . Always the charismatic leader, with intimate personal control of his productions, Disney closely identified with his company. Late in life, when asked about his most rewarding experience, he responded, 'The whole damn thing. The fact that I was able to build an organization and hold it.'"

Disney's success as a Style 1 leader is based in part on the fact that he had the goods. As the creator of Mickey Mouse, he demonstrated that he knew what kids liked and how to communicate with them. But more important, he knew how to make adults feel like kids again, thus making him the ultimate patriarch. The fact that 80 percent of those who visit the Disney theme parks are adults emphasizes the importance of this ability to take people back to their childhood. If you doubt the power of this effect all you need do is visit "Mickey's Birthdayland," at which there is a perpetual birthday party taking place for the famous mouse. Seeing all those adults gathered around giant screens singing "Happy Birthday" to their beloved mouse is the greatest testament to Disney's ability to transport adults back to their younger days.

This patriarchal presence also gave a *dominating* aspect to the Disney dynasty, playing itself out particularly in Disney's relationship to his employees. "Disney's most important control was that which he exercised over his subordinates. He may have appeared avuncular to the public, but on the job, he played the stern and powerful father. Animator Ward Kimball was one of many who explicitly acknowledged this relationship: 'Walt was our father figure. We both respected and feared him. He ran the studio as a sort of benevolent and paternal dictatorship. He was the total boss. . . , but we all knew he was a genius whose tough demeanor seemed to stimulate and bring out the best in all of us. . . . We were inwardly proud to be part of his organization" (Croce 1991, pg.99).

While it would be difficult to argue with the success of the Disney phenomenon, one can also learn about the downside of such an approach by examining the ways in which Disney's patriarchal style created limitations for those affected by it. According to close associate Kimball, in the early days, "There were lots of newcomers around, but Walt just laid them over an anvil and beat the Disney style into them.' With Disney setting the tone, his workers could express little of their individuality in animation, acting, or directing." But even more potentially problematic is the effect of such control on the consumer of the Disncy product. Social critics like T.D. Allman and Robert Sklar contend that the impact of Disney's highly controlled approach diminishes individual imagination and creativity. Critics contend that the Disney approach to entertainment through its carefully choreographed theme parks leads to *imagineering*—essentially the control and engineering of one's imagination. Because of the predictability and passivity that the parks induce, visiting one is, according to Allman, "like watching TV." (Allman 1987).

Whether you love Disney theme parks or agree with the more cynical views expressed by the social critics above, there is no question that Disney's Style 1, *directing* approach, has been successful in creating a vacation experience that is unparalleled—and a success story that is unprecedented.

CHOOSE HEALTH OR ELSE

Another highly effective Window 1 leader is a public-sector figure, former Surgeon General C. Everett Koop. Koop was by many accounts the first person to transform the position of surgeon general from that of a figurehead political appointee, to one of an authoritative proponent of public health. He did it by using a distinctively Style 1 approach.

Not one to mince words, Koop tackled every major health issue in the country from AIDS to condoms to smoking in public places—and did so by issuing directives and dictums about what was and what was not acceptable in no uncertain terms. Perhaps more than anyone in the public eye in recent years, Koop maintained both a public and private persona that exemplified a *directing* approach to leadership. Whether talking to millions of people over the television airwaves or one-to-one in an intimate encounter, Koop's message—and his approach to conveying that message—was the same: Do everything in your power to influence people to change their health habits.

Consider the image of a Style 1 leader conveyed in this news magazine article (Winn 1988, p. 26): "One fateful evening last spring Frances Epstein, a dressmaker in Riverdale, N.Y., lit a cigarette, flicked on her TV and found herself face to face with C. Everett Koop, Surgeon General of the United States. Dressed in a dark blue military uniform, bearded, huge, unsmiling, looking for the life of him like a vengeful biblical patriarch, the 71-year old top doctor of the nation looked directly at Frances Epstein in Riverdale and asked, 'Why do people continue to smoke despite the known health hazards?'

"Frances inhaled deeply. She had been asking herself that question for years. 'The answer,' the surgeon general said, 'is that cigarettes are addicting.' Moreover, he continued, standing before a poster board display of nicotine absorption in the rat brain, speaking portentously into a messy ganglia of microphones connected to a phalanx of television cameras, 'the pharmacological and behavioral processes that determine tobacco addiction are similar to those that determine addiction to drugs such as heroin and cocaine.'

"Heroin and cocaine! That did it. Frances, a longtime pack-a-day smoker, threw away her last pack of Dunhills and quit. It was not the first time. This time she hoped it was forever."

Perhaps what's most striking about Koop's Style 1 approach is his total commitment to influencing people in both his public and private life. Consider this exchange reported in an article in *U.S. News and World Report* (Lynn 1988) between Koop and a cigarette smoking train conductor he encountered: "'I tried quitting,' says the man, 'gained 40 pounds.'

"'Then quit again,' says Koop, drilling him with a steely look.

"'Nothing works,' says the conductor, adding that his wife hates his smoking. Wordlessly Koop signs an autograph to the man's wife: 'To Kathy,' he writes, 'Keep after Hank to quit.'"

CONTROLLING THE GAP

At a time when the retail clothing industry is experiencing tremendous losses, Mickey Drexler, president of the enormously successful retail chain, The Gap, exemplifies the power a Window 1 leader can wield—if he or she is right. Like all successful Style 1 leaders, Drexler has a compelling vision that drives every aspect that contributes to his company's staggering success—and it *is* staggering. In the fiscal year ending January 1991, a period in which many retail clothing chains recorded record losses, The Gap and its offshoots (GapKids and Banana Republic) showed increases in earnings near 30 percent over the past year and increases were expected to be even greater than they have been in the past three years (with an average growth of 43 percent). Part of Drexler's vision was to create a network of stores that provided consistent products of good style, good quality, and good value, a network of stores that would be appealing to many markets including children, teenagers, young adults, and baby boomers. What Drexler did to create a corporate culture where consistency ruled was to focus on two principles: simplicity and control.

Consider this description of Drexler's actions soon after his taking charge of The Gap: " . . . Drexler handed out signs with a single word in white letters on gray background: Simplify. He meant not just the clothes, but the whole way The Gap does business. He got rid of executives who relied on complicated quantitative research. Instead, he hired people who understood his approach of quickly testing his fashion intuition in new products. . . ." (Mitchell 1992).

Drexler's penchant for maintaining consistency through control can be seen throughout his organization, from the way the clothes are manufactured, to the way the stores are managed. ". . . the company has 200 quality-control inspectors working inside factories in 40 countries to make sure specifications are met right from the start. Because The Gap designs its own clothes, chooses its own materials, and monitors manufacturing so closely, it can keep quality high and costs low" (Mitchell 1992) While this highly systematic, methodical approach ensures consistency of product, it's the way the stores are managed that assures the consistency of service that completes the loop.

"The tight control extends to the stores themselves. There's no more room for creative expression at a Gap store than there is at McDonald's—maybe less. Gap merchandise goes through a major shift about every two months, and store managers receive a book of detailed instructions that tell them exactly what clothes go where" (Mitchell 1992).

Perhaps the most telling view of Drexler's Style 1 approach can be seen by looking at his day-to-day activities: "Drexler once oversaw every major design decision, and he still keeps a close watch. He visits stores constantly and rarely comes to rest at headquarters. A typical day at The Gap's San Francisco office finds Drexler roaming the halls, popping in unexpectedly on staffers to praise or criticize dozens of projects in design, advertising, and merchandising. . . . Insiders say newcomers either adapt easily to Drexler's vision—or they quickly walk" (Mitchell 1992).

It is clear to all who work with and for him that this high control leader is determined to maintain the control that has been so good to him and his company: "Drexler's opinionated style comes through at a meeting in San Francisco. About 30 merchandisers are showing the proposed fall collection for GapKids to Drexler. The woman in charge of jackets holds up a hooded design cut to look very puffy. Everyone holds a collective breath while Drexler eyes the jacket: 'I hate it,' he says." The design is killed.

As with any Style 1 approach, the danger (more on this later) for Drexler and The Gap is that as the company grows, the ability and benefits of maintaining such tight control come into question. Signs that the efficacy of Drexler's *directing* approach may be beginning to wear thin are evidenced by merchandiser Kay Vewrmeulen, who recently left the company: "'The Gap," she says, "has gotten so big you have to go through several people to get anything done. You have to sign off with this department and that department" (Mitchell 1992). Whether Drexler's unquestioningly successful approach so far will continue to serve him well, or whether he'll have to become more inclusive and less proprietary remains to be seen. His ability to make the best decisions about what to control and what to defer to others may very well determine the future success of his company.

LOSING CONTROL

The view of the ineffective leader through Window 1 is equally striking. Consider the case of the 1992 visit of the big three car dealers to Japan. Anyone who understands the nature of influence at all would wonder at the motives of Lee Iacocca when he conveyed to the Japanese that they'd better hear our message or else. In attempting to get the Japanese to buy more American cars, Iacocca chose to be directive at a time when what was needed was more of a collaborative approach. Consequently he came across as *dominating* and was totally ineffective.

The ripples of that failed trip continue to be felt throughout the American automotive industry. Iacocca is an interesting case because he has long projected himself as the consummate team player, working with others, asking for a lot of input, building consensus, and generating team spirit. Yet those who work closely with him describe him as *dominating*. He loves to be in the limelight, they suggest, and say that with Lee it's "his way or no way."

A far more extreme example of a *dominating* Style 1 leader is Iraqi dictator Saddam Hussein. There is little doubt that Hussein's intent is to be in total control of every aspect of his dictatorship. He controls the military, the economy, the educational system, and every cultural aspect imaginable. He aggressively tells Iraqis, Kurds, Kuwaitis, and everyone else in the world exactly what he wants and threatens consequences if people don't do what he wants. His decision-making style leaves no room for input from others, his communication is exclusively downward, and his reward system clearly emphasizes compliance: You do it his way or you get shot.

WINDOW 1 BEHAVIORS

If you analyze the above situations with regard to the key leadership behaviors—decision making, communication, and recognition—you can begin to see how The L4 System works.

In the case of Ray Kroc, he was an effective Style 1 leader because he retained decision-making power in a situation where the most important goal was delivery of a consistent product. He relied primarily on downward communication rather than two-way since the realization of his vision was what was important to him. And he built a reward system based on employees' abilities to meet his specs, or follow his rules. Disney employed many of the same strategies. The vision of delivering a consistently predictable experience kept the decision making in his hands, conveying that vision led to almost exclusively downward communication, and rewards were given for adhering to designated roles.

Koop's Style 1 approach was based in the belief—and often the reality—that he had exclusive access to information regarding public-health concerns, and that the most effective use of this information power coupled with his ability to get his message heard through mass media created conditions that were best served by a directive approach.

In the case of Iacocca's trip to Japan a very different picture unfolds. Iacocca was in a position to influence a collaborative alliance between the Americans and the Japanese—a task requiring a great deal of give and take in which there was a sharing of ideas and problem solving. Instead of taking an open position and engaging in joint decision making, Iacocca presented an ultimatum, a mistake unless you're ready and able to deliver on it—which he clearly wasn't. Instead of opening two-way channels of communication he spoke down to his Japanese counterparts, thus diminishing the chances of any serious dialogue occuring. Since Iacocca had no real power to reward or recognize, this factor did not come into play in a significant way. However, while he certainly didn't have the power to reward in a directive leadership role, had he engaged in a more cooperative approach he could have recognized any successful joint problem solving and rewarded his Japanese counterparts with kind words of appreciation—something highly valued in Japanese culture. Instead, he chose a heavy hand which resulted in furthering the gulf between these two superpowers and lessening the chances of any true collaboration.

Hussein's *dominating* Style 1 behavior has certainly not served him well. While he is still in power, he now rules over a country in shambles. His unilateral decision making has caused his people untold suffering. His inability to take and use input from others has caused him humiliation and disgrace. And his heavy hand has alienated him from his people to the point where he is in constant fear for his own life.

THE WINDOW 1 LEADER: DIRECTOR OR DOMINATOR

As you can see, the success of the Style 1 leader lies in the ability to make decisions unilaterally, communicate those decisions unequivocally, and reward behaviors that are in line with the leader's wishes directly. These leaders tend to be focused on their own goals and are not particularly concerned with the attitudes or developmental needs of followers (except of course in the case of Koop, whose life's work has been the welfare of followers). They tend to maintain a high degree of control around decision making and task management. They rely on motivating subordinates by imposing punishments and penalties for lack of compliance, and reward followers primarily for following their directions.

The Style 1 leader's top priority tends to be to get the job done as he or she believes it should be done. They are most effective when they have a vision that they want others to implement, and they are willing to take full responsibility for the results of that implementation. Some advantages to this approach are that the leader has control over completion of the task, knows precisely how things are going, and can readily identify and respond to problems as they emerge. Some disadvantages to this approach are that the leader has to be highly involved at all times, limits problem-solving capacity to his or her own abilities, and carries the burden of success or failure on his or her shoulders exclusively.

ERRORS IN AEROSPACE—A CASE STUDY

Herb was the manager of a small plastics factory. One of his key accounts was with an aerospace company for whom his company manufactured plastic parts for jet engines. Over several weeks Herb received an inordinate amount of returns on a particular part cited by the customer company as not meeting specifications. Since the part was to be used for a precise instrument, it was essential that it meet exact specifications.

Herb's usual approach with his employees was to present them with clear instructions and leave them alone. He knew the job had potential to be boring, so he encouraged them to be creative in developing ways to do the work. As long as quality work was getting done on time he didn't mind that employees frequently socialized while operating their mold machines. To motivate people he would keep track of production output and occasionally announce how the shop was doing. If overall production was low, he would reprimand the group and suggest they find new ways of operating; if production was high, he would praise them and urge them to keep up the good work. As long as the work was getting done, Herb felt his hands-off approach worked well.

As it became clear to Herb that problems were emerging with the quality of the work being produced, he let the workers know and engaged in conversations with them about what they might do to change. After a few days of observation, Herb grew increasingly concerned that the problem was not "fixing itself." In an attempt to remedy the problem without getting heavy-handed, Herb started making suggestions as to how to improve the quality of the work. He was surprised when he found the workers resistant to changing their patterns and became increasingly concerned as the delivery date for the new shipment rapidly approached.

Herb realized that in order to remedy the problem he needed to take increased control of the situation. He knew he could not afford to spend much time on the problem since competition was fierce and his contract could be jeopardized if there were any other delays. Thus, time was of the essence. Herb decided to get tough and be a directive leader. He quickly let his people know that under no circumstances would he continue to tolerate the production of substandard parts. He announced that there would be no more distracting conversation on the shop floor and began frequent inspections of parts to insure quality. As soon as he began seeing improvements in quality, he voiced his approval to those responsible. For the next several days the tone of the plant was conspicuously sober. Any employees not producing high-quality, high-yield products were carefully scrutinized and monitored. At the end of a four-day period, the job was completed, and the parts were delivered and accepted. Eventually the plant returned to its pre-crisis state. However, the message was clear that poor-quality work would not be tolerated. Herb went back to his less controlling style but knew that if production problems arose again he would not hesitate to return to his *directing* appoach. His crew knew it, too.

As seen in the above examples, the *directing* style can be quite effective when used with the right people in the right situations at the right time—and can be quite powerful and rewarding as evidenced by the success of a Ray Kroc, Walt Disney, or Mickey Drexler. Style 1 also carries with it great potential for influence as evidenced by the impact of Surgeon General Koop on the nation's health consciousness, and entrepreneur Disney on the entertainment industry.

The key to Style 1's effective use is having a clear vision of what it is you're trying to accomplish, a keen understanding of how you are going to accomplish it, and an unwavering commitment to achieving your desired results.

REFERENCES

Allman, T. D. *Miami: City of the Future.* New York: Atlantic Monthly Press, 1987, 259–267.

Croce, Paul Jerome. "A Clean and Separate Place: Walt Disney in Person and Production." *Journal of Popular Culture*, 25, no. 3 (Winter 1991): 91–103.

Labich, Kenneth. "The Seven Keys to Business Leadership." *Fortune*, 24 October 1988, 58–66.

Mitchell, Rusell, "Inside the Gap." *Business Week*, 9 March 1992, 58–64.

Moser, Penny. "The McDonald's Mystique." *Fortune*, 4 July 1988, 113–114.

Ola, Per, and D'Aulaire, Emily. "Sixty Billion Burgers and Counting." *Reader's Digest*, September 1987, 39–44.

Rosellini, Lynn. "Rebel with a Cause, Koop." *U.S. News and World Report*, 30 May 1988, 55–63.

Winn, Marie. "The Legacy of Dr. Koop." *The New York Times Magazine*, 9 October, 1988, 26.

Chapter **4**

Window 2: The Leader as Problem Solver

With every company challenging itself to improve quality, straining to become more customer-oriented, and trying to find better ways to involve employees in top level decisions, problem solving is a critical tool for every leader. The view through Window 2 will show you a number of effective leaders who are good at *problem solving*, skilled at managing the balance between openness and decisiveness.

Window 2 will also show you some leaders who rely too heavily on problem solving and therefore come across as *overinvolving* themselves or others in the decision-making process. As you will recall from the discussion of the *problem-solving* style in chapter 2, a key aspect of this leadership style is that the leader retains control of the decision-making process, as distinguished from the Style 3 approach where the leader supports followers with their decision making in a way that develops their future problem-solving capability.

As you read this chapter, think about the choices you made on the cases in chapter 1. Is Window 2 the one you like the best?

MANAGING CRISIS THROUGH PROBLEM SOLVING

Jim Burke, the former CEO of Johnson and Johnson, is a good example of someone who effectively employed the *problem-solving* style of Window 2 during the Tylenol scare of the early 1980s. When traces of cyanide started showing up in bottles of

Tylenol, leading to some deaths and more near deaths, most people thought that the life span of the popular painkiller was coming to an abrupt end.

What prevented Tylenol's seemingly inevitable demise was Burke's leadership in handling the crisis. Rather than merely relying on his own instincts in what was a very complex matter, Burke called on the combined brainpower of everyone around him and solicited their input on handling the problem. According to *Fortune* magazine (Labich 1988) Burke utilized his staff's expertise to solve the problem. "Relying on his staff's sometimes noisy advice, Burke seized the initiative when seven people died from cyanide-laced Tylenol capsules in 1982. He recalled some 30 million Tylenol packages and sent out new ones with elaborate safety seals.

"When a poisoner struck again in 1986, Burke pulled all capsules off the market and sold the pain reliever only in tamper-resistant tablet and caplet form. . . . [H]e stayed cool in numerous media appearances in which he explained his efforts and soothed anxious consumers. All the while he was entertaining often sharply differing opinions about what he should do, and he believes he made better decisions as a result. Recalls Burke, 'People yelled and said what they thought and I synthesized it all. We had a tremendous fight over whether we should go on "60 Minutes."' Burke allowed CBS cameras into crucial strategy sessions, winning further public support of his efforts to contain the crisis."

What the above shows is a typical Style 2 approach in which a leader, after considering all alternatives, made an informed decision that led to surprising results and the resurgence of the product as a viable, safe choice for pain relief. This effective *problem-solving* approach should not be underestimated since, as the above example illustrates, it can mean the difference between success and failure. At the time of the Tylenol scare, most industry analysts were proclaiming the death of Tylenol as a pain-relief product. What Burke was able to do by inviting ideas from all his staff, no matter how divergent, was to make decisions that led to unlikely success and averted almost certain failure.

BUILDING ALLIANCES—THE LEADERSHIP OF POLITICS

George Bush provides another good example of a Window 2 leader, as long as you focus on his presidency in terms of foreign policy. If you focus on domestic policy, his view was not through Window 2 at all, but you will read more about that side of Bush in the next two chapters.

Bush's greatest successes as president came in the international arena. Early in his administration, he pushed for the invasion of Panama to capture accused drug lord Manuel Noriega. Using a *problem-solving* approach, Bush gathered the input of knowledgeable military advisors, ignored the political counsel of those who said that such an invasion would violate the international sovereignty of Panama, and went forward with the plan. This gathering of expert opinion and subsequent decision making based on that informed opinion are hallmarks of the *problem-solving* leadership approach.

Some accused him of grandstanding in order to overcome the "wimp" image that had haunted him during the campaign against Michael Dukakis. Others accused him of trying to silence Noriega, who supposedly knew too much about Bush from his CIA days. But most people saw Bush as a strong leader who was willing to use force in pursuit of his agenda which, in this case, was the "interdiction" of large-scale drug trafficking from Latin America. In fact, the biggest criticism of the Panama invasion was that Bush should have been more decisive when he got input that Panamanians were holding Noriega. Better use of *problem solving* might have saved lives and helped the Panamanians at the same time.

Later, when Saddam Hussein became a threat in the Middle East, Bush seemed to have strengthened his ability to use Style 2. Before and during Operation Desert Storm, Bush was masterful in his ability to build a strong coalition with other world leaders, including several from the Middle East whose countries had been in conflict for centuries. He also used the United Nations skillfully by persuading that international body to pass the resolutions which he fully intended to enforce. He was also very adept in his timing as he picked the right moment to bring the issue before the United States Congress.

Throughout the conflict with Iraq, Bush spent incredible amounts of time in ongoing communication with other world leaders, in part to keep the coalition alive, but also to get continuous input to his decision-making. He also listened closely to advice from the military. Most important, the perception of George Bush throughout Desert Storm was that he was a leader who could forge solid alliances, would listen to input from all key people, and still be the one in charge. Bush was a perfect

Style 2 leader in this situation, and his popularity in the polls was higher that any president had received since the polling game began.

Ironically, Bush's powerful use of Style 2 in the foreign policy arena actually hurt him a year later when he was running for reelection. We will say more about that in the next chapter.

FROM WAFFLER TO WINNER

In 1992, the successful presidential campaign of Bill Clinton illustrated how a Style 2 strategy can work to combat accusations of ineffectiveness. Perhaps the biggest threat to Clinton's successful race to the White House was the accusation by the Bush campaign that Clinton was a waffler—indecisive and *overaccommodating*. Ads showing two faces of Bill Clinton filled the airwaves, and the suggestion by Bush that Clinton could not be trusted seemed to be cutting into Clinton's lead just weeks before the election. Indications were that the Bush campaign had struck a nerve, that perhaps Clinton's Achilles heel was his inability to be decisive and his tendency to be overly compromising (more on this later).

What Clinton managed to do in response to this threat was to shift from what by most observers' accounts had been an overly solicitous, crowd-pleasing approach, laden with generalities about change, to a very focused, specific deliniation of what he would do if he were president. Concrete, well-thought-out directives about his plans to overhaul the health-care system, rebuild the nation's infrastructure of bridges and highways, and revitalize the government's approach to employment and training led to a dramatic shift in perception that Clinton was not just a smooth talker, but an active *problem solver* with a plan.

Many political observers believe that it was Clinton's attention to the issues both during and after the debates, while Bush continued to focus on the nebulous issue of character, that led to the Democrat's victory.

Most important, Clinton was able to keep the focus on the domestic agenda or, in the words on his campaign wall, "It's the Economy, stupid!" Knowing that Bush's strength was in foreign policy and that his weakness was the sluggish economy, Clinton had to convince the voters that he was the leader to turn the economy around. Whether or not he really convinced people is not clear. Many people expressed serious doubts about all of the 1992 candidates right up to Election Day.

What Clinton was definitely able to do was convince the masses that he would be more likely to use Style 2 on economic issues than George Bush. His message was that he would listen to a much broader constituency than Bush had been paying attention to, and that he would be much more decisive in responding to their concerns. Then he specifically defined his constituents as everyone making less than $200,000 which, of course, included most people who could vote. To demonstrate his willingness to be decisive on their behalf, he promised to raise taxes on that same upper-income group which had profited during the Reagan–Bush years. He also promised not to allow taxes to be raised on the people making less than $200,000.

By election time, it was almost irrelevant whether his policies would work or not. As a leader, he had dodged a bullet by not letting Bush's accusations stick him with the *overaccommodating* waffler label. He was able to convince the public that he would listen to them, then make the tough decisions as the Style 2 leader of the downtrodden masses.

Defining himself as a *problem solver* has been a struggle for Clinton from the outset of his presidency. His first stake in the ground after his inauguration was about gays in the military, an issue where his attempts to please everyone made him appear extremely *overaccommodating*. Another one of his earliest actions was his economic summit which looked like rampant *overinvolving* to most of the public and the press. Before his first year was half over, he looked so wishy-washy that he added David Gergen, a former Reagan advisor, to his staff specifically to improve his image. Gergen's job was to help Clinton appear more decisive. Within a few weeks, *Newsweek* ran a lengthy article about a typical presidential day in which Clinton came across as open but very decisive. We were reassured that he always had been solving problems, but we didn't know it. A few weeks after that, Clinton used all of his political muscle to get his deficit-reduction budget passed and again was back in the driver's seat.

Is this image or reality? That may be the core issue that determines his effectiveness.

EQUAL TIME FOR THE INDEPENDENT CANDIDATE

While we are on the subject of the 1992 presidential election, it is only fair to give a little press to Ross Perot. After much deliberation, we have decided to include his profile here in the Window 2. We put him here because we believe that if you were to ask Ross Perot about his leadership style, he would probably describe himself as a *problem solver*. What was his answer to almost any tough problem facing the nation? His plan was to assemble some of the best experts on that particular subject, listen to their opinions, then make the tough decisions. His biggest criticism of traditional Washington decision making was the endless debates and horse trading. He often said during the campaign, "We don't need any more plans running around Washington. They've got plans for everything. What we need is someone who will pick the best plan and then just do it."

We also decided to include Perot in Window 2 because no one should forget that he is one of the best businessmen in the country. His ability to succeed at IBM, then build EDS from scratch, then start over again with Perot Systems is clear evidence that he is able to take input from key people and make good decisions. There are also many people who have worked with him who tell stories of bringing proposals to the boss and getting his approval.

The reason that we deliberated about where to put Perot is that, even though he sees himself as a good listener who hears other people out before he moves ahead, not everyone sees him that way. Yes, he listens. But he processes the information so rapidly and responds so quickly that he doesn't appear to reflect on other people's perspectives. Then, when he responds, his answers are so full of detail that he can overwhelm others with his point of view, facts, and figures. He comes across as a salesman (which he once was) who listens just enough to get his foot in the door, then launches into his pitch.

In business, this has probably served him well and may even enhance his reputation as a *problem solver*. But, in the political arena, many observers saw Perot as more of a Window 1 leader. His supporters saw him as the *directing* type, a strong-willed and decisive leader who makes up his mind and then charges full steam ahead. He was their candidate to clean up the gridlock in American politics. If anyone could break the old system, Perot could.

His detractors also saw him as Style 1, but more on the *dominating* side. They told tales of his controlling ways of managing his companies, and tried to make him out to be a paranoid megalomaniac. Being the strong and decisive person he is, Perot gave them plenty of evidence to work with. He often came across as *dominating* discussions by talking on at great length and then crossly reprimanding reporters who would ask a focusing question. He would chide them, "Are you gonna let me finish?" His firing of campaign advisors also fed this perception, as did his seemingly unilateral decisions to get into and out of and into the race again.

When it came to the election, many people still saw him as the guy to shake up the establishment and tackle the deficit. Most voters saw him as overly focused on one issue and too much of a loner to be effective under the intense public scrutiny of the presidency.

WHEN HANDS ON IS OFF BASE

Window 2 leaders are not always effective. Sometimes they operate out of Window 2 too much, leading to accusations of *overinvolving*.

An historical case in point was President Jimmy Carter, whose grasp of the details turned his *problem solving* strength into an *overinvolving* handicap. Carter was a voracious reader who would absorb so much information that people used to joke that he knew who was using the White House's tennis court at any hour of any day. To many, Carter's downfall as a president was caused by his inablility to know when to allow others to take the reins.

The most glaring example of this was the abortive attempt to rescue American hostages who were being held captive in Iran. After that mission failed, Carter himself said that he should have listened better to the military advisors. Instead, by his own admission, he got too involved and made a lousy decision.

Imagine what would have happened if that mission had succeeded. Carter probably would have been a hero and most likely would have been reelected. So, this is a strong example of how a leadership style can impact one person's career as well as world history.

Ironically, Carter's *problem solving* style, which he demonstrated superbly during the Camp David meetings between Anwar Sadat and Menachem Begin, has served him well in his postpresidency as a hands-on leader of the low-income housing organization, Habitat for Humanity. In this situation, his willingness to get his hands dirty and to personally involve himself in the details has inspired many others to participate in solving one of the nation's most pressing problems.

THE BEST OF TIMES AND THE WORST OF TIMES

Another example of a politician who fits the profile of a Window 2 leader is John F. Kennedy. Even when he was in office, long before he had been elevated to mythical status, Kennedy was admired as a leader who surrounded himself with the best and the brightest advisors. He was known for being able to absorb tremendous amounts of information and was certainly willing to be decisive in pursuit of his agenda. He is still highly regarded for the commitment he made to the National Aeronautics and Space Administration (NASA), a commitment which included his compelling vision to put a man on the moon. His handling of the Cuban missile crisis is still reviewed as the textbook for showdown diplomacy.

Kennedy also provides a good demonstration of how a leader's greatest strength can also become a liability. The most glaring example of his ineffective use of Style 2 was the *overinvolving* that precipitated the Bay of Pigs fiasco. A classic case of ineffective decision making, the Kennedy team's process was the subject of a chapter in *Victims of Groupthink* by Irving Janis.

Janis' book paints a vivid scenario of Kennedy as both an ineffective Style 2 leader and then (a year-and-a-half later), as an effective Style 2 leader and provides us with a compelling portrait of that style in action.

First, some background. In January of 1961 President Kennedy and his leading advisors were briefed by the CIA and the Joint Chiefs of Staff about a plan hatched by the Eisenhower adminstration to overthrow the Cuban government of Fidel Castro by secretly placing a small brigade of Cuban exiles on a beachhead in Cuba. According to Janis, Kennedy and his top advisors assumed that "use of the exile brigade would make possible the toppling of Castro without actual aggression by the United States." (Janis 1967, p.15)

The plan proved to be what historians describe as a perfect failure. In examining the leadership approach in this situation we can see, with the help of Janis' analysis of the decision-making process, a classic case of *overinvolving*. According to Janis, group norms had developed within Kennedy's inner circle of advisors around the belief that they were, in fact, the best and brightest. Janis refers to mindguards and an aura of invincibility as two of the traps that cloaked their discussions.

Discussing issues without full debate is another symptom of *overinvolving*. Janis writes, "Whatever may have been the political or psychological reasons that motivated President Kennedy to give preferential treatment to the two CIA chiefs Dulles and Bissell, he evidently succeeded in conveying to the other members of the core group, perhaps without realizing it, that the CIA's baby should not be treated harshly. His way of handling the meetings, particularly his adherence to the extraordinary procedure of allowing every critical comment to be immediately refuted by Dulles or Bissell without allowing the group a chance to mull over the potential objections, probably set the norm of going easy on the plan. . . . Evidently, the members of the group adopted this norm and sought concurrence . . . without looking too closely into the basic arguments for such a plan and without debating the questionable estimates sufficiently to discover that the whole idea ought to be thrown out." (Janis 1967, p. 48)

More specifically, at one point in the debate, in an attempt to resolve the crisis Kennedy pressured his cabinet to comply with his views on what should be done. As a result of this pressure, decisions were made that led to near disaster.

When interviewed after the fact, several of Kennedy's chief aides said that they felt uncomfortable stating their true opinions because the charismatic, influential Kennedy was so adamant about what should be done. In this case the retention of control that is characteristic of the Style 2 leader clearly led to his *overinvolvement* and lack of ability to tap the formidable talents of his staff.

Interestingly, it seems in retrospect that Kennedy learned from his mistakes. A year-and-a-half after the Bay of Pigs incident, the Kennedy administration was faced with another challenge, the Cuban missile crisis. In this instance Kennedy once again acted as a Style 2 leader; however, this time he was an effective *problem solver*.

Again, some background. One of the outcomes of the Bay of Pigs fiasco was the establishment of a deal between the Soviet Union and Cuba to set up nuclear bomb installations on Cuba targeted at the U.S., establishing Cuba as a powerful military satellite of the Soviet Union. The result of this action was the Cuban missile crisis, considered by most historians to be the greatest risk to mankind since the advent of nuclear weapons. The crisis spanned a period of thirteen days during October 1962. Speculation had been growing that in spite of Cuba's insistence that it was doing nothing more than reinforcing its own air defense system, it was in fact building an arsenal of deadly missiles aimed at the U.S. On October 16, 1962, that speculation was confirmed by photos taken by a U-2 plane over Cuba and the crisis began.

JFK's initial response to the threat was to launch air attacks against Cuba, but rather than go with his own inclination he decided, given the stakes involved, to once again call on his panel of experts. However, this time he employed the effective *problem solving* approach of Style 2. Rather than ride herd over his cabinet and risk stifling their problem solving capacity as he did in the previous incident, Kennedy intentionally took actions designed to lead toward the best possible solution.

Consider the following analysis of Kennedy's actions, ". . . instead of inducing the group at the opening session to focus on the air-strike action he favored, President Kennedy emphasized the need to canvas alternatives. His message was that 'action was imperative' but he wanted the members to devote themselves to making a 'prompt and intensive survey of the dangers and all possible courses of action.'" (Janis, p. 149–50) In addition, reports Janis, he called on outsiders to get their opinions as well, such as U.N. representative Adlai Stevenson, representatives from other government agencies, and distinguished outsiders. So committed was Kennedy to avoid contaminating the *problem solving* process with his own *overinvolvement*, that he even absented himself from cabinet meetings for two days, leaving instructions that communicated his desire to hear all the divergent views and recommendations from those most capable of helping him solve the problem. Many observers believe that the actions taken as a result of this strategy led to the aversion of a major military confrontation.

In this case, Kennedy found a way to remain in control, and be seen as the final decision maker, while encouraging his team members to give him their most complete and uncensored advice.

FROM DUKE TO DISASTER

A more recent example on the political front is the fascinating case of Michael Dukakis, the former Massachusetts governor and failed presidential candidate. Dukakis was another Style 2 leader who used that style to both advantage and disadvantage.

As governor, Dukakis used a classic Style 2 approach. He surrounded himself with knowledgeable advisors, yet always maintained control over the decision-making process. For example, early in his second term as governor, Dukakis decided to take on the welfare system to remedy previously failed programs. He successfully launched the Employment and Training Choices Program for welfare recipients. To do so, he retained the help of outside social service advocates—people who were potential opponents of the program—and asked them to work with him to draw up the plans for the new program. This *problem-solving* strategy worked extremely well, and Dukakis was able to demonstrate results—and get extremely good press along the way.

Many political analysts suggest that this same style of involving experts but retaining control is the very thing that caused his undoing as a presidential candidate. While the Republicans played hardball using every tactic they could find, Dukakis refused to listen to his advisors who urged him to fight back, and instead followed his own instincts to "walk the high road." Many believe that his *overinvolving* himself in this strategic decision made his campaign fail miserably.

INTERNATIONAL WINDOW 2

Sometimes the very nature of the political arena demands a certain style of leadership. Consider the case of Israel. Whether or not you agree with its policies, a study of its political structure can be enlightening in terms of the way that Style 2 leadership can work.

From David Ben-Gurion to Golda Meir to Yitzhak Rabin, Style 2 emerges as the predominant style in this wide-open democracy. The Israeli Knesset probably has more open and free-wheeling debates than any other parliamentary body in the world. Israeli leaders tend to be strong-willed and outspoken. They represent a multitude of small special-interest parties which must be brought into a coalition for any of the major parties to form a government. All the successful leaders have been able to take input from a wide range of sources who often hold differing points of view and formulate policy that the various splinter groups are willing to follow.

In Israeli politics any leader who is not a good *problem solver* would have a very difficult time surviving. In fact, Menachem Begin and his successor Yitzhak Shamir were both strong Style 2 leaders, but they chose to take input from different groups of constituents than their rivals in the Labor Party had done. In time, Shamir's steadfast refusal to accept input from the forces seeking a resolution of hostilities with the Palestinians led to the perception that he and his party were not focused on *problem solving*. As a result the Labor Party and its leader Yitzhak Rabin were returned to power with a platform based on a *problem solving* style that would include input from the Palestinians. The key to their continued power will be the extent to which they demonstrate the ability to listen to all points of view and forge a dominant coalition.

WINDOW 2 SOVIET STYLE

While we're on the subject of international politics and culturally acceptable leadership styles, the former Soviet Union offers an interesting leadership story. From Lenin to Stalin to Kruschev to Brezhnev to Kosygin and Andropov, the Soviet Union experienced a series of very strong Style 1 leaders who were every bit as *dominating* and ruthless as the czars whom they replaced.

Finally, when Mikhail Gorbachev came into power, a truly different breed of leader had come to the top of the Communist party. Gorbachev was far more willing to listen to input from within his country and from foreign sources. He was far more tolerant of open dissent and candid debate than any of his previous leaders.

Like many leaders, his strength also became his undoing in the long run. He also provides a good illustration of what can happen when a leader says one thing and does another.

When Gorbachev began negotiating with the Eastern European satellites about a new relationship with the Soviet Union, he began the discussions using Style 2. He wanted to listen to their concerns but made it clear that he (and the Soviet Union) were in control of the final decisions. However, as the negotiations proceeded, he did more listening than controlling. As a result, he allowed the satellite leaders to make their own decisions with his advice and counsel. To the Western media, he came across as Style 3, *developing*, and was hailed as a new age leader who was willing to listen. To his constituents, he came across as Style 3, *overaccommodating*, and was seen as open, democratic, but potentially weak.

Shortly thereafter, the Baltic states began their own negotiations to restructure their relations with the Union. In this situation, Gorbachev was inconsistent again. He began the negotiations with Style 3, saying that he would listen, be supportive, and work with them to find a mutually agreeable solution. In practice, however, he drew back to Style 2 by making decisions which did not reflect the input from the Baltic leaders. The hard-liners praised him for listening to their input and saw him as *problem solving* while the Baltic states accused him of *overinvolving*; going through the motions with them while accepting too much input from the hard-liners.

Beyond these foreign-policy decisions, Gorbachev's gravest problem was the Soviet Union's staggering economy. Here, too, he walked an ambiguous line. His main style was Style 3. He wanted open debate and believed that good solutions would emerge from listening. On the other hand, he followed a strong tradition of strong-willed Style 1 leaders who listen to no one. The masses wanted input, but they also wanted strength at the top. The politicians also required a strongman at the helm. As a result, Gorbachev had to use more Style 2 than he wanted and came across as an ambivalent leader in the process.

With his style changes, the people turned to the streets, ousted their local Communist party officials and turned to the outside world for recognition as independent states. As Gorbachev attempted to retain power, the union crumbled beneath him.

It is interesting that the leader who followed Gorbachev, Boris Yeltsin, actually is more of a Style 2 leader than Gorbachev, even though his political views are more liberal.

Yeltsin is a very strong anticommunist and a very strong advocate of free-market forces, who was quite willing to dismantle the Soviet Union to get a fresh start with those countries who truly wanted to be in a union by choice not force. As a leader, because he was much stronger and willing to be more decisive, he actually was able to gain more respect within the Soviet Union. His use of Style 2 was a smoother transition from the centuries of *dominating* leadership to an acceptable level of *problem solving*.

Thinking of the Soviet Union as a huge organization, the gradual transition from Style 1 to Style 2 left the country with the structure and security that large groups of people seem to require. Yeltsin's ability to maintain that control while accepting enough input from the left-wingers and the hard-liners will be his biggest challenge. Russia will move toward more Style 2, but the person at the top may change a few more times before the dust settles.

ENTERTAINING EXPERTS: TWO WOMEN AT THE TOP

While a Window 2 approach can work well in the political arena where both control and access to experts provide a balanced approach that many have utilized, it is also evident at the upper echelon of the entertainment industry. Consider the cases of two dynamic high-profile women at the top—Oprah Winfrey and Madonna.

Both are enormously successful entertainers—and business women—with net revenues in the millions (39 million and 23 million respectively for 1991). And both, it seems, are essentially Style 2 leaders. According to an article in *Working Woman* magazine (Goodman 1991) both women run carefully controlled operations where they retain all the important decision making, utilize a select group of advisors, and reward people for helping them make sound judgments and business decisions.

"In an industry where stars traditionally turn business matters over to others and wealth is measured by how much money isn't bilked each year, Oprah and Madonna are notable for their independence. Each charts her own course and keeps her hand firmly on the corporate tiller, putting in long hours managing her holdings, investments and public image. As businesswomen, they share one important trait: both are control freaks."

However, since they are both entertainers first and business moguls second, each seems to recognize the need for expert advice. For example, Madonna has a stable of the best business people helping her manage her affairs—Bert Padell, the leading music industry accountant, Paul Schindler, a well-known entertainment attorney, and Liz Rosenberg, considered one of Warner Brothers' top publicists. In true Style 2 form, Madonna uses these independent experts in accounting, law, and publicity to help her make decisions, rather than hire a group of lesser talent that she could more readily direct. This strategy allows her to maintain a hands-on approach while still benefitting from the wisdom and experience of others.

According to a *Forbes* magazine cover story (Schifrin 1990), "She has a very strong hand in dealmaking and financing of her enterprises. Nothing gets done without her participation," says Jeffrey Katzenberg, the chairman of Disney Studios, who dealt with her during the production of *Dick Tracy*. He adds that she uses her lawyers, accountants, and advisers "as aides in making her own judgment, as opposed to having them run her life."

Oprah's dynasty uses a similar Style 2 formula for success,

although she relies heavily on one person, Jeffrey Jacobs (one of only two of Winfrey's full-timers). Consider the following from a *Ms.* magazine article on Winfrey (Gillespie 1988). "Winfrey describes Jacobs' presence in her life as a gift. 'He helped me to see that I really could have control and didn't have to be simply a talent.' Jacobs insisted that she be 100 percent in charge of her business. 'It's my job to present research, options, and opinions to her,' he says. 'We discuss them and then she makes the decisions. I work for her and with her,' he adds, 'and because of that, we've built an organization where she knows exactly what's going on at all times. She signs the checks, she makes the decisions. I protect her and look at things from a legal as well as business standpoint, but she understands this organization from top to bottom.'

"With Jacobs' help, Winfrey operates similarly to Madonna, utilizing panels of experts to provide input into her decision making. Says Jacobs, 'I tried to find the best and the brightest people in the financial and banking communities here in Chicago. . . . We all meet periodically and come up with a consensus opinion. Sometimes Oprah sits in the meetings and sometimes— because of her travel schedule—she can't. But she's always presented with the information, and then she makes a decision. So she's really in control of her money.'"

THE STYLE 2 LEADER: PROBLEM SOLVER OR OVERINVOLVER

What the previous examples allude to is the centrality of information gathering and assimilating that is key to the Style 2 leader. Like the Style 1 leader, this type of leader retains control over decision making, but unlike his or her Style 1 counterparts, this leader pays close attention to what others have to say. This style of leadership can be particularly effective in situations where others have access to key information but are not in a position to make the decision.

In a classic study of the difference in effectiveness between a Style 1 leader and a Style 2 leader, industrial psychologists Robert Blake and Jane Mouton tell of a situation which highlights the potential effectiveness of *problem solving* and the potential liabilities of *directing*. The case has to do with a major airline that was experiencing an inordinate amount of "near misses" by their pilots. The airline decided to bring in consultants to train the pilots to be more decisive. After the decisiveness training, airline officials were puzzled by the lack of reduction of near-miss incidents. With the help of the consultants, they came to the realization that they were operating under a false assumption—that the problem *was* one of decisiveness. What they learned after studying these crisis situations was not that the pilots were indecisive, but rather that they were underutilizing the resources in the cockpit. In other words, when faced with a quick but crucial decision, pilots were using a Style 1 approach and making unilateral decisions without consulting the other members of the cockpit crew.

What finally led to a reduction in near misses was training the pilots in how to more effectively gather information from other crew members, synthesize that information, and then make an informed decision. They needed to be better *problem solvers*, not quicker unilateral decision makers.

Like the political leaders discussed earlier, the pilots in this situation had to learn to be better listeners and information processors. The role of the Style 2 leader is to take in as much information as possible, sort it, and act as a result of a full understanding of the parameters of the situation. When this style is used with the right people in the right way it can be a powerful tool for any leader for whom responsibility and control are primary.

What it offers a leader is the opportunity to utilize the knowledge and experience of followers. The advantage of a Style 2 approach is that the leader taps the talents of followers yet still maintains control over the process and the end result. The disadvantage of this approach is that it can result in a time-consuming process in which followers or the leader can be more involved in making decisions that could be more efficiently made in another way.

FROM CRUNCHING NUMBERS TO CREATING QUALITY—A CASE STUDY

Dick had just become the manager of human resources for a large computer company. He had been part of the organization, working in the accounting department. The shift, although unusual, made sense since he had been studying human-resource development in graduate school and had been a loyal employee of the organization.

More important, he was seen as someone who was very decisive and was good at working with other people.

Dick had an advantage moving into his position since he was an insider and had thus seen the operation from that viewpoint. He knew coming in that he was going to make some changes. The human-resource department, in his opinion and in that of his superiors, was "soft." The training they offered was focused primarily on self-development and it seemed apparent that the management of the department emphasized the development of the human-resource staff itself as a priority.

Dick was brought in after the previous manager of human resources was let go amid complaints that there was no consistency in the training coming out of the department, and that there was no way of measuring the effectiveness of the department's work. In management's view, the department had become a "consensual free-for-all" where no one was accountable and no one was at the helm.

Upon arrival in the department, Dick announced to his new staff that all programs currently in progress would be halted immediately, and that he would spend the next month entertaining proposals for training programs. He stressed that he would be making the final decision on whether or not a program would run, but encouraged staff members to present their most creative and innovative ideas for consideration. Programs would be judged, he informed staff, on the extent to which they were measurable and clearly tied to the goals of the organization. Each new proposed program, he stated, would have to pass his rigorous requirements and would have to be viewed by managment as worthwhile and substantive.

For the next four weeks, Dick maintained an open-door policy and spent most of his time listening to and evaluating proposals. He made a point of informing people of the status of their proposals as soon as possible. Those that passed his strict criteria were given the go-ahead to develop their programs, those that didn't were told what was lacking and were encouraged to revamp and resubmit their ideas.

Within a couple of months, Dick's *problem-solving* leadership style had turned the department around. Enrollments in the department's classes were up and there was a general feeling throughout the company that training was now a viable professional development department that added value to employees' repertoire of skills.

As with any shift in leadership, there were some problems. Several trainers, frustrated with the new controls exerted over them, quit, while others complained to top management about the changes. (Since Dick had the sanction of his superiors, this was not a problem). He eventually lost some staff to transfers to other departments, but he was able to replace the people he lost with new staff who were willing to comply with his approach.

In addition, the people who survived were happy to work in a department that could demonstrate measurable results. To not be under the gun as a department, as they were with their previous manager, was quite a relief.

While Dick feels the pressure of shouldering the responsibility for the department's accountability, he is pleased with the company's shifting view of human resources from one of a questionable contributor to one of a department that gets things done. And he is confident that once some of his senior trainers establish their footing, he can begin delegating some of the decision making to them.

REFERENCES

Gillespie, Marcia Ann. "Winfrey Takes All," *Ms.* November 1988, 50–54.

Goodman, Fred. "The Companies They Keep . . . (Madonna and Oprah Winfrey)" *Working Woman*, December 1991, 52–57.

Janis, Irving L. *Victims of Groupthink*, Boston: Houghton Mifflin, 1967.

Labich, Kenneth. "The Seven Keys to Business Leadership," *Fortune*, 24 October 1988, 58–66.

Schifrin, Matthew, with Newcomb, Peter. "A Brain for Sin, and a Bod for Business," *Forbes*, 1 October 1990, 162–166.

Chapter **5**

Window 3: The Leader as Developer

Perhaps the leadership style that receives the most lip service in some of today's more forward-thinking organizations resides in Window 3. Many leaders attempting to meet the demands of an increasingly sophisticated workforce adopt a *developing* approach by listening to people, implementing job rotation strategies, and offering skill-building and other career-enhancement opportunities. This developer approach can be a powerful leadership tool at the right time; however, it can be disastrous if used with the wrong people at the wrong time.

At its worst, it creates a perception that the leader is unwilling to take a stand and is *overaccommodating*, trying to listen to every point of view and to make everybody happy.

As discussed in Chapter 2, the key to understanding the *developing* approach is in looking at the ways communication, recognition, and perhaps most important, decision making play themselves out in this style. In Style 3, the leader is primarily on the receiving end of communication, listening actively and helping the follower sort things out for him- or herself. Recognition is provided to the follower for asking the leader's help in solving his or her own problems. This leads us to the primary distinction between a Style 2, *problem-solving* approach and the Style 3, *developing* approach. The difference is, and it's an important one, that the shift from Style 2 to Style 3 involves a fundamental change in the way decision making gets handled. In Style 3, the leader defers responsibility for solving the problem to the follower and thus becomes someone who assists and supports the other person in solving the problem but does not, as in the case of Style 2, solve the problem him- or herself. Keep this distinction in mind as you read this chapter and it will help you better understand the essence and distinct nature of the *developing* window.

Again, as you read about these people, think about yourself. In what ways do you resemble these Window 3 leaders?

EMPOWERING SELECTIVELY

A good example of a *developing* leader is Warren Buffett, CEO of the holding company Berkshire Hathaway. Buffet is not your typical acquisitions mogul. He only buys companies that he believes in and can get behind; then he gets behind them. What he does as a developer is quite simple. Periodically, he sits down with the top people of a newly acquired company and listens to them—using his experience to help them sort out their own problems. He can be quite pointed in his advice if he needs to be, but his preference is to help others solve their own problems.

In fact, Buffett functions as a kind of consultant to those in his charge. "His operating managers can call him whenever they wish with whatever concerns they have, and none pass up the opportunity to draw on his encylopedic knowledge of the way businesses work" (Loomis 1988).

This accessible but nondomineering approach is the hallmark of a Style 3 leader in that it emphasizes Buffett's preference for supporting people rather than controlling them—and it pays off in many ways to those charged with running Berkshire Hathaway's companies. For example, Ralph Schey, chairman of Buffett's Scott & Fetzer Company, says that working with Buffett has provided him with more autonomy and support than he's experienced anywhere else. "If I couldn't own Scott & Fetzer myself," says Schey, "this is the next best thing" (Loomis 1988).

There can be a downside to this type of hands off approach, suggest some who work for Buffett (although he is almost unanimously praised by all who report to him). Robert Heldman, who runs Fechheimer Brothers, a Cincinnati manufacturer and distributor of uniforms, also under Buffett, reluctantly suggests that there are times when he would like to see Buffett be a little more hands on. " '...he never second-guesses us. Maybe he should do more of that.' Buffett roars upon learning of this complaint:

'Believe me, if they needed second-guessing—which they definitely don't—they'd get it' " (Loomis 1988).

One of the keys to Buffett's success as a high-support leader is that when buying companies he not only looks for quality in the company, but quality in the managment as well. He is often quoted as saying that what he looks for is "wonderful businesses run by wonderful people." According to *Fortune* (Loomis 1988) that was one of the main reasons he bought Fechheimer Brothers, a company smaller than his usual acquisitions. Robert and George Heldman, owners of Fechheimer, according to Buffett, "seemed so completely the kind of managers he looks for— likable, talented, honest, and goal-driven."

Perhaps the key to Buffett's success, aside from having a gift for smart investing, is that he finds people who know what they are doing and helps them do it.

He also rewards them for making good decisions that lead to improved performance. Many people had never heard of Buffett before he was asked to become CEO of Salomon Brothers. "Just two years after the Salomon scandal brought the firm to the brink of collapse, Wall Street's preeminent trading house has been thoroughly reformed. Buffett's secret: stressing two themes critical for running any business—proper allocation of capital, and mangement incentives tied to producing shareholder value.

"You can't pay for performance unless you really measure it—and pre-Buffett, Salomon didn't. . . . Accordingly, they allocated expenses to the business units, and since compensation is now linked directly to each operation's earnings, managers are inspired to squeeze out costs" (Fisher 1993).

While Buffett's predecessor at Salomon, "John Gutfreund had exercised absolute power and ran the business more like a clubby partnership than the gigantic publicly held company it has become," Buffett shifted decision-making responsibility downward and rewarded managers for seeking whatever input would enable them to impact the bottom line. This is one more hallmark of a *developing*, but certainly not *overaccommodating*, leader.

SURROUNDED BY EXPERTS

Another high-profile business leader who has used Window 3 successfully is Apple Computer chairman John Sculley. When Sculley first came to Apple after having been a marketing vice president for PepsiCo, his knowledge of personal computers was severely limited. In order to become an expert in his new business he had to spend a lot of time listening to those in the know. He understood that for him to lead this organization effectively, he first needed to pay close attention to those around him who had the expertise to produce products that would eventually dominate their industry.

He also knew that he had to be careful. He was walking into an environment that, under the leadership of Steve Jobs, had become *overaccommodating* to its employees. Jobs had created a culture that enjoyed teamwork, engaged in free-spirited brainstorming, and was extremely open-minded. Had Sculley entered this highly collegial environment with a heavy-handed, highly controlled approach, he no doubt would have met with formidable resistance. Instead, he effectively met the technically savvy workforce on their own terms and was able to learn from them in a way that led to the development of his own expertise. He was careful, as are most *developing* leaders, not to take decision making away from those who knew more about the decisions to be made then he. As a result, eventually he was able to take greater control once he knew more about the nature of the game.

In fact, when it came to a showdown between Sculley and his predecessor Jobs, Apple's board of directors chose Sculley— even though he lacked Jobs' technical wizardry—for his business sense. By listening to his people and supporting their decision making around technical issues, he was able to make some tough business decisions, like letting go of some employees and forming a partnership with archrival IBM.

After several years, Sculley felt that he knew enough to assume technical leadership of Apple, and shifted to more Style 2 as he challenged the company to breakthrough *problem solving* on state-of-the-art technology. Then, after ten years as CEO, he passed the baton to Michael Spindler.

What's next for Sculley? Hopefully, a position that allows him to go back to doing what he does best—supporting followers with their decision making.

ELECTRIFYING THE RANKS

Perhaps the most surprising high-profile Window 3 business leader is Jack Welch, CEO of General Electric. Most observers of this CEO of one of the largest corporations in the world would not guess that this tough-as-nails corporate leader who demands excellence in every corner of his organization would be a champion of a style which suggests words like listening and employee involvement. Certainly his reputation as "Neutron Jack" implies more of a Style 1, *dominating* approach than a Style 3, *developing* orientation. But even if Welch used to be a hard-nosed driver, he has certainly changed his tune in recent years.

Jack Welch also explodes the "soft" or "touchy-feely" mythology that often distorts people's ideas about Window 3. On the contrary, Style 3 can and should be highly demanding of those who are charged with doing the work. Jack Welch understands this and has taken on—as his way of leading one of the most powerful companies in the world into the twenty-first century— the enormous task of transforming a company steeped in traditional approaches to management into one that runs on the premise that those in the trenches have the know-how to create change and ought to be listened to carefully.

Consider the following from an article on Welch in *Fortune* (Stewart 1991 p. 41): "'We've got to take out the boss element,' Welch says. By his lights, twenty-first-century managers will forgo their old powers—to plan, organize, implement, and measure—for new duties: counseling groups, providing resources for them, helping them to think for themselves." This shift reflects, in every way, the hallmarks of a Style 3 leader—one who listens to followers and helps them to solve their own problems.

Welch's approach to Window 3 is the brainchild of James Baughman, head of faculty at GE's Management Development Institute in Crotonville, New York. The approach is called Work-Out. In its typical format a group of 40 to 100 people, increasingly coming from the lower ranks of the organization, spend three days with each other talking, with the help of an outside facilitator, about problems and how to solve them. At the end of the three days those in the Work-Out present their recommendations to superiors who are charged with doing one of three things: saying yes, saying no, or asking for more information. The distinction between the Work-Out and the typical two- or three-day retreat is that those participating in the Work-Out are empowered to make decisions, so much so that there are serious consequences for those at the top for not "driving decision making down" and for not following through on the decisions that get made during the Work-Out.

As is characteristic of a Style 3 approach, decision making is handed down the line to the lowest possible level, and accountability is maintained at that level. Welch has gone to great lengths to institute culture-wide change at GE to support this high-participation notion, from informally sending the message that not supporting Work-Out Teams is bad for your GE career to formally building evaluation of support for Work-Outs into formal annual reviews.

One result of this *developing* approach has been increased success for GE's operations. In addition, this has made GE one of the best training grounds for CEO's of other companies. After being an executive at GE, you would be ready to lead most corporations.

WORKING TOGETHER FOR CREATIVE ENTERPRISE

Perhaps the most renowned Style 3 leader of the corporate world is the late Sam Walton, founder of the Wal-Mart dynasty. Walton built his unparalleled retail chain (over 1,650 stores) on the basis of involvement and participation, beginning with his family, who comprise the board of Walton Enterprises and make all major decisions by consensus.

While modest about his role in the making of Wal-Mart's strong participatory culture, it is clear that Walton's folksy style and his insistence on maintaining the corporation as a partnership were in great part responsible for bringing that culture to life. "We don't pretend to have invented the idea of a strong corporate culture. We're constantly doing crazy things to capture the attention of our folks and lead them to think up surprises of their own. We like to see them do wild things in the stores, things that are fun for the customers and fun for the associates. If you're committed to the Wal-Mart partnership and its core values, the culture encourages you to think up all sorts of things to break the mold and fight monotony" (Sam Walton 1992).

What's critical to Walton's approach—and the success of his corporation—is that he built in mechanisms for problem solving that recognized the importance of openness, involvement, and shared responsibility. "At Wal-Mart if you have some important business problem on your mind, you should be bringing it out in the open, so we can try to solve it together. . . . From the very start we would get all our managers together once a week and critique ourselves . . . and it worked so well that over the years, as we grew and built the company, it just became part of our culture" (*Fortune*, June 29, 1992).

The best way to understand Walton's commitment to a Style 3 approach is to take a look at the principles by which he guided the business and the rules he went by in playing out those principles. First, he placed a high value on communication occurring up, down, and across the entire organization. Consider this excerpt from Walton's memoirs, regarding his abiding principles. "Communicate, communicate, communicate: If you had to boil down the Wal-Mart system to one single idea, it would probably be communication because it is one of the real keys to our success. What good is figuring out a better way to sell beach towels if you aren't going to tell everybody in your company about it."

He also focused on pushing responsibility down through the ranks. Walton believed that the people on the frontline, the department managers, those who stocked the shelves and talked with customers, were the ones who should make as many decisions as possible—and he supported their doing so. "What sets us apart is that we train people to be merchants. We let them see all the numbers so they know exactly how they're doing within the store and within the company; they know their cost, their mark-up, their overhead, and their profit. It's a big responsibility and a big opportunity" (Huey 1991).

This sharing of responsibility with the people in the trenches created a dynamic within the network of stores that made those managing the stores realize they they really did have responsibility for their own success. Walton was also very careful to always acknowledge success and use one person's accomplishments to achieve greater success system-wide. For example, he took ideas that would emerge from the ranks and would spread them throughout the company, creating a dimension to problem solving that he would call "bubbling up"—true Style 3 form, involving careful listening and support of others' decisions. Walton became notorious for his store visits, traveling around the country, dropping in unannounced, looking for good ideas to support.

Consider the following scenario as reported in a cover story in *Fortune* (Huey 1991): "On store visits, Walton's 'primary tool of empowerment' is his tape recorder. 'I'm here in Memphis at store 950, and Georgie has done a real fine thing with this endcap display of Equate Baby Oil. I'd like to try this everywhere.' Georgie blushes with pride."

Some observers of Walton's style have been critical of his open approach, suggesting that this sort of broad-based access to information for everyone in the organization creates a vulnerability to outsiders that can be damaging. Walton counters those accusations by suggesting that any corporation serious about gaining commitment from employees can ill afford the secrecy that many corporate leaders engage in. "Communicate every thing you possibly can to your partners. . . . If you don't trust your associates to know what's going on, they'll know you don't really consider them partners. Information is power, and the gain you get from empowering your associates more than offsets the risk of informing your competitors" (Walton 1992).

WHEN PLEASING THE MASSES SPELLS DISASTER

Window 3 clouds up when the perception of those around the leader is that the leader is more concerned with being popular than being effective. This brings us back to George Bush, the domestic policy leader. During his reelection campaign, Bush received a great deal of criticism from both ends of the political spectrum for failing to articulate a clear, strong position on many key issues confronting the nation. Conservatives in his own party accused him of being too wishy-washy on issues like abortion and support for religious schools. Liberals, on the other hand, saw him as bending over backwards to *overaccommodate* the Pat Buchanan side of the Republican coalition at the expense of issues like health care, education, and, most important, the economy.

This really should not have come as a reelection year surprise. When Bush ran for the presidency the first time, he told the American public that he wanted to give us a "kinder and gentler" form of leadership. His hope was to use the power of the presidency to encourage the private sector (the businesses that had been making huge profits during the Reagan years) and the volunteer sector (the "thousand points of light") to come forward and solve the social problems facing the country.

Even George Will, a staunch conservative, said very early in Bush's term in office that George Bush couldn't make a decision without consulting four or five polls. The man was trapped by the fear that he might offend one of his constituencies. He preferred to step back and let the natural forces of the market-place bring prosperity to everyone.

This apparent tendency to *overaccommodate* everyone is typical of the ineffective side of Window 3. Most analysts agree that part of Bush's downfall was his inability during the 1992 campaign to shift to a more directive style and demonstrate his ability to solve the country's economic problems.

Instead he tried to paint Bill Clinton as more *overaccommodating* than he was. The clear message was that if people thought Bush was bad, they should know what was coming if they elected a "pork-barrel, rainbow-coalition, misery-index Democrat."

Unfortunately for Bush, he was already seen as so *overaccommodating* to the wealthy that it was easier for Clinton to make the "trickle-down economics" label stick to Bush than for Bush to stick the "Waffle House" image to Clinton.

THE RAZORBACK PRESIDENCY

While we are still learning what type of president Bill Clinton is, one can get a view of his leadership style as governor of Arkansas.

Despite the fact that toward the end of the campaign trail he appeared to be a Style 2 *problem-solving* leader, examination of his gubernatorial style reveals a strong Style 3 approach. According to John Brunnett (*Newsweek*, July 20, 1992, p. 40) an Arkansas journalist who covers Clinton, "First he gives great lip service to his proposals. Then when the bill comes in and the legislators and lobbyists chip away at it, he says, 'That's okay, that's okay.' In the end, it's watered down to forty percent of what it was, and he declares victory."

This *overaccommodating* approach is the result of overusing a Style 3 approach. A Style 3 strength that Clinton brings to the White House is that he carries with him a formidable list of policy experts that history suggests he will use broadly.

Illustrative of this was his acceptance speech at the Democratic convention of 1992. If you were to dissect that speech, you would find that it was peppered with language that reflects the thinking of a wide range of pundits on everything from economics to social psychology to pop music. The speech was in fact a carefully woven presentation of many people's ideas, another hallmark of a Style 3 approach.

Many analysts believe that candidate Clinton was served well by a Style 3 approach. Consider this excerpt from a *New York Times* front-page story (September 13, 1992): "If a man is known by the company he keeps, Bill Clinton is clearly a left-leaning liberal. Also, a right-leaning moderate. In foreign policy he is a United Nations multinationalist and an America-first interventionist. In a city where every Democrat suddenly wants to be a 'friend of Bill,'" Mr. Clinton is a man for all advisers."

According to those who carefully follow the presidency, the same approach that served him well in his campaign—and was workable for him as the governor of a small state—could spell disaster for the leader of the world's last and only superpower. Consider these words from Leslie H. Gelb (1992) in the editorial section of the *New York Times* on the Sunday following Clinton's electoral landslide of 1992 regarding the threat of Republicans who would like to weaken Clinton's power early in his first term: "If the President-elect is to avoid being weakened even before he steps into the Oval Office, he had better cut off the poisoners at the knees now. He must send out the word that he knows who they are—and that he will settle accounts soon.

"Republicans have played the game just as hard in past transitions. Democrats should do no less. It is the only way to survive and govern in Washington. It is also the best way to let foreigners know that they, too, will pay for gratuitous opposition and personal attacks.

"Washington has become almost totally unruly. The town is saturated with left- and right-wing ideologues, officals and lobby-ists with independent power bases. They do not respond well to persuasion. But they do appreciate fear and power. The question is whether Mr. Clinton has the stomach for such combat. . . . He will not be able to please everyone. He will need to put a harder edge and thrust on his advocacy—and break some knuckles."

While "breaking knuckles" does not fit into any of our four windows of leadership, the message expressed above—which is held by many other observers of Clinton's style—is that if he is to be successful in holding the White House for the the Democrats for more than one term, he needs to take and maintain control over the executive branch of government by shifting into a position of greater control than is characteristic of Bill Clinton—an approach that resides more likely in Window 2 than in his comfortable, facilitative Window 3.

TOO MUCH POWER TO THE PEOPLE

The ascendancy of Corazon Aquino to the presidency of the Philippines provides an enlightening view of the dangers of overusing a Style 3 approach. Cory Aquino defeated Ferdinand Marcos, a very strong tyrant and a *dominating* Style 1 leader who controlled every aspect of government including the electoral process and the military. He ruled the Philippines in much the same way as the first mayor Daly ruled Chicago, with an iron fist and a lot of patronage.

Like many *dominating* leaders his ruthless behavior eventually caught up with him. The execution of Benigno Aquino (Cory's husband) proved to be Marcos' undoing. He seriously underestimated Aquino's widow, who eventually unseated him in a popular uprising against the dictatorship.

When Cory Aquino was elected president of the Philippines, it was on a power-to-the-people platform. In her first days in office she opened the presidential palace to the public, put Imelda Marcos' ostentatious collection of shoes on display, and tried to share her power with as many people as possible. She wanted to be the antithesis of Ferdinand Marcos, whose main style was *dominating*. In contrast, Aquino listened to her constituents, supported their cause, encouraged them to openly express themselves, and invited her supporters to take on substantial responsibility. In other words, her main style was a Style 3 approach of *developing*.

Unfortunately the honeymoon didn't last long, and her effectiveness with Style 3 *developing* diminished rapidly. The Philippines has a long tradition of power-dominated leadership, and Mrs. Aquino had a rebellion on her hands within a few months of taking office. Apparently some of her cabinet and many of the military leaders felt that she was *overaccommodating* to the people and some of her political adversaries.

She and her allies were able to squelch the coup and, as a result, she learned that she needed to be much stronger. She decided to be more selective in whom she trusted and more careful about whose input she used. She realized that in order to survive in a nation coming out from under Marcos' strong domination she had to become tougher.

And that's exactly what she did. She started taking input from a close-knit group of trusted advisors who were very powerful in their own right. She listened to their recommendations but made it clear that she was making the bottom-line decisions.

As a result of her becoming more decisive and regaining some control, she was able to provide a more democratic form of leadership than her predecessor while still demonstrating her ability to be a strong leader of her nation and its competing factions.

She even used her hard-learned *problem-solving* skills to take herself out of office. In 1992, she went against the wishes of many of her supporters who wanted her to run for office again. The history in the Philippines would have permitted her to become as benevolent a despot as Marcos had become a self-serving one. Instead, Aquino refused the temptation of perpetual power. She preferred to use her power to guarantee a smooth transition from her to her strongest supporters with the result that her candidate won the election. Not only did her party remain in power, but a small victory for democracy was achieved as well. Aquino is a good example of someone who shifted from an ineffective Style 3, *overaccommodating* approach to a more effective Style 2, *problem-solving* approach that was best for her country as she envisioned it.

THE STYLE 3 LEADER: DEVELOPER OR OVERACCOMMODATOR

Perhaps the greatest difference between the Window 3 leader and the Window 1 and 2 leaders is a shift in responsibility. For the Style 3 leader, decision-making is transferred to followers, communication is more upward than downward, and followers are valued for using the leader as a coach, not for following orders or going off on their own. In order for this to work, timing is critical.

We can see this from both the postive and negative cases discussed above. John Sculley used a Style 3 approach to effectively gain the trust and knowledge of followers when he needed them to help make decisions for which he was accountable. Cory Aquino used the same approach at a time when followers needed an unwavering decision-maker at the top, and it almost cost her the presidency.

The Style 3 leader is decidedly more follower-centered than the previous two. This leader considers the development of followers as the key means to an end. The Style 3 leader supports followers' decision making by asking lots of open-ended questions, listening actively, and praising them for asking for assistance. Primarily, the Style 3 leader promotes followers' development of their own problem-solving abilities. He or she does this by helping followers define their own problems, clarify their own goals, generate alternatives, evaluate and choose among alternatives, build action plans, and monitor and evaluate those plans.

The Style 3 approach works well when the leader is prepared to share significant responsibility with followers and followers are prepared to take it. The advantages of Style 3 are that leaders get to share the burden of responsibility with followers, chances of success are often optimized because all human resources are utilized, and there is often a high commitment to the task on the part of followers resulting from a sense of ownership over the work.

The disadvantages of this approach are that the leader gives up control over the process, has to tolerate followers' moving in directions not necessarily consistent with the leader's desires, and that the leader may have to accept decisions made by followers that differ from his or her own.

LEADING IN A LEARNING ENVIRONMENT— A CASE STUDY

Julie was the new president at a university where her predecessor was described as someone who ran a "tight ship." In her first meeting with faculty and staff, she quickly discerned that there was a lot of frustration with the tough, hands-on approach that the former president had used to run the school. The school was, she learned early in her first week, a place that attracted a large number of nontraditional students. Many of those who attended were adult students returning to school after several years in the workforce; others were homemakers returning to school after their children had grown; others were seeking skill upgrading in their jobs. At a meeting with this diverse, sophisticated student body she learned quickly that they too had been feeling the constraints of an overly controlling administration.

Julie decided to take the feedback she was getting from faculty, staff, and students and do something about it. She knew that the school had been overmanaged from the top down and that the best way to change things was from the top down. She met with the three executive deans individually and informed them that she intended to change the way the school was run.

Beginning today, she announced to each, the deans would be responsible for making decisions in their areas. She would be available to them to lend her support and advice if they wished, but each of them would be charged with making the key decisions in their areas. Further, she suggested that they might want to pass their authority down the line to those who could handle making lower level decisions that they felt should not be the domain of the dean.

At first, the three deans were shocked with their new level of authority. Within a few days two of them expressed their excitement personally to the new president over their newfound freedom. The president reminded them that she still intended to be involved with the decisions they were making, and was simply shifting decision-making power for their overall responsibilities to each of them. The third dean was less enthusiastic about his newfound freedom—and responsibility. He expressed his concern to the president, and she assured him that he was not on his own in these matters, but would have all the support he needed from her. Since he was less enthusiastic about the new setup, the president decided to set up a regular meeting schedule with him to help him develop and feel secure with his own problem-solving process.

While there was some initial confusion about who was accountable for what, the high-support style established by the president with her deans eventually took and she was able to spend most of her time dealing with her board of trustees and handling big-picture concerns of the university.

The three deans, including the reluctant one, eventually learned to model their own behavior on that of their president and began appropriately deferring decision making down the line, often offering high support to their charges, particularly in the early stages of the shift in authority when those with the new responsibilities felt somewhat hesitant to take control. As time went on it became clear throughout the system that the president's preferred way of operating was to share responsibility down the organizational hierarchy to the lowest reasonable level for any given set of decisions. What also became clear was that her way of creating this shift away from what she called "top-down gridlock" was to offer those engendered with new responsibilities all the support necessary for them to take on those responsibilities. As a result of this careful, thoughtful approach Julie was able to retain her control over the overall direction of the university while empowering those charged with meeting the goals of the organization with the authority and support to do it.

REFERENCES

Alter, Jonathan. "How He Would Govern." *Newsweek*, 20 July 1992, 40–42.

Fisher, Anne B. "Buffett's School of Management." *Fortune*, 14 June 1993, 116–118.

Gelb, Leslie H. "Is Clinton Tough Enough." *New York Times*, Op.Ed. Section, 8 November 1992, 17.

Huey, John. "America's Most Successful Merchant." *Fortune*, 23 September 1991, 46–59.

Loomis, Carol J. "The Inside Story of Warren Buffet." *Fortune*, 11 April 1988, 26–34.

Walton, Sam. "Sam Walton in His Own Words." Book Excerpt. *Fortune*, June 29, 1992, 98–106.

Stewart, Thomas A. "GE Keeps Those Ideas Coming." *Fortune*, 12 August, 1991, 41–49.

"Clinton: The Company He Keeps." *New York Times*, 13 September, 1992.

Chapter **6**

Window 4: The Leader as Delegator

One of the most common approaches to leadership in lean times, when resources of all sorts, human and otherwise, are becoming increasingly scarce, is that reflected in Window 4. So many companies, in the face of increased global competition, are flattening hierarchies, widening spans of control, and *delegating* increased responsibilities. In many cases, the leaders then try to wrap these changes in the mantle of empowerment. Our research consistently suggests that employees in these "empowered" organizations feel that the people above them are just downloading responsibility without providing the accompanying assistance required for them to truly be empowered.

What leaders often don't realize is that the downward shift of authority only results in effective *delegating* when the next level down the hierarchy feels that the expanded responsibilities make sense in light of organizational goals and offer greater opportunities. Giving people increased authority may just as likely be perceived as the *abdicating* of accountability when it doesn't serve either the needs of the individual or the best interests of the organization.

GIVING UP TOO MUCH

A highly visible example of both the upside and downside of Window 4 can be seen by examining the presidency of Ronald Reagan. Reagan was a popular president and an effective *delegator*. While he was very directive in establishing the foundation and ideology of his presidency, he was a consummate *delegator* once he chose the people who would carry his banner. The model for his presidency was to find competent people to do the work that needed to be done and, provided their values and agenda matched his, let them do it.

Perhaps to avoid repeating the mistakes of his predecessor, Jimmy Carter, whose excessive hands-on approach was partially responsible for the demise of his presidency, Reagan maintained a decidedly hands-off approach to the day-to-day management of the government. He was praised in the media for his skills as a communicator and a manager. Especially during his first term in office, and early in the second term, there were articles all over the business magazines telling us what we could learn from Reagan the manager. He was touted for his ability to define a value-based vision and then get out of the way and let his people have the authority to run their departments as they saw fit. Despite the occasional reprimand like when he scolded David Stockman for being too open with the press, Reagan always handled people in a gentle, avuncular manner and was an expert at letting go.

As with any leader who views his role primarily from a single window, this myopic view got him into trouble. From the outset, his detractors accused him of being too laissez-faire or *abdicating* on critical issues. Some said that he spent too much time at the ranch. Others claimed that he let his wife Nancy make too many decisions. And rumors circulated that he would often doze off during cabinet meetings.

The peak of dissatisfaction with his Window 4 leadership style came during the Iran–Contra scandal when his claim not to know what Oliver North was doing raised concerns about his competence. He doggedly maintained that he was not aware of what was going on. Interestingly enough, it seemed that most people who followed the Ollie North hearings did not mind the fact that North had been given so much authority. Where they drew the line was with the president's attempt to dodge accountability for his role as commander in chief. Consequently, the press hounded him mercilessly until one day he finally accepted full accountability for what had happened under his leadership. Of course, in the next breath, he still insisted that he didn't know.

An interesting footnote on Reagan's presidency is how the public's perception of him has shifted over the years. When he was in office, and we asked audiences about his style, we always heard vehement arguments about whether he was a *delegator* or *abdicator*. After Reagan retired and Bush was at the height of his popularity during the Persian Gulf War, most people we talked to described Reagan as a leader who had done too much *abdicating*. Then, when Bush's popularity waned, many Republicans started longing for the good old days, and Reagan's reputation as a *delegator* returned to the discussions.

Ultimately history will judge the effectiveness of Reagan's presidency. Nonetheless, he serves as a good study of both the pluses and minuses of Window 4 leadership: Reagan's strength in *delegating* was also his weakness when it turned into *abdicating*.

A FINAL NOTE ON GEORGE BUSH

In the last chapter, we talked about the label-slinging battle between "Trickle-Down" Bush and "Waffle-House" Clinton in the 1992 election. One reason Bush couldn't make the Waffle-House label stick was the way Clinton positioned himself as the Style 2 leader of the masses. A second reason was that Bush was already seen by many people as *overaccommodating* a much smaller and wealthier constituency.

A third reason was Bush's own success in foreign policy. Since he had clearly demonstrated during the Persian Gulf War that he knew how to build a strong coalition, listen to divergent points of view, and mobilize a well-coordinated effort to combat worldwide problems, Bush left himself open to the criticism that he did not care about the economic woes of poor and middle-class Americans. It wasn't that he didn't know how, he was simply choosing not to.

So his penchant for *overaccommodating* on the domestic front, colored by his skill at *problem solving* on the international front, actually created the perception that he was *abdicating*. Many people saw him as using Style 4 in a noncaring, aristocratic manner, aloof from the problems of the real world, leaving the homeless and the jobless to fend for themselves. And, of course, his adversaries took full advantage of the opening he gave them.

BROADCASTING LEADERSHIP

Perhaps the most visible Window 4 business leader is CNN's Ted Turner. Turner, named *Time* magazine's man of the year in 1992 for his leadership in catapulting CNN into the ranks of the world's leading news outfits, has a knack for *delegating* responsibility that few leaders can parallel.

One key to his success, aside from his willingness to take risks and to dream, is his willingness to forego control of the day-to-day operation of his empire to others who are more equipped to do so. He has thus effectively managed to *delegate* to a small group of journalists responsibility for decision making on world events, and has created a cadre of what some say is now the world's most influential group of journalists. In doing so, Turner has created an organizational structure that consistently outperforms its network counterparts.

By eliminating the bureaucracy that plagues and inevitably slows down reporting of the news at the networks, Turner has created a culture that defies and consistently outperforms the competition. Consider this observation from CNN executive producer Simon Vicary regarding a fast-breaking news story (Henry 1992). "My counterpart at ABC would have to go through 15 committees. I can just turn my head around and get a decision made."

From a leadership perspective, what Turner did in building his organization was to surround himself with experts in their field and give them the power and authority to do the job. While he still makes important decisions around overriding issues and overarching goals that determine the direction of the network, he lets those in the know make the decisions that lead to producing consistently high quality-programming.

Ed Turner (no relation), executive president in charge of news gathering, executive producer Bob Furnad, and CNN president Tom Johnson essentially run the network, making all the important tactical decisions on an ongoing basis. While this triumvirate of news hounds, unlike their leader, takes a decidedly hands-on approach concerning what gets aired, Turner's penchant for *delegation* seems to have rubbed off on how they work with people. Says Johnson, a refugee from the print medium (Henry 1992): "I'm not going to try to become an expert in TV technology. I want to surround myself with people who are better than I am in the various disciplines. My job is to lead."

Perhaps the most striking thing about Turner's *delegator* approach and its impact on CNN's "product" is that it gets carried down to the consumer. Unlike its network counterparts it does not tell viewers what to think about events. Says G. Cleveland Wilhout, professor of journalism at Indiana University (Henry 1992), "Ideological critics of the media, left and right, agree on one thing—that the press is too arrogant, too ready to tell people what to think. By its very structure, CNN is populist. It provides the raw materials of the story and lets the viewers form their own opinions." People watch CNN because they get far more information than can be provided in a half hour of soundbites, and are left to sort out and interpret that information for themselves.

VIEWING LEADERSHIP AT MTV

Interestingly enough, another highly successful media mogul, Sumner Redstone, also brings a decidedly Style 4 approach to th∖ ∖anagement of his growing media empire. Redstone, less known, but no less impressive than his CNN counterpart Turner, is the owner of 76 percent of MTV, which currently is viewed in twice as many households as CNN.

Perhaps it's the nature of the business, or the diversity of the holdings (Redstone also owns 100 percent of National Amusements, a movie theater chain, as well as controlling interest in the children's network Nickelodeon), or the entrepreneurial leanings that these two giants have in common, that leads them to defer direct control of the management of their enterprises to others. Whatever the reason, it is clear that in their industry, under their circumstances, it works.

One of the keys to Redstone's success—and to that of most effective *delegators*—is the ability to surround themselves with good people and let them do what they know how to do. For example, when Redstone took over Viacom International Inc. (the parent company of MTV, Nickelodeon, and Showtime) he kept key operating executives Thomas E. Freston, chairman of MTV Networks, and Nickelodeon president Geraldine Laybourne on board and encouraged them to keep doing what they had been doing (which was working). He also brought on Frank J. Biondi to be Viacom's CEO rather than take the position himself.

In a *Business Week* article (Landler 1992) on Redstone's takeover of Viacom, Biondi, who formerly headed Viacom's archrival Home Box Office, imparts that Redstone's pledge to him as his boss was that he would not interfere with him, and Biondi contends that Redstone indeed gives him a great deal of room. Says Biondi, "Unlike any other chairman I've worked for, he's enormously deferential."

STYLE 4—DELEGATOR OR ABDICATOR

Delegating as a primary leadership style can be tricky to grasp because, on the surface, it looks like the classic laissez-faire approach whereby the leader defers to followers and appears indifferent to what goes on. However that is definitely not the case with the truly effective *delegator*.

One of the hallmarks of the Style 4 leader is that he or she respects and acknowledges the personal vision of followers. This does not, however, mean that one's own vision becomes irrelevant in the leader/follower relationship. Consider for a moment the two cases that opened this chapter—Ronald Reagan and Ted Turner. While you might argue with Reagan's policies as a leader, you would be hard-pressed to argue with his ability to effectively choose people who were aligned with his vision and delegate responsibility to them. Nor could you find fault with Ted Turner's ability to select people who would carry out his vision of a "thinking person's" news network, a place where people can come for information and make their own judgments about that information.

The point is that effective Style 4 leaders don't *abdicate* responsibility, they merely empower others who share their vision to orchestrate the realization of that vision. They find others who are ready and able to run with the ball and let them, always continuing, however, to keep their eye on the ball as well.

CREATIVE AUTONOMY

Consider the case of another highly successful entertainment industry leader, Alan Ladd, who was president of Twentieth Century Fox Film Corporation. In a recent book on creativity and management, Harvard Business School professor John J.

Kao documents how Ladd left Fox to create his own motion picture company that would foster optimum creativity in the film-making process. In so doing, Kao also paints a picture of a masterful Window 4 leader.

The case is a particularly compelling study for an industry that is normally dominated by people with strong egos and strong control needs—people far more likely to exhibit Style 1 characteristics than Style 4. Consider the following observations made by Kao about the film industry as background for understanding the significance of Ladd's approach.

"It is a highly speculative business where stakes are in the millions. Two out of ten make money, two break even, and the rest lose money. The production process is complex and depends on a diverse group of creative and technical people. In the 18 months to two years needed to complete the cycle, public taste may change, or the competition may have already released a similar product. People in the industry use gambling analogies to describe their successes and failures. They assert that charts and graphs led nowhere; Lady Luck, magic, and pure mysticism explained events just as well. You give the people what they want and they still don't come."

Considering the volatile, uncertain nature of the film industry, one might suspect that those at the head of production companies would respond to this uncertainty by imposing a measure of control and direction more reflective of a Style 1 or Style 2 leader. The case of Alan Ladd is a good example of how someone could effectively use the power of delegation to prosper in the context of uncertainty.

According to Kao, the first thing Ladd did, which set the groundwork for the Window 4 organization he would create, was to handpick a group of proven performers to start his venture with him. These included such people as Jay Kanter, his senior vice president of worldwide production, and Gareth Wigan, his vice president of worldwide production, as well as half a dozen other industry veterans who collectively were responsible for garnering 33 Academy Awards in 1978. They had produced *Star Wars* in 1976, and backed five critically and popularly successful "women's films" in one year: *Julia, The Turning Point, An Unmarried Woman, Norma Rae,* and *The Rose.*

In assembling such an illustrious cast of characters, what Ladd was doing was setting the stage for his Style 4 approach by staffing his organization with experts who knew what they were doing and creating the conditions for letting them do it. Observes Kao, "Production requires a sensitively and efficiently coordinated effort of subgroups—office people, technical crew, and talent groups—making full use of available technical resources for creative problem solving." Adds Wigan, "If things are going well, and the principal individuals are people who like to be left alone, then your personal contact can be slight. It's a question of judging between not nagging and at the same time appearing not to be disinterested" (Kao 1991).

This snapshot of Ladd's corporate culture suggests the hands-off approach characteristic of an effective Style 4, while sustaining the limited involvement necessary to avoid the threat of *abdication* present in the ineffective form of this style.

Another indication of Ladd's Style 4 approach can be seen by looking at the way day-to-day activities occurred. According to Kao, decision making took place all the time, anywhere people gathered. Though there was one person with primary responsibility for each project, everyone else was involved, and anyone could step in and become the project's spokesperson at any time. And consider these observations by Kao regarding Ladd's open, *delegating* style regarding meetings: Meetings simply evolved and included long silences which Ladd seemed comfortable with. There was often no agenda—people spoke when they had something to say and decisions got made "by dissolve." Ladd was totally accessible to everyone in the company, all of whom he trusted completely—they would not be there otherwise. Certain people needed to be at certain meetings, but others weren't kept from coming. Whoever wanted to attend a particular meeting could. While this scenario might sound like chaos, and very well could be under the wrong circumstances, it highlights the need for the leader to let go of control when using the *delegating* style.

According to Kao, one of the main incentives people identified for wanting to work with Ladd had to do with his tendency and preference for leaving people alone and letting them do their work. He seemed to use this aproach even when things were not going well. Says Ladd, "Well, there's leaving people alone and leaving them alone; the difference is how you approach your involvement . . . you don't say, 'I'm right and have all the answers, because they may be right too.'"

As with most effective CEOs, Ladd's style was echoed by and evident in the approach of his key charges. Consider these words by Ladd's vice president, Gareth Wigan, "If things start not to go well—it gets behind schedule, or you don't like the material—then it becomes much more difficult. It doesn't help to be sitting on top of the creative person's back. You can't tell him or her what to do, exactly, and if you're standing there with a stopwatch, it can be counterproductive.

"It's very important with creative people to join them, and not to challenge them. It's always easy for them to turn around and say, 'You don't understand, you're not a filmmaker.'"

This perspective on working with people in a delegating way even when the going gets tough is probably the greatest testament to Ladd's commitment to a Style 4 approach. Finally, consider these words by Ladd himself, regarding his philosophy, "As long as you trust the people you're working with and feel that they are responsible, then you don't ask a lot of questions." While the volatility that is inherent to the motion picture industry has caused Ladd to move on to other ventures, he continues to be a major player in the American film industry.

WHEN THE SHOE DOESN'T FIT

While finding and surrounding yourself with good people to delegate to, like Ladd, Turner, and Redstone have done, choosing the wrong people to delegate to in the wrong situation can spell disaster. Consider the case of Paul Fireman, chairman of athletic shoe giant, Reebok International Ltd, which since its inception has been battling for the top of the sneaker heap with Nike.

In 1987, according to *Forbes* magazine (Meeks 1990), Fireman reconceived his vision of Reebok from that of a shoe company to that of a consumer products company. To further his vision he brought in experts from other specialties—Joseph LaBonte, formerly president of Twentieth Century Fox, Mark Goldstone, formerly president of Faberge, and Frank O'Connell, formerly CEO of HBO Video—to run his operation. According to *Forbes*, and to Fireman himself, his strategy of *delegating* control of the company to outsiders who were a bad match for Reebok's client base failed miserably and, as a result, looked more like *abdicating*.

Says *Forbes*, ". . . the shoe business wasn't show business. The strategy flopped. Shoe retailers liked dealing with people who knew about shoes, and resented flashy Hollywood types. 'I really abdicated responsibility,' concedes Fireman."

The difference between the successful Style 4 approach used by Turner, Redstone, and Ladd, and the failed Style 4 approach of Fireman—who has since reestablished himself as the driving force of the company with great result—is that his counterparts in the entertainment industry recognized the need for finding the right people to delegate to in the right way at the right time.

LETTING EXPERTS BE EXPERTS—A CASE STUDY

One of the times when *delegating* can be most effective is when you're dealing with someone who knows far more than you do about a particular problem and how to solve it, and is willing to tackle it. For example, in this age of rapidly advancing technology, it is entirely possible that someone who reports to you is more adept in a particular area under your purview than you are. Many managers resist this notion; nervous about their own accountability, they maintain control over things they know little about and end up decreasing their effectiveness along with the effectiveness of their reports. However, you'll see from the following example that it is possible to delegate and retain your accountability at the same time—and the rewards for both you and those who report to you can be considerable.

Roger was a senior manager in a medium-sized research lab specializing in software development for the microelectronics industry. He took great pride in the fact that his research group functioned as a team and always shared responsibility for both their successes and their failures. Roger was extremely knowledgeable in most of the technical areas his group encountered, so it was reasonable that he used a hands-on approach most of the time, working closely with his team to make sure their motivation and results were as strong as possible. Roger's personality was such that he liked this hands-on approach and enjoyed the control over his team's results that it afforded him.

His greatest challenge as a manager came one Friday when he was assigned a new employee, Steve, and the same day was assigned a project in an emerging technology he knew little about. The new hire, it turned out, was an expert in this emerging technology. The assignment was to create a software program employing the new technology, and to do it fast.

That Friday afternoon, Roger met with Steve to begin to establish their working relationship. He began by explaining to Steve that their unit worked as a team and that he prided himself in being a team leader who recognized that everyone on the team had a contribution to make, and that he saw his role as one that integrated everyone's contributions.

During the conversation Roger noticed that Steve seemed decidedly disinterested in what he was saying. As soon as Roger was done talking about teamwork, Steve began asking him questions about the technical resources that would be available regarding the new project. As Steve talked Roger grew increasingly uncomfortable, realizing that Steve was not a team player and that he seemed to know a great deal more about the upcoming project than Roger or anyone else in the group. Rather than bring up his concerns, Roger decided to spend the weekend thinking about the situation before attempting to address them.

That weekend Roger realized he had a dilemma. If he used his typical participatory style with Steve he would likely end up slowing the progress of the project which was up against a tight deadline, but if he let Steve have free rein, he ran the risk of alienating the rest of the group who were used to working together on everything under his leadership.

By the end of the weekend, Roger developed a strategy that he was hopeful would work. He decided that since Steve was the most qualified to take the lead on this project, he would try *delegating* responsibility for the project to him. That would solve the first problem—not slowing down the project. His second problem was the team and their expectations around involvement and their comfort in following Roger. He knew from his initial discussion with Steve around teamwork that it was unlikely that Steve would be an effective team leader. Perhaps the best thing to do, he thought, was to encourage Steve to work on his own, with assistance if he needed it, while the rest of the group worked on other projects.

On Monday morning he called Steve into his office, told him of his plans to delegate responsibility for the new project to him, and suggested that he let Roger know if he would need any assistance. Meanwhile, he told Steve, he would be talking to the rest of the team about what they would be doing while Steve worked on the new technology project. Steve seemed excited about being able to dig right in and admitted he had been nervous all weekend about having to work with a group that might slow down his progress. Roger pointed out that at some point Steve would have to accept that he was in a team environment and that when the circumstances warranted he would be expected to work more cooperatively with the rest of the group.

As a result of Roger's careful *delegating* of responsibilities, he managed to get the project completed on time without disrupting the team spirit he so cherished.

REFERENCES

Henry, William A. III. "History As It Happens." *Time*, 6 January 1992, 24–31.

Kao, John J. *Managing Creativity.* New Jersey: Prentice Hall Press, 1991.

Landler, Mark, with Smith, Geoffrey. "The MTV Tycoon: Sumner Redstone is Turning Vicacom Into the Hottest Global TV Network." *Business Week*, 21 September 1992, 56–62.

Meeks, Fleming. "The Sneaker Game." *Forbes*, 22 October 1990, 114–115.

Chapter 7

Your Personal Window of Leadership

By now, you should have a good understanding of the leadership styles of The L4 System. You know what they look like in terms of direction and support. You understand the decision-making methods, the communication skills, and the recognition strategies that are associated with each window. You also have many well-known leaders to use as a frame of reference. There should be no doubt in your mind as to what the four windows look like.

As you have been reading about the styles and famous people who use them, we have asked you several times, "Which leadership styles do you tend to use?" Now it is time to find out the answer to that question.

This chapter will help you interpret your responses to the cases from Chapter 1. First, you will see which styles you selected on each case. Then you will see the overall mix of styles that you chose. Finally, as you read about your main, back-up, and limited styles, you will get a clear picture of how you see yourself as a leader.

In the matrix on the next page, enter your responses to each of the cases in Chapter 1. You will notice that the four actions have been reorganized into columns that reflect the leadership styles that you selected. Be careful to get your answers in the right spaces.

	S1	S2	S3	S4
CASE 1	B____	A____	D____	C____
CASE 2	C____	A____	B____	D____
CASE 3	C____	D____	A____	B____
CASE 4	D____	B____	C____	A____
CASE 5	A____	D____	B____	C____
CASE 6	B____	C____	D____	A____
CASE 7	D____	C____	A____	B____
CASE 8	A____	B____	C____	D____
CASE 9	C____	D____	A____	B____
CASE 10	B____	C____	D____	A____
TOTALS	____	____	____	____
PERCENTAGES multiply by 2	____	____	____	____

Add each column to determine the total number of points you assigned to each style. The four totals should add up to 50 points.

Finally, multiply each column by two to find out what percentage of each style you selected. The four percentages should add up to 100 points.

Your main style is the one with the highest percentage. It is the style you used most often in these cases. If two styles are equally high, think of them both as main styles.

Any other style with 15 percent or more is a back-up style. You can have any number of back-up styles. These are the styles that you use frequently but probably don't overuse.

Any style with less than 15 percent is a limited style. Again, you can have any number of these styles. These are the ones you don't use very often, if at all.

Now, read the charts on the next two pages for a more complete look at your leadership profile. You may want to highlight the borders of those paragraphs that pertain to you. That will make it easier to get a full view of your leadership profile.

The following sections provide a more complete interpretation of your Window of Leadership. The first section is for people who have one main style that stands out as their clear preference. The second section is for leaders who have two predominant styles and two styles that are used on a more limited basis. The third section describes leaders who use three styles with some degree of frequency as well as one limited style. The fourth section is for people who use all four styles.

You don't need to read every section—you will probably be most interested in the one that pertains to you.

There is a fourth section that will enable you to compare the percentages you assigned to each style with some industry averages that we have compiled over the years.

ONE-STYLE PROFILES

Style 1

If your clear preference is Style 1, Directing, and you use the other three styles on a limited basis, you are the type of leader who likes to make decisions on your own, gives explicit instructions to team members, follows up with close supervision, and values followers who comply with your wishes.

Your strength is your clarity about what you want, when you want it, and how you expect it done. You like being in control and are good at providing structure in situations that call for someone to take charge. You are particularly good at pointing people in the right direction.

Your weakness is that you tend to overuse Style 1. As a result, you come across as dominating to people who like to take some initiative or think for themselves.

Your reluctance to use Style 2 puts you at a disadvantage in situations that call for you to take input to your decisions. So there are times when you make decisions that are not well-

	STYLE 1	**STYLE 2**
MAIN STYLE	DIRECTING is your strength. You are decisive and don't need a lot of input to make a decision. You are good at giving clear directions and full explanations. You follow up to make sure work is done properly and value people who do exactly what you want. Your weakness is that you can be DOMINATING when people already know what to do or want more responsibility.	Your strength is involving people in the PROBLEM SOLVING process. You are good at listening to team members' problems and making decisions based on their recommendations. You are also good at opening your problems to input from others. Your weakness is that you can be OVERINVOLVING by getting yourself or others into the process unnecessarily.
BACK-UP STYLES	You can be DIRECTING when you need to be. Even though this is not your main style, you are good at making decisions on your own, giving team members clear assignments, and providing them with close supervision if it's necessary. You may come across as DOMINATING at times if you tend to use this back-up style in situations when less directing is needed.	You are willing to involve yourself or others in the PROBLEM SOLVING process whenever it is necessary. While this is not your main style, you are good at opening up problems, inviting input, and getting closure on decisions if you need to. You might come across as OVERINVOLVING at times if you use this back-up style in situations that call for less participation.
LIMITED STYLES	DIRECTING is not your favorite way of leading. As a result, you may not be as decisive as you should in situations that don't permit time for deliberation. You also may not be as clear as you could about what you want and how you expect it to be done. On the other hand, you are not likely to be DOMINATING unless you use this style at times when people don't need it.	PROBLEM SOLVING is not your most comfortable way to work with people. Consequently, there may be times when you don't get others involved enough with your decisions. You also may not involve yourself with followers' decisions as quickly as you should. You are not likely to come across as OVERINVOLVING unless you use this style at the wrong times.

STYLE 3	**STYLE 4**

DEVELOPING people is your strength. You are good at giving followers challenges that let them stretch and grow. You listen well and are good at helping them think through problems without undercutting their sense of responsibility. Your weakness is OVERACCOMMODATING by listening too much and letting followers make decisions that you should make.	DELEGATING is your strength. You are good at giving followers meaningful responsibilities, then letting go and allowing them to handle their assignments on their own. As long as your team members are prepared for this much authority, they see you as a challenging and trusting leader. When they feel overwhelmed, they are more likely to accuse you of ABDICATING.	**MAIN STYLE**
DEVELOPING is something you can do when you need to. While this is not your main style, you know how to support followers with their responsibilities when it is necessary. You can listen well, ask challenging questions, and offer helpful suggestions. On the downside, you may slip into OVERACCOMMODATING if you let followers call the shots when you need to decide.	When DELEGATING is needed, you are comfortable giving followers full authority. While you prefer some level of involvement, you are willing to let team members handle significant responsibilities in certain situations. Although this isn't your main style, you may come across as ABDICATING at times, especially if you are not available when people need you.	**BACK-UP STYLES**
DEVELOPING is not what you do best. You may leave followers alone to make some decisions, but when you get involved, you like to be the one who decides. As a result, you may miss some chances to give followers the support they need to handle their responsibilities. You aren't likely to be seen as OVERACCOMMODATING unless you use this limited style at the wrong times.	DELEGATING is not easy for you. You are more comfortable with some level of involvement. Consequently, you may not give team members full authority as often as you could and may keep yourself more in control then you need to be. You are not likely to come across as ABDICATING unless your limited use of this style occurs when people need something from you.	**LIMITED STYLES**

received, or have trouble getting followers to buy in to your way of thinking.

Your limited use of Style 3 handicaps you at times when you should listen to followers and support them with their decision making. Consequently, you do not create as many opportunities for developing followers as you might.

Your tendency to avoid Style 4 makes you reluctant to let team members handle some responsibilties on their own. This leaves you unable to delegate as much as you should.

Style 2

If you have a clear preference for S2, Problem Solving, and a limited use of the other three styles, you are the kind of leader who enjoys getting others involved in helping you make tough decisions. You bring issues to the members of your team (and sometimes to peers, superiors, customers, or consultants) so that you can get as much input as you can on the problems you are trying to solve. You also feel important when other people bring their problems to you so that you can tell them what needs to be done.

Your strength as a leader is your willingness to roll up your sleeves and get your hands dirty to solve problems. You like to meet with people, one-on-one or in groups, to identify and fix whatever needs fixing. You are good at listening to diverse points of view, finding areas of agreement, and getting closure when there is disagreement.

Your weakness is that you may overinvolve others in discussions that they would rather not participate in, or you may overinvolve yourself in decisions that others could resolve, either on their own or with a little support.

Since you don't use much Style 1, you may appear indecisive to those who believe that you already have the relevant facts. You may also give unclear or incomplete directions when you have made up your mind.

Your limited use of Style 3 can make you come across as a poor listener in situations where others don't feel that you fully understand their point of view. It also limits your opportunities for developing followers by helping them think through tough decisions.

Finally, your reluctance to use Style 4 can make followers feel that you don't trust them to handle meaningful responsibilities. By not delegating you actually reduce the possiblity that followers would accept authority at times when you might want them to.

Style 3

If you have a definite preference for Style 3, Developing, and use the other three styles on a limited basis, then you are the type of leader who excels at giving followers responsibility and supporting them as the need arises.

Your strength is your ability to listen in a way that makes team members comfortable approaching you with problems they can't resolve on their own. You ask good questions, encourage others to fully explain the problems and their ideas for solving them, and are more likely to reflect back others' viewpoints than to express your own. Most important, you give people opportunities to stretch their skills while knowing that you will back them up when they need it.

Your weakness is that you can spend too much time listening. Sometimes you become overaccommodating by wanting everyone to like you. You can also make yourself so available for assisting others that you don't have time for your own work.

Since you don't use much Style 1, you may appear incapable of making your own decisions. You may also give incomplete or unclear directions when you have made up your mind.

Your reluctance to use Style 2 puts you at a disadvantage in situations that call for you to make decisions based on others' input. There are times when you try so hard to please that you listen too much or are swayed to the point of view of whomever talks to you last.

Your tendency to avoid Style 4 makes you reluctant to let team members handle some responsibilties on their own. Your desire to be supportive may actually hamper your ability for delegating and may also limit followers' full capacity for growth.

Style 4

If you have a clear preference for Style 4, Delegating, and a limited use of the other three styles, then you are the kind of leader who likes to let followers handle major responsibilities on their own.

Your strength is your willingness to let others take full ownership of their assignments. You are comfortable letting go, staying out of the way, and letting team members make decisions as they see fit. You don't feel the need to give followers your perspective or to check in to see how they are doing.

Your weakness shows up when followers find that they need your involvement. Often they find you unavailable. If they can find you, you will probably be unwilling to let the responsibility shift back to you. Either way can make you come across as abdicating.

Since you don't use much Style 1, you may appear indecisive to those who believe that you have all the information you need to make a good decision. You may also give unclear or incomplete directions when you have made up your mind.

Your reluctance to use Style 2 makes you less than effective in situations where you need to make decisions based on follower input. Your preference to keep hands off may convince them to turn to other leaders when they need timely decisions from above.

Your limited use of Style 3 can make you come across as a poor listener in situations where others don't feel that you fully understand their point of view. It also limits your opportunities for developing followers by helping them think through tough decisions.

TWO-STYLE PROFILES

S1–S2

If you use mostly Styles 1 and 2, Directing and Problem Solving, you are definitely a hands-on type of leader. You like being in charge, you are comfortable with decision making, and you are good at telling people what you want, when you want it, how you want it, and why. Sometimes you seek input from others to make sure you fully understand a problem situation and have the benefit of their thinking before you make up your mind. You also like people to bring problems to your attention so that you are aware of what's going on and can make the right decisions.

The strength of this profile is your ability to be decisive, your willingness to be the focal point of decision making, and the fact that decisions will be made with a high degree of consistency based on the principles that you believe will drive your team to success.

The weakness of this profile is that you don't give followers much in the way of meaningful responsibilities. Consequently they don't get many opportunities to think for themselves or to develop their capabilities. The other side of that coin is that your desk stays cluttered with decisions that everyone waits for you to make.

Your reluctance to use Style 4 may give others the message that you don't trust them or that you don't like the way they handle responsibilities. Your lack of delegating not only keeps the monkey on your back but it makes team members hesitant to accept authority at times when you might want them to.

This lack of trust is reinforced by your preference for Style 2 over Style 3. When you try to offer support, you only listen until you have made up your mind about the right course of action. As a result, when you are genuinely trying to be helpful, others are more likely to see you as checking up on them to be sure they are doing things your way as opposed to developing their skills.

S3–S4

If you use mostly S3, Developing, and S4, Delegating, you have a definite preference for giving followers responsibility. You are comfortable letting them make decisions and do not feel the need to control their actions. As a result, you are particularly good at leading people who like to think for themselves.

Under your leadership, these types of people feel challenged as they take on increased amounts of responsibility and stretch themselves to handle them as well as they can. They will accept the authority that you delegate in part because of who they are, but also because they know you will back them up with support when they need it.

The downside of this leadership profile is that there may be times when you need to step up to the plate and make some tough decisions or give followers clear directions. Under these circumstances, you may not come across as the kind of strong leader that people look to for decisiveness and action.

Since you don't use much Style 1, you may appear indecisive to those who believe that you have all the information you need to make a good decision. You may also give unclear or incomplete directions when you have made up your mind.

Your reluctance to use Style 2 makes you less than effective in situations where you need to make decisions based on follower input. Your preference to keep hands off or to help others decide may convince them to turn to other leaders when they need timely decisions from above.

S2–S3

If you have a preference for Styles 2 and 3, Problem Solving and Developing, you are the kind of leader who likes to be involved. You value talking to followers, peers, and superiors about problems that need to be addressed. You like participating in discussions and appreciate being asked to give your ideas to others.

Your strength is that you enjoy the problem-solving process. When you need to make decisions, you will seek out input from other people. When others are looking for input to their decision making, you are quite willing to share your best thinking.

Your weakness is getting caught up in too many meetings, endless discussions, and fruitless debates. You can be too quick to make others' problems your problems and involve yourself more than they would like. At times you may be giving followers support that they aren't ready to hear or don't feel they need. At other times you may try to make decisions that others were expecting to make.

Since you don't use much Style 1, you may not do as much directing as you should and may appear incapable of making your own decisions. You may also give incomplete or unclear directions when you have made up your mind.

Since you don't use much S4, you are also not likely to let followers make decisions on their own. Consequently, you may not delegate as frequently as might be appropriate for the ability and motivation of the people working for you and may involve yourself more often than is truly necessary.

S1–S4

If you use mostly Styles 1 and 4, Directing and Delegating, you have a preference for using the low-support, low-involvement leadership styles. For you, the question of who is responsible for decision making is black and white. If the ball is in your court, you just decide. If the ball is in someone else's court, you stay out of the way and let him/her decide. You don't seek a lot of input to the decisions you have to make and you don't feel the need to provide a lot of input to decisions that others have to make.

The strength of this profile is very efficient decision making. You and the other people around you don't get caught up in lots of meetings, endless discussions, or fruitless debates. Either you make the decision or they make the decision, and you get on with it.

The weakness of this profile is that since decisions are not based on other people's thinking, they are not always the best ones that could have been made. Consequently, decisions you make may not have the full backing of those who have to live with them. There also times when you don't fully endorse other people's decisions simply because you don't understand their perspectives.

Your tendency to underuse Styles 2 and 3 can make you seem aloof and uninvolved. People may not seek you out to ask for support because they have learned not to expect it from you. They are more likely to take their problems to others who will offer them support and who will value their recommendations when tough decisions have to be made.

S3–S1

If you use mostly Styles 1 and 3, Directing and Developing, you tend to be decisive in those areas where the decision-making responsibility is yours. You know what you want, you know how you want it done, and you are quite clear with the people who work for you about the directions you would like to have followed.

When your team members are responsible for making decisions, you will listen and offer support when they need it. You are comfortable giving them responsibility but like to stay close to the situation to help them stay on course. If they are unable to make good decisions, even with support, your tendency is to take over completely. You will reframe the project to your own way of thinking and redirect people in the way that you think is most appropriate.

With this profile, you have the potential for being a very effective leader if you use Style 1 to give clear directions up front and then use Style 3 to provide support after people have had a chance to handle responsiblities on their own. Since you are less inclined to use Style 4, the challenge for you is to let go enough so that team members feel some sense of authority over their work. Without that, your attempts to support may come across as hovering.

With this profile, you also have the potential to hinder performance. If you are overaccommodating in the beginning, you may spend too much time helping followers discover their own path. Then, when time is running short, your tendency would be to switch to Style 1 and undercut their sense of responsibility.

A leader who is more comfortable with Style 4 might let followers wrestle with the problem on their own for a longer period of time before taking over. A leader who uses more Style 2 would take control less abruptly by using followers' input to their decision making.

S2–S4

If you use mostly Styles 2 and 4, Problem Solving and Delegating, you are good at giving followers meaningful responsibilities. You trust them and are comfortable letting them make decisions on their own. When you do get involved, you tend to jump in with both feet. Your inclination is to listen to problems that staff bring to your attention and then outline the best course of action for them to solve the problem.

Since you don't use much Style 3, followers don't experience you as someone who listens with a great deal of patience or who wants to fully understand their analysis of the situation. Instead, you listen only to that information which fits your perspective on the matter. As soon as you have heard enough, you will make your decision and move on. Consequently, your desk stays cluttered with other people's problems. Your tendency to take the monkey off a follower's back and put it on yours may be overstressing yourself, while simultaneously you may not be helping others make the tough decisions.

Since you don't use much Style 1, you may also be sowing the seeds for problems to return to your desk by making assignments without giving adequate directions. The result is that people come looking for you sooner than they might have if they had clearer expectations. Then, when they do seek you out, you move into the problem-solving mode and reclaim the problem.

THREE-STYLE PROFILES

S2–S3–S4

If you use Styles 2, 3, and 4 with some frequency, you are the kind of leader who is comfortable with problem solving, developing, and delegating. You are good at leaving followers on their own to handle significant areas of responsibility. You are equally effective at listening to them and providing support when they need some assistance. You are also willing to make tough decisions based on their input when necessary.

Because you use a limited amount of Style 1, Directing, others may perceive you as lacking vision or decisiveness. They may see you as unable or unwilling to make a decision on your own. When you are in charge, they may see you as giving inadequate instructions or clear enough directions so that they can implement decisions in a way that meets your expectations or achieves the necessary results.

S1–S3–S4

If you use Styles 1, 3, and 4 with some frequency, you are the kind of leader who is comfortable with directing, developing, and delegating. You are good at giving team members clear outlines of what you expect. You are also good at leaving followers on their own to handle significant areas of responsibility and are equally effective at listening to them and providing support when they need some assistance.

Since you use a limited amount of Style 2, Problem Solving, you may be perceived as the kind of leader who does not like to receive input to your decisions. It is rare that you will seek out others' analysis of a situation before you make up your mind about what needs to be done. When you are in charge, you make up your mind and tell followers what to do. When others are in charge, you let them handle it on their own. If they need support, you are happy to provide it, but you are reluctant to take followers' recommendations and make decisions that they cannot or will not make. In addition, you are unlikely to bring problems to their attention and ask them to support you with your decision making.

S1–S2–S4

If you use Styles 1, 2, and 4 on a regular basis, you are the type of leader who is willing to use directing, problem solving, and delegating. You are good at telling team members what you want, when you want it, how you want it, and why. You are also willing to get out of their way and let them handle their responsibilities in the ways they consider most appropriate. When they get stuck and come to you for support, you are happy to listen to their problems and advise them about the best way to solve them.

Since Style 3, Developing, is limited in your profile, you come across as an impatient listener when followers discuss the problems they're wrestling with and the possible actions they are considering. While you are good at leaving people on their own to handle responsibilities as they see fit, once you get involved and begin to listen, ownership transfers quickly from them to you. In your mind, you may be doing the most efficient thing by shifting from Style 4 to Style 2, but from your followers' perspective you are undercutting their sense of responsibility.

A leader who is more comfortable with Style 3 would listen better and get a more complete understanding of the other person's situation. Listening often keeps the monkey off their backs. More important, from a long-term perspective, these leaders are developing followers' potential for dealing with tough problems and finding good solutions.

S1–S2–S3

If you use Styles 1, 2, and 3 on a regular basis, you are the type of leader who is willing to use directing, problem solving, and developing. You are good at telling team members what you want, when you want it, how you want it, and why. You like asking them to bring problems to your attention so that you can solve them and truly value their input to decisions you need to make. You are equally comfortable helping them think through decisions they are wrestling with and giving them your best thinking without undercutting their sense of responsibility.

Since Style 4, Delegating, is limited for you, your major weakness as a leader is not being able to let go. While you are comfortable giving followers assignments, your preference is to stay in close contact so that you can support them and assure the quality of their decision making. You are less comfortable giving them the authority to make decisions and handle their areas of responsibility on their own.

People experience you as being a very involved leader, and since you use a lot of Styles 2 and 3, they will see you as open and communicative. Since you use a lot of Styles 1 and 2, they will also see you as being decisive and clear about what needs to get done. What they won't get is a feeling of being trusted to handle meaningful responsibilities or empowered to make decisions on their own.

A FOUR-STYLE PROFILE

If you use fairly even amounts of all four styles without having a clear main style, your leadership profile reads like a set of backup styles. At times, you are willing to tell team members what you want, when you want it, how you want it, and why. You are also willing to listen to people's problems, take their recommendations, and give them timely decisions. Sometimes you ask questions and offer support to help them think through decisions they are wrestling with. You are also capable of leaving followers on their own to handle significant areas of responsibility as they see fit.

The most unique aspect of this profile is that you don't overuse or underuse any of the styles. While this may make you more flexible than other leaders, your effectiveness will still be determined by your ability to use each style with the right people at the right times.

HOW DO YOU COMPARE TO MOST LEADERS?

Another way to think about yourself as a leader is to compare your percentages to the averages and ranges that we have compiled over the years. These averages enable you to see if your use of each style is typical of most managers or if you stand out from the pack by using some styles more or less than your counterparts. If you are above or below average, the ranges will let you see how extreme your scores are.

These comparisons can help you understand other people's reactions to you as a leader. Their perception of your leadership actions comes in the context of other managers they have worked for or seen in action. So, the way you come across is not just a question of what styles you use. It is a question of what you use in comparison to what other leaders use.

More specifically, when you look at the percentages you selected in the 10 cases, even though you may have selected all four styles, if your use of any one style is outside the norm, that could color people's perception of you. For example, suppose you selected an even 25 percent of each style. Even though you chose all four styles equally, you would be on the high end for Style 1 and, therefore, could easily be seen as dominating. And you would be on the low end for Style 3 and might not be providing as much developing as people really need.

AVERAGES	S1	S2	S3	S4
Accounting	19	22	51	08
Consulting	18	19	52	11
Hi Tech	17	20	47	16
Insurance	16	20	47	17
Manufacturing	14	17	48	21
Pharmaceuticals	20	22	41	17
OVERALL	17	20	47	16
RANGE	0—60	0—53	5—94	0—57

As you can see, the averages vary somewhat from industry to industry. They also fluctuate within an organization's hierarchy. In general, higher-level managers in every industry tend to use more Style 3 and Style 4 than frontline supervisors, who tend to be more hands-on with Styles 1 and 2.

The overall average for Style 1 is 17 percent, with a range of 0 to 60. That means that with Style 1, if your score is below 17 percent, you see yourself doing less directing than the people around you. If your score is above 17 percent, you see yourself doing more directing than others. If you are near the low end of the range, you probably aren't doing as much directing as you should. At the high end of the range, you are likely to be perceived as dominating.

For Style 2, the overall average is 20 percent, with a range of 0 to 53. If your score for Style 2 is below 20 percent, you see yourself doing less problem solving than the average manager. If your score is above 20 percent, you see yourself doing more. At the low end of the range, you are probably not doing enough problem solving, while at the high end you could be overinvolving yourself or others in decision making.

The average for Style 3 is 47 percent, with a range of 5 to 94. If your score is below 47 percent, you see yourself doing less developing than most people in the room. If your score is above 47 percent, you see yourself doing more. With a very low score, you may not be giving people enough support or creating opportunities for developing them. With a very high score, you may be perceived as overaccommodating.

For Style 4, the overall average is 16 percent, with a range of 0 to 57. If your score is below 16 percent, you see yourself as delegating less than most managers. If it is above 16 percent, you are more inclined to delegate to others. At the low end of the range, you are apt to come across as lacking trust in your team. At the high end, you may be perceived as abdicating.

Looking at all of these averages combined into a composite profile, you can see that most people selected Style 3, Developing, as their main style. In every industry, most managers think of themselves as giving their direct reports a lot of responsibility while being available to provide them with support.

All of the other styles are used as back-up styles to varying degrees. This does not mean that everyone has a similar profile. In reality, it means that the other three styles are selected as back-up styles by a large percentage of managers.

So it could be your back-up style that distingushes you from other leaders. How do you balance your preference for giving responsibility and support? With trusting delegation of full authority? With a tendency to tell people how to solve their problems when they appear stuck? Or with new directions to remind people what is expected?

If you overuse any one of these back-up styles, you will be standing out from the pack and that, as much as anything else, can affect your reputation as a leader.

THERE'S MORE TO COME

In the next chapter, you will get some more feedback about how you responded to the the first eight cases in chapter 1. Did you put the styles in the best places? Did you use the same styles with the women as you did with the men?

In chapter 11, you will get feedback about your responses to the last two cases. How did you decide to handle the two situations that involved groups? Did you use the best styles to get them focused and keep them productive for the long haul?

Keep reading. There's more to come.

MORE FEEDBACK

Beyond that, if you want to find out more about the mix of leadership styles that you actually use and the right combination of styles that you should use, the best way is to get feedback from people who work with you. At Charter Oak, we compile L4 Self and L4 Other profiles for the leaders we consult with. The L4 Self tells them what leadership styles they think they use. The L4 Other tells them what styles they actually use, and the styles that followers ideally need so that they can perform to the best of their potential.

Let us know if you want to find out what your people have to say about you.

Chapter **8**

Through the Working Glass: Viewing Followers through Their Window of Potential

Now that you have an understanding of your own Window of Leadership and the strengths and weaknesses of your leadership profile, you're ready to move on to the next crucial step for effective leadership, which involves taking the focus off of your own style preferences and focusing on the needs of the people you're leading. Understanding what good leaders do and becoming skilled at doing those things is what the *science* of leadership is all about. Knowing when to do what requires the use of your analytical and intuitive abilities and is what the *art* of leadership is all about.

To help you fine-tune your diagnostic skills and develop your effectiveness as a leader, this chapter will show you the *Window of Potential*, a device for assessing the performance potential of those you wish to lead and a way to determine which main style to use under which circumstances.

The Window of Potential is based on four key characteristics of ability and four key characteristics of motivation. The ability factors are: technical skills, interpersonal skills, job knowledge, and organizational power. The motivation factors are: interest, confidence, willingness, and alignment with organizational goals. By assessing ability and motivation you can accurately diagnose performance potential and can align your Window of Leadership with the Window of Potential of the people you are trying to lead. Once the two windows are aligned, effective leadership is almost guaranteed because the odds are high that, if you follow through on your diagnosis, you will be providing the people you want to lead with what they need. Once you establish which window is needed, all you need to do is provide what that window calls for. Just be sure you pay attention to the fact that as conditions change, any window can suddenly close on you, requiring you to open another one that offers a better view of the new situation.

In order to accurately diagnose the needs of a follower's performance potential, you must fully understand the concepts of ability and motivation. Ability is crucial in these rapidly changing times, because if one of your team members is in over his or her head, that individual's chances of realizing his/her full potential without the appropriate leadership are minimal. Equally important these days is understanding followers' motivation. Gone are the days when a leader could motivate employees by offering job security and career advancement. Anyone paying attention to the shifting corporate landscape knows that employee motivation is based on far more immediate issues than hypothetical opportunities down the road. Being able to accurately diagnose a person's motivation is key to effective leadership.

Let's take a look at the four ability factors and four motivation factors so that you can get a better understanding of the concept of performance potential.

WHAT IS ABILITY?

When you think about ability, there are four factors to consider. Unfortunately, in most organizations, when leaders think about followers' ability, they only think of the first factor, *technical skills*—a person's education, training, and experience. Then they assume that all of the other ability factors are present.

Assumptions are always dangerous, especially here because the other three factors are equally important.

The second factor is *interpersonal skills*. These include the skills for leading downward with people at lower levels, the skills for leading upward with your boss, as well as the skills for developing effective relationships with peers, vendors, customers, and so on. In sales or service jobs these skills are essential, and the higher a person rises in any organization, the more important these skills become.

The third factor is *job knowledge*. One of your followers might have impeccable technical skills and outstanding interpersonal skills, but if that person doesn't know your expectations or doesn't understand customer requirements, he/she really doesn't know what the job is all about. Without that, how can this person be expected to deliver the necessary results?

The fourth factor is *organizational power*. In order to have the power to deliver results, a follower also has to understand the back alleyways and hidden channels of the organization. He/she needs to have a network of people to call on in order to cut through the red tape and get things done. This applies to your organization, but also to your customers' organizations. Your people need to know how to get in and out and through these organizations in order to get things done.

WHAT IS MOTIVATION?

When you think about a follower's motivation, there are also four factors to consider. The first factor is *interest*. This is important because, if a team member is not interested in the work itself, then he/she will not be very enthusiastic about it. But in most organizations, interest is monitored in a very superficial way, focusing on how early people come in, how late they stay, and how willing they are to work on weekends. Interest is important but motivation is more complicated than the hours your people put in.

The second factor is *confidence*. This is extremely important, especially when organizations and the people in them are facing increasingly difficult challenges. Have you ever worked with people who have great skills but lack the self-confidence to use them? Or have you ever been in a situation where you weren't totally confident of your skills? Without confidence, how motivated will any person be to take on increased responsibility?

The third factor is *willingness to assume responsibility*. Most often, willingness is a function of a follower's skills, interest, or confidence, but not always. These days, it is not uncommon for people to be skilled, highly interested, and very confident, but so busy and stressed that they're reluctant to take on new responsibilities. So, if someone is going to motivate them, there is going to have to be a very strong incentive, whether it's a carrot dangled in front of the nose or a stick applied to the rear end, to encourage them to take on new responsibilities.

The fourth factor is *alignment with organizational goals*. If a team member's goals are not consistent with the organization's, the result will be frustration and conflict. There are some highly motivated people in every organization who are motivated for all the wrong reasons. They will do anything and will walk over anyone to accomplish their own agenda. If their efforts are not in sync with the organization's values and your department's mission, their commitment may do more harm than good. Alignment is also a critical factor when an organization is going through a major change. If people aren't sure where they fit, where the organization is going, or what management expects, their motivation is hindered. Consequently, they may not be willing to take on as much responsibility or to commit their time and energy without more frequent check-ins to be sure they are on track.

ABILITY + MOTIVATION = THE WINDOW OF POTENTIAL

So what do you do with these factors of ability and motivation? Focusing on a specific task or job responsibility, use them to assess a team member's ability and motivation as high, moderate, or low. Based on that assessment, then assign two points if it's high, one point if it's moderate, and zero points if it's low. How do you make that assessment? By thinking about the four factors for ability and the four factors for motivation.

If all four factors for ability are present, give ability two points. If you have any question marks about any factor, give ability one point. And if you have several question marks about these factors, give ability zero points. The same assessment takes place for motivation. If there are no problems, give motivation two points. If there are any concerns, give motivation one point. And if you have several concerns, give motivation zero points.

So, use the four factors to assess ability and motivation as high (2 points), moderate (1 point), or low (0 points). Then, all you do is add those assessments together to determine this person's performance potential for the specific task or job responsibility that you are focusing on, as shown in Figure 8.1.

Remember, this is not an overall assessment of the person. It is a diagnosis of his/her ability and motivation to perform certain aspects of his/her job.

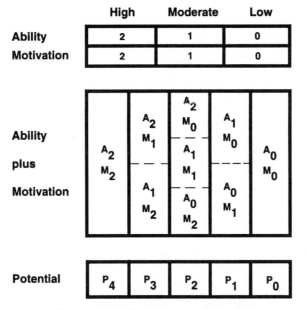

Figure 8.1   The Window of Potential.

A2 + M2 equals P4. High ability plus high motivation gets you to the highest level of performance potential.

A2 + M1 or A1 + M2 equals P3, the next highest level of potential. In these situations, followers are very capable but there's one factor missing from either ability or motivation. It could be anything on the list—technical skills, interpersonal skills, job knowledge, organizational power, interest, confidence, willingness, or alignment. Whatever it is, P3 is still a very high level of performance potential.

There are three ways to get to P2. The most common one is in the middle, A1+ M1, moderate ability and moderate motivation. But the two extremes also occur at times. One is A2 + M0, when someone is very capable and experienced, but disinterested or burned out. The other is A0 + M2, when a person is new to a job and not very experienced, but is overly confident and out to set the world on fire. All these cases also add up to P2, a moderate level of performance potential.

Any combination of 1 plus 0 adds up to P1 which is a relatively low level of potential.

The math, when you get down to the end, is very simple, A0 + M0 = P0, the lowest level of potential.

WHAT'S YOUR WINDOW OF POTENTIAL?

Would you like to have some fun? Before you try diagnosing your team members' performance potential, it is important to apply this concept to yourself first. So take a few minutes to think about your own Window of Potential. As you think about these five levels of performance potential and the nine combinations that make them up, think about how they apply to you. Think about your job, the goals you're accountable for, and the huge range of tasks you have to perform to achieve those goals. Now try to think of some tasks that will fit into each level of performance potential.

Can you think of some tasks that are P4? Can you think of some tasks that are P3 or P2? Are there any that are P1 or even P0? Take a few minutes to think about your job and how you'd classify some of the different tasks you have to do.

If you were able to identify some part of your job as P4, high ability and high motivation, that's normal. Everybody has some part of their job that is A2M2. If you didn't have any P4 situations, you probably would have been fired a long time ago.

Did you classify some parts of your job as P3? Most people do. Usually everyone has some P3 tasks where they could use a little help with some aspect of their work.

How about the P2 level? You certainly aren't alone if you have some P2 situations. In a typical department of any organization, about 75 percent of the people have some P2 situations.

What about P1? This category is more common than you may think. It is very normal to have some responsibilities for which you have only a little ability and, consequently, little or no motivation. At least 30 percent of a typical group has some P1 cases.

Did you find any P0 parts of your job? Don't feel alone if you did. It is not unusual to have a task or two that you are lousy at doing and that you avoid like the plague. In a normal group, about 10 percent of the people will admit publicly to having some P0 situations. In private, we suspect that everyone has some. We certainly do!

The main purpose for asking you these questions is to drive home a very important point. What is normal for you is normal for most people. When most people look at their jobs and the range of tasks that are required, they need to use the full Window of Potential to assess themselves.

It's important to keep this in mind as you think about matching your leadership styles with your followers' potential. Do not get caught in the trap of labelling people as P4, P3, P2, P1, or P0. Instead, always remember that you are assessing their task specific potential. You're diagnosing situations, not pigeonholing people.

MATCHING YOUR STYLES TO A FOLLOWER'S WINDOW OF POTENTIAL

Figure 8.2 below shows you how to match your leadership styles to followers' performance potential. You can see that the five levels of potential are at the bottom and the four leadership styles are at the top. Where the dotted lines intersect with the diagonal, it shows you which style you use for each level of potential.

Use Delegating in P4 Situations

In a P4 situation, the best style is S4, Delegating. The person has the ability and the motivation to accomplish the task. So, in a P4 situation, delegate the responsibility and the authority, then let

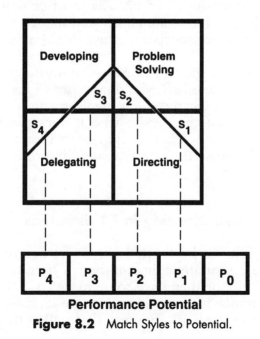

Figure 8.2 Match Styles to Potential.

the person run with it. Just keep yourself informed so you don't lose your own accountability.

Use Developing in P3 Situations

In a P3 situation, you should use Style 3, Developing. The potential is strong. There are just one or two factors missing in either ability or motivation.

Whatever it is that's missing, your job is to provide support. That could mean technical advice, interpersonal coaching, clarification of job knowledge, or use of your organizational power. Support could also mean sharing your own interest in a priority area, hand-holding to bolster confidence, arm-twisting or carrot-dangling to get people to take on more responsibility, or signing off to assure alignment with organizational goals. Whatever it is, you're giving people the support they need to succeed with their responsibilities.

Use Problem Solving in P2 Situations

In a P2 situation, the best style is S2, Problem Solving. Remember, there are three forms of P2. The most common is A1M1. When a person has moderate ability and moderate motivation, it's common sense to incorporate their thinking into your decision making.

It is also true in the two extremes. With the person who is very capable but turned off, you don't want to lose their expertise, so you should structure their involvement in your decision making. How about the person who is very green and over-confident? You want to channel that motivation in appropriate directions. Encourage their participation but offer frequent advice and feedback.

Use Directing in P1 Situatons

In a P1 situation, the best style is S1, Directing. In these situations, you are essentially doing on-the-job training. The people have some ability or they have some motivation, but there are many performance factors which they are lacking. It is important to structure the work in a way that makes them feel challenged without being overwhelmed. You should give them clear directions and complete explanations. Frequent feedback will keep them on the right track while helping them develop the skills and confidence to move into the P2 category as soon as possible.

What about P0 Situations?

You have probably noticed that we have run out of leadership styles and P0 is still dangling off the end of the chart. This is not an accident. The leadership styles are powerful tools, but they will not solve all of your people problems. As shown in Figure 8.3, to make The L4 System work, you have to integrate leadership with human-resource management strategies.

In a P0 situation where people have low ability and low motivation, don't waste your time or exhaust their patience with increasingly detailed directions and increasingly tight supervision. Instead the best response is human-resource mangement.

The first human-resource management strategy is training. One efficient way to change a P0 situation is to increase a person's technical skills, interpersonal skills, job knowledge, confidence, willingness, and alignment through training.

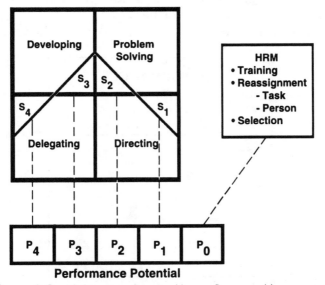

Figure 8.3 P0 Situations Require Human Resource Management.

The second human-resource management strategy is reassignment. In a P0 situation, the most common strategy is to reassign the task to someone who likes it and can do it. It is also common to reassign a person to another job within the department. Job posting is a technique that many organizations use for relocating people to other parts of the company. Sometimes it is necessary to simply cut your losses. We used to call that firing people—now it is called *outplacement*.

The main point in reassignment is to help people find a good fit between their potential and a job description. You are not doing your department or the individual a favor by leaving a person in a job where they consistently fail.

The last human-resource strategy is selection. If you have a bad fit, you should be more proactive the next time in selecting the right people with the ability and motivation to be top performers.

The main point is this. If you're going to lead a high-performing team, you have to select the right people, assign them to the right jobs, and give them proper training. That gets them onto the playing field. Then, you have to use all four styles on an ongoing basis in a way that matches their Window of Potential.

ARE YOU ADDING VALUE?

So what do you get by matching leadership styles to follower potential? The answer is performance!

Figure 8.4 illustrates this point. Think of the horizontal line

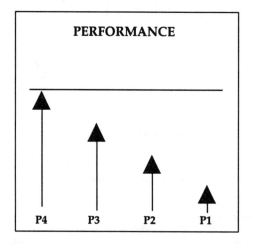

Figure 8.4   Performance Potential vs. Performance Expectations.

as a performance line. It represents the standards for excellence in your organization. The arrows represent individuals at different levels of performance potential.

In P4 situations, if you leave people alone, they will hit the line. In P3 situations, if you leave people on their own, they will come close to the mark. In P2 situations, people will get about half way on their own. In P1 situations, they can just get started.

Figure 8.5 shows that your job as the leader is to make sure performance is on target. It's your job to make sure that everyone hits the line. To do that, you have to provide the value-added leadership that guarantees performance. It's your role to close the gap between expectations and potential.

That means that in a P1 situation, your role is to give clear assignments with complete instructions, provide close supervision and frequent feedback. This use of the directing style results in the on-the-job training that is needed to achieve the desired performance levels in this type of situation.

In a P2 situation, your job is to listen to the follower's problems and solicit his/her recommendations about what needs to be done, then make the decisions that will ensure performance. Your use of the problem-solving style takes advantage of the ability and motivation that they bring to the situation without letting them flounder.

In a P3 situation, your job is to provide the type of support that will make this a developmental opportunity. The person has strong performance potential, and with a little help from you

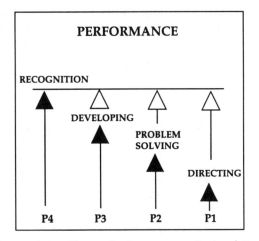

Figure 8.5 Closing the Expectations–Potential Gap.

should be able to hit the performance line. Just remember that support means different things to different people in different situations.

In a P4 situation, even though the individual is quite capable of hitting the performance line without any help, don't forget to give him/her recognition for the outstanding work. If you don't give your top performers appreciation for their efforts and the results they produce, they may not be your top performers for long. Either their motivation will drop off or they will start looking around for someone else to work for.

This approach is different from what passes for supervision in most organizations. Typically, employees are lucky to know what the performance standards are. Whether or not they do, they are most likely to be left on their own to try to hit the line. Their managers have their own jobs to do. They don't have time to help their employees. Instead, the role of their manager is to fill out forms once a year which pass judgment on how close their people have come to hitting the mark.

Usually, this type of performance-management system also claims to reward the best performers and get rid of the worst. In reality, all that happens is that people feel judged and threatened. Under those conditions, who do you think eventually bails out? Of course, the best ones do. They've got the credentials and the confidence to move on. Then the organization is worse off than it was before. Organizational performance drops, then people on the low end are laid off, and a smaller and less talented work force is left to keep the ship from sinking.

If your organization operates in this way, you are probably not getting the most out of your people. And you may be sowing the seeds for disaster. Leaving people alone and then judging them is a far cry from being clear about expectations and then using all 4 Windows of Leadership to help them realize the full results of their Window of Potential.

HOW GOOD ARE YOU AT MATCHING STYLES TO POTENTIAL?

Remember the cases you read in Chapter 1? The first eight cases involved individuals and there were two cases for each level of performance potential. In the next four sections, you can see how effective (or ineffective) your responses were at each level of follower potential.

Start with the P1 Situations

The two cases that follow were P1 cases. In each situation, the follower's performance potential was relatively low. Put your answers in the spaces below to see how much of each style you used in these cases.

After adding each column, multiply your totals by 10 to find out what percentage of each style you used in these P1 situations. Then to calculate your effectiveness score, multiply the totals for the best style by 10 and the next best style by 5, then add those two products together.

	S1	S2	S3	S4
CASE 1	B ____	A ____	D ____	C ____
CASE 8	A ____	B ____	C ____	D ____
TOTALS	____	____	____	____
PERCENTAGES x totals by	____ 10	____ 10	____ 10	____ 10
EFFECTIVENESS x totals by	____ 10	+ ____ 5		=____

In these P1 cases, you should have chosen mostly S1. By using Style 1, you would be directing two people who need instructions and frequent feedback. By providing specific directions, you can keep them focused on achievable tasks. Close supervision should enable them to perform satisfactorily while developing skills and confidence.

If you didn't select Style 1 with Tom in case 1, you probably weren't recognizing his need for clear directions to help him get oriented to the new assignment. Until he fully understands the job, he won't appreciate your point of view that his skills are all right. And until he knows that, his confidence and willingness will remain low.

With Megan in case 8, the situation is quite different, but still requires you to step in and take charge. She knows what she has to do and knows that she is not very good at it. The job requires more attention to detail than she has the technical skill or interest for. As a result, she is not willing to accept more responsibility and is more aligned with looking for another job than doing this one. You should encourage her to find another position, but until she can move on, you need to direct her work and monitor her closely so that your department doesn't suffer while she looks.

If you used a lot of Style 2, you were overinvolving these team members. Getting their input may be meeting your needs but is probably not helping them. Right now, Tom needs to get fully oriented to the job at hand. When that has occurred, he might have some meaningful suggestions to make. And since Megan is a bad fit for her job, her input would not help you much and might delay her moving on. At least you picked the second best choice, because Style 2 still leaves you in control which is important in these two cases.

If you used a lot of Style 3 with these two people, you were overaccommodating. You may be trying too hard to give these people developmental opportunities when they are not ready for decison-making responsibilities. They probably view you as friendly and may appreciate your offers of support, but they are not getting enough direction to make them productive.

If you selected Style 4 in these cases, you were definitely abdicating. It is not appropriate to give these people so much responsibility. They need direction and close supervision. Without this, they will flounder, feel discouraged, or direct their efforts to the wrong places.

Look at the P2 Situations

Write your answers to cases 2 and 5 in the spaces, then complete the calculations.

In the P2 cases, if you chose S2 answers, that's good. With these two people, your best response is problem solving. They have some ability and some motivation, so it is appropriate to involve them in the decision-making process. By doing this, you are helping them learn the critical issues that impact problem solving in this line of work. You are also benefiting from their skills and/or enthusiasm while making them feel involved and appreciated.

	S1	S2	S3	S4
CASE 2	C ____	A ____	B ____	D ____
CASE 5	A ____	D ____	B ____	C ____
TOTALS	____	____	____	____
PERCENTAGES x totals by	____ 10	____ 10	____ 10	____ 10
EFFECTIVENESS x totals by	____ + 5	____ 10		= ____

In case 2 with Susan, she has good skills and the confidence to use them. Her performance has suffered because she lacks job knowledge and is out of alignment with the norms of your team. By listening to her ideas, you can make her feel valued; that should make her more likely to listen to your point of view. She also can learn a lot about the job and the organization through these discussions.

With Ted in case 5, he has his own narrow perspective of the department's goals. Coupled with some rough interpersonal skills, he is not performing as well as someone with his skills and experience could. By seeking his input you can broaden his understanding of the organization while letting him know that you still appreciate what he can offer to the team. Also, by letting him see you in action, maybe he will learn some better ways to work with people.

If you selected a lot of Style 1 in these cases, you were too dominating. If you just tell Susan what she needs to do differently without showing respect for what she can do, she may not be receptive to the reorientation she needs. In Ted's case, if you don't acknowledge his capabilities, he may feel too discouraged to keep trying.

If you chose Style 3 actions in these cases, you were over-accommodating. Since each person has some performance-related problem, you should not leave them in charge of making critical decisions right now. Too much responsibility might make their situations worse than they have been. Take their input for now. If improvement becomes noticeable, then you can acknowledge that with increased opportunities.

If you used a lot of Style 4 in these situations, you were guilty of abdicating. They do not understand how their actions are affecting organizational performance. Until that happens, they should not be left on their own. If they are, they are likely to create some problems for themselves and others.

Look at the P3 Situations

Put your responses to cases 3 and 6 in the spaces, then complete the calculations.

	S1	S2	S3	S4
CASE 3	C ___	D ___	A ___	B ___
CASE 6	B ___	C ___	D ___	A ___
TOTALS	___	___	___	___
PERCENTAGES x totals by	10	10	10	10
EFFECTIVENESS x totals by			___ + 10	___ = ___ 5

In the P3 cases, S3 was the best response. If you chose S3, you were developing. By listening, you are helping these followers think through their own decisions in their areas of responsibility. Your support helps them handle challenging assignments while developing their skills and confidence in the process.

In case 3, Joe just needs an orientation period to fully understand how to apply his skills most productively. Unlike Tom in case 1, Joe is highly motivated and raring to go. A little coaching from you at critical moments should be all he needs.

Martha, in case 6, had all the ability and motivation she needed to handle the original assignment. Some immediate support from you should help her regain her confidence to handle the new time constraint. Some empathy should also reduce her strong reaction so that she can refocus on the organizational need.

If you used a lot of Style 1 in these cases, you were too dominating. If you are directive with these people, they will feel smothered and will be discouraged from taking initiatives. Telling them exactly what to do would undermine their willingness to assume responsibility without giving enough regard to their ability.

If you selected a lot of Style 2 in these cases, you were overinvolving yourself in the decision-making process. You should not need to exercise this much control with either Joe or Martha. They are quite capable of making good decisions with a little support from you. At least this style is better than Style 1, since you do get them involved.

If you chose Style 4 in these cases, you were abdicating. It is appropriate to give Joe and Martha responsibility so they will feel challenged, but it is too soon to give them authority to make decisions on their own. They might do all right but they could also make some serious mistakes. To make these situations developmental, you need to talk with them at critical checkpoints to make sure they are in alignment with your expectations and offer some coaching if they are not.

Look at the P4 Situations

Write your responses to cases 4 and 7 in the spaces, then complete the calculations.

	S1	S2	S3	S4
CASE 4	D ____	B ____	C ____	A ____
CASE 7	D ____	C ____	A ____	B ____
TOTALS	____	____	____	____
PERCENTAGES x totals by	____ 10	____ 10	____ 10	____ 10
EFFECTIVENESS x totals by			____ 5 +	____ 10 = ____

In the P4 cases, you should have chosen S4. If you did, then you were effectively delegating to people who were capable of handling these situations on their own. Since both Jane and Barry are high on ability and high on motivation, it is appropriate to give them the authority to make decisions on their own. In situations like this, team members usually thrive on responsibility and are motivated by the opportunity to take charge.

In Jane's case, she is performing very well and does not appear to need any support from you. Your only reason for getting involved is to remind her that she still works for you and is not totally independent. Your best way to do that is to give her plenty of appreciation for the good job she is doing without distracting her from her work. With some recognition for the way that she handles her responsibilities, Jane will value you as her boss and continue to perform for you.

In Barry's situation, the reason to consider intervening is based on mounting organizational pressure. Often it is good to anticipate that pressures can require some support from above, but you should not make the assumption that Barry cannot handle his responsibilities on his own. He always has and there is every reason to believe that he will now. Be alert and stay sensitive to his situation, but don't jump in if you don't have to. By waiting, you may discover that all you need to do is give him recognition for a job well done.

If you used mostly Style 3 in these situations, you were overaccommodating. You would probably come across as helpful and friendly, but your support is not really needed. In fact, you may be slowing these people down by taking them away from their work at a critical moment. At least with this approach, you are not undercutting their sense of responsibility and listening to them will probably not cause any serious damage.

If you selected a lot of Style 2 in these P4 cases, you were overinvolving. There is no reason for you to take over responsibility for decision making. With Jane, if you redirect her, you would be overinvolving yourself. And in Barry's case, if you get into problem solving with his situation, you would be overinvolving him. In both situations, you would be taking these top performers away from the tasks they need to complete.

The worst response to these cases is Style 1. If you chose the Style 1 actions, you definitely would come across as dominating.

You would be giving specific directions and close supervision to people who have been handling major responsibilities on their own. Instead of smothering these people and frustrating them, you should be giving them praise for their accomplishments and staying out of their way.

HOW EFFECTIVE WERE YOU?

Before you go on, take a minute to look back at all four levels of potential. What were your effectiveness scores for each level? The best score is 100. Anything less than 80 means that you should think about your real cases at that level of potential. Ask yourself if you are making the same mistakes at work as you did with these hypothetical cases. If you are, keep reading. Chapter 9 will give you some more ways to improve.

ARE YOU READY FOR SOME MORE FEEDBACK?

When you responded to the cases, you may or may not have noticed that there were distinctly male and female names in each case. We did that on purpose to let you see if there are differences between the type of leadership you provide to men and women.

To see how you responded to the male and female cases, just look at the last few pages and copy the numbers from the P1, P2, P3, and P4 cases into the matrix on the next page. Then add the numbers in each column and multiply by 5 to see what percentage of each style you used with each group.

As you look at these scores, you need to take them with a grain of salt. Sometimes when people respond to the questions, they don't even notice the names. Even if you did read the names, one case might have been about a particular problem that made you think of somebody who was, in fact, the opposite sex of the name that was in the case. So it is important not to look at this feedback as an absolute statement about you.

Small differences don't mean much. But if you find some significant differences between the styles you used with the two genders, you might want to ask yourself why. Is it the men and women you work with? Are their needs different? Or is it inside you? Might you be giving one group what you think they need

	S1	S2	S3	S4
CASE 1	B ____	A ____	D ____	C ____
CASE 5	A ____	D ____	B ____	C ____
CASE 3	C ____	D ____	A ____	B ____
CASE 7	D ____	C ____	A ____	B ____
TOTALS	____	____	____	____
x 5	____	____	____	____

MALE PERCENTAGES

	S1	S2	S3	S4
CASE 8	A ____	B ____	C ____	D ____
CASE 2	C ____	A ____	B ____	D ____
CASE 6	B ____	C ____	D ____	A ____
CASE 4	D ____	B ____	C ____	A ____
TOTALS	____	____	____	____
x 5	____	____	____	____

FEMALE PERCENTAGES

instead of what they really need? Or giving them what you want whether they need it or not?

As you look at the two sets of percentages, if a clear pattern appears, you should think about it.

For example, in one department of a company we studied, every manager had dramatically different responses to the men and the women. It turned out that their professional staff was all men and the only women in their department were secretaries. These managers were, in fact, treating those men and women in very different ways not because they were all discriminating against women, but because the department's norms for recruiting, hiring, and promoting staff were out-of-date and clearly prejudiced. What followed was a very productive discussion about some strategies for correcting this organizational inequity, not a discussion about leading men and women differently.

Another interesting case is a general manager who was participating in an L4 training program with several levels of his management team. When he looked at his overall leadership profile, he had 70 percent in Style 3. This man was beaming ear-to-ear and said he couldn't wait to take his questionnaire home to show his wife, since she frequently accused him of being Attila the Hun. But when he looked at the differences between his male responses and female responses, his smile started to fade. With the men, he had used all four styles and used them pretty much in the right places. But with the women, he had used 100 percent Style 3. Regardless of the situation, he was more driven by his comfort level with women than their needs in task-specific terms.

When he saw the discrepancy, he asked the women who worked for him for some feedback about his interactions with them. They said he was always very friendly and very supportive but not as straight with them about what they were doing wrong. Also, they thought that he didn't trust them as much to call their own shots.

Later, he was still troubled about this and asked us what he could do differently. We said that it was very obvious. He needed to be nicer to his wife so that she would stop calling him Attila the Hun. Then he would be less afraid of getting in trouble with the women at work and could start treating them as individuals instead of as a group to be handled with kid gloves. He thought the advice might be a little hard to swallow, but did say that he would consider it.

These two stories are extremes, and you should be cautious about overinterpreting your responses to the eight cases. However, if you see some strong patterns in the scores, think about them.

Do you use the full range of styles at the right levels of performance potential? And are you objective about your people's needs without letting gender or ethnic background get in the way?

These are tough but important questions if you are going to be a good leader!

KEEP YOUR WINDOWS OPEN

Remember, the most important point of this entire chapter is that to be an effective leader, you need to be open to using all four styles all of the time while being as open as possible to recognizing which style is the primary approach to take in each situation.

Chapter 9

Window Wisdom: The Name of the Game Is Leadership by Anticipation

If all you had to do to be an effective leader was figure out an individual's performance potential and use the style that matches that potential, then a lot more people would be effective as leaders. Obviously, leadership is not that simple.

That's because the real world is not that simple. Real problems don't come at you like still photos that capture a single moment and freeze it in time. The real world is more like being in the middle of a very fast-paced movie. Working with people is a constantly shifting process requiring continuous adjustment and adaptation. Being able to anticipate and respond to changing follower needs is one of the great challenges of effective leadership.

While no one can anticipate everything, you can and should anticipate the need to change leadership styles before the need is pressing. Matching your Window of Leadership to a follower's Window of Potential is a good first step, but you need more Window Wisdom than that to make quick style changes in smooth and predictable ways.

The core of this Window Wisdom is what we call *leadership by anticipation*. There are four predictable leadership-by-anticipation patterns that will help you anticipate how to make style changes: development, intervention, frustration, and empowerment.

The *development* and *intervention* cycles will help you anticipate shifts in the main style you use with an individual. Development shows you how and when to make smooth transitions upward through the styles. Intervention teaches you how and when to make smooth transitions downward through the styles.

The *frustration* and *empowerment* cycles will help you anticipate shifts in the way you lead people on a day-to-day basis. The frustration cycle helps you avoid one of the most common traps of ineffective leadership by showing you one style change that you do not want to make. And empowerment, which we think is the most important of these four cycles, teaches you how to make style changes the way the best leaders do.

Empowerment is a guaranteed formula for real-world, day-to-day leadership. It teaches you a style sequence that will make your use of any main style successful. Any style can be the right general approach to a given situation if it is implemented with the wisdom of empowerment. And without this Window Wisdom, your use of any main style runs the risk of failure.

DEVELOPING TOP PERFORMERS

One of your most important tasks as a leader is to develop the people who are working for you. Leaders who have the most power are the ones who have people in their departments who can take over their jobs at any time or who can move on to other positions of power in other parts of the organization. Leaders who have little or no power are immobilized, stuck in dead-end jobs because they have never developed anyone in their department who could take over if they moved on.

Development is not just a nice thing to do for your people. It is an important key to organizational strength and it is an important key to your own career mobility.

When they created Situational Leadership Theory, Paul Hersey and Ken Blanchard (1982) enabled managers to understand how leadership styles can be used for development. Development is a pattern of styles that enables you to gradually turn over responsibility to members of your team. It enables your people to take on increasing amounts of responsibility and control as their performance potential steadily increases.

The development cycle is shown in Figure 9.1.

This pattern for using the four leadership styles helps you

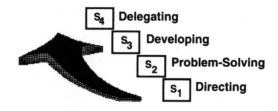

Figure 9.1   Development Cycle.

understand the main style that you should use with a person over a period of time. It shows you how to gradually make the transition from Style 1 to 2 to 3 to 4 as the individual strengthens his/her ability and motivation. As the person's performance potential increases, you should anticipate the need to move upward one step at a time.

This cycle makes a lot of sense when you think of a new person entering an unfamiliar job. Initially, you should anticipate giving a lot of directions, complete explanations, a clear picture of the payoffs and pitfalls associated with the job, plenty of advice, and frequent feedback. The person requires clear assignments and frequent checkpoints from you to help him or her get oriented to the job. Basically, you are doing on-the-job training.

As the person gains some experience, his/her technical skills usually start to improve as does his/her job and organizational knowledge. In addition, confidence, willingness, and alignment begin to increase. Consequently, you can begin to ask for input about problems and invite recommendations to your decision making.

In time, as the ability and motivation factors continue to increase, you can assign responsibilities while anticipating the need to provide support. You shouldn't leave the person totally alone, but with a little guidance he/she can perform very well.

Eventually, you can delegate the authority to go along with the responsibility. By this time, ability and motivation have increased to the point that the person can function independently.

In general, the development cycle advises you to look for opportunities to give increased amounts of responsibility as a person's performance potential gradually increases. Just think of it as gradually letting out the string of a kite. By doing this, you keep people motivated, challenged, and productive.

INTERVENING TO AVOID PROBLEMS

While the development cycle offers a logical sequence for moving through the four styles of leadership in a gradual way that promotes growth and increased autonomy for followers, managers are frequently confronted with circumstances that demand the opposite response. We call this response the *intervention* cycle.

Intervention is needed whenever a follower's performance potential is diminishing, a circumstance that can be caused by a variety of factors. When demands such as increased complexity, accelerated change, and increased time pressure reduce a follower's potential, you need to respond with intervention. By using this pattern of styles, you can limit the damage by responding to and adapting to drops in potential before they cause drops in performance.

Intervention is the flip side of development, as you can see in Figure 9.2. Instead of taking place over time, this progression often takes place in a matter of hours or minutes.

Intervention is important whenever you have been leaving followers on their own, whether it is from conscious delegation or by default. As a leader, sooner or later you have to leave people on their own, and when you do that, it is also inevitable that problems will arise that someone can't handle alone.

As problems surface, you need to anticipate moving gradually down the styles, one at a time. Think of gradually reeling a kite back in. If you pull too hard on the string, you either break the string or send the kite into a tailspin. If you reel it in steadily, you can fly it again another day.

With people, the first step is to help the person be objective about the responsibilities he/she is handling and develop his/her own action plan for turning the situation around. You should

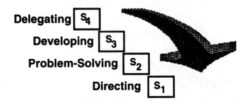

Delegating S_4
Developing S_3
Problem-Solving S_2
Directing S_1

Figure 9.2   Intervention Cycle.

use the developing style to ask questions, listen carefully to your team member's analysis of the problem situation, and find out what possible solutions he/she is considering. By doing this, you may discover that all you needed to do was listen and sign off on the action plan. You may also find out that other types of support are needed but that, with your support, this person can still handle the responsibilities and solve the problem.

Sometimes, as you listen to the problem and the alternatives that are being considered, you realize that all the support in the world will not enable this person to solve the problem. When that happens, the next step is to make the decision yourself based on the team member's analysis and recommendations. When this is necessary, usually the person will have given you many hints or outright requests (in some cases, demands) that you are the best one to make this decision. So when you do step in, the person is grateful and relieved. From your perspective, you are intervening with full information and therefore not simply shooting from the hip. More important, you are not overriding the person who was previously given the responsibility. And by totally including the follower in your decision-making process, it will be easier for him/her to reclaim the responsibility so that you don't get stuck with it.

Finally, intervention requires that, as a last resort, if the person is unaware of the problem and has no recommendations to make, you may have to move to the directing style and make the decisions on your own. However, unless the ship is literally sinking or the proverbial theatre is really on fire, you usually don't have to get this direct and are better off using the problem-solving style to take charge while capitalizing on the team members knowledge of the situation.

So that's the intervention cycle, a gradual shift from Style 4 to 3 to 2 to 1.

Why would you need to intervene like this? Sometimes intervention is caused by personal pressures. A person is getting married or divorced. Someone is having a baby or has a parent who is terminally ill. A car accident, a drinking problem, an office romance—there are all sorts of reasons why an individual's motivation might drop off.

More often than not, it is organizational pressures, not personal pressures, which cause you to intervene. In our work with a wide variety of organizations, these four factors are most frequently cited as causes for intervention: change, increased complexity, sudden visibility, and time.

Any major change can create ambiguity about job knowledge and organizational goals, and that ambiguity can impact people's confidence and willingness to assume responsibility. As major corporations have been downsizing, many employees have also experienced ambiguity about job expectations. Others talk about loss of power as their contacts for cutting through the organizational red tape have left or relocated to other divisions. And almost everyone seems unsure about his/her alignment with organizational goals because the goals themselves have become unclear as changes have taken place.

Increased complexity, like having a wider span of control, or expanding your product line, or any other version of "do more with less" will also impact performance potential. There are countless examples of excellent performers whose performance has deteriorated when their jobs were automated. You also hear lots of stories about salespeople who went from one product line that they knew well to four or five that they barely understood, or whose territories expanded from one state to half the country. These types of changes often require new technical skills, interpersonal skills, job knowledge, or organizational knowledge. And these dropoffs in the ability factors can also precipitate problems with the motivational factors of interest, confidence, or willingness to assume responsibility.

Visibility can also put pressure on people. If a major customer starts to complain, or senior management starts looking closely at your numbers, this can easily distract people from their work. Or what about having the auditors show up? Or a government regulatory agency? Or suppose the press turns your operation into a cover story? In these circumstances, interpersonal skills often get pushed to the limit as do confidence and willingness to assume responsibility. And if your organization is in the wrong, the alignment factor gets challenged in a big way.

Last, but not least, is time. Imagine that a very capable woman named Mary works for you. An important project has hit your desk and it is due in four weeks. Mary has the ability and the motivation to complete the project, so you decide to use mostly Style 4 and delegate the responsibility to her.

The next day you find out that there will only be three weeks to complete the project. So, you might need to use Style 3 as the main style to help Mary think through the new situation and make her own game plan with your listening and support.

Then your boss tells that the project has become a top priority and you only have two weeks to do the same project. Now you may need to use predominantly Style 2 to get input from Mary about the other objectives she is handling so you can make decisions about priorities and advise her about how to proceed.

Of course, as soon as that is settled, (you guessed it) the customer calls you directly and pleads to have the project done in one week. Forget propping up Mary. Now you have to take charge of it yourself. Assemble your team, tell each person including Mary explicitly what he or she can do to help you get the project completed, and coordinate the effort yourself.

The point is that in each scenario Mary is the same person and the project has the same requirements, but the time factor could make any one of the four styles appropriate.

RAISING THE PERFORMANCE BAR

Remember the discussion in the last chapter about matching your leadership styles to followers' potential? A diagram similar to the one in Figure 9.3 illustrated the need to provide the added value that guarantees that followers will hit the performance line.

In this new diagram, the bar has been raised. That's normal. Organizations always raise the bar. And they should. That's what keeps them competetive.

For you and the people who work for you, the intervention cycle will make life a lot easier and work more productive. When

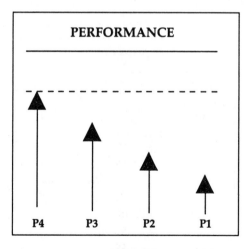

Figure 9.3 Raising Performance Expectations.

management raises the bar by increasing performance standards or asking you to do more with less, they have upped the ante and you have to intervene one step at a time to be sure your team handles the changes.

In these situations, you have to be careful to avoid the trap of trying to do it all yourself. Many managers do just that. When the bar gets raised, they come in earlier, stay later, spend every minute of drive-time on their car phones, have a computer at home so they can keep going at all hours of the night, and try their hardest to fill all of the gaps. In the end, they can't do it. Instead, they just do themselves in.

Smarter managers realize that they can't do it all themselves, and that their people have to be empowered to take on more responsibilities. It has become conventional wisdom that you have to drive the responsibility down into your organization. And everyone is talking about empowering their employees to handle these new responsibilities. But, in most cases, employees aren't feeling empowered at all. Instead they are feeling buried. If you drive responsibility down to the members of your team and then leave your people alone with these increased duties, you aren't empowering anyone. You're just unloading the dump truck on their shoulders.

When you push responsibility down, you are raising the bar for your people. And you have to anticipate how the performance line looks from their perspective, as illustrated by Figure 9.4. That means that you have to prepare yourself to do more leading than you have ever done before.

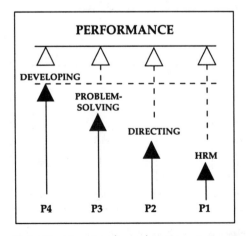

Figure 9.4 Do More Leading when Expectations Increase.

In a situation that used to be P4, you now should use Style 3, Developing, to help people hit the new line with your support.

In a previous P3 situation, you now need to use Style 2, Problem Solving, listen to their problems and recommendations, then make the tough decisions that they may lack the confidence or alignment to make.

In situations that used to be P2, you may not have the luxury to involve staff in your decision making now, and simply need to use Style 1, Directing, to get them pointed in the new direction.

And in situations that used to be P1, you probably can't afford to keep up the on-the-job training, and need to consider human-resource management strategies. Basically, you need to fish or cut bait.

If you are going to fish, training is one option which helps people meet new standards by improving their technical skills, interpersonal skills, job knowledge, interest, confidence, and willingness to assume responsibilities. Organizations that do a good job with change management are usually prepared with training programs designed to help their people handle new and increased responsibilities.

All the training in the world won't save you from the reality that in some cases, you may have to cut bait. The leaders of major changes consistently tell us that their greatest challenges as leaders come when they have to counsel people into lower status jobs or out of the organization. It isn't pleasant, but doing it well can make the difference between success and failure.

HERE'S A LITTLE MORE REALITY FOR YOU

On that sober note, let's talk a little more about reality. They say beauty is in the eyes of the beholder. Reality is also based on individual perceptions, which means that your reality may look quite different to other people.

Even so, when most people look upward at their managers, the reality that they typically describe is illustrated in Figure 9.5.

Most people in most organizations, when they talk about the leadership styles they receive on a day-to-day basis, say that they get told what to do (Style 1) and then left alone to do it (Style 4). If your people like the way you do it, if it's appropriate for them, they give you credit for delegating. If they don't like it, if it's not working for them, they accuse you of abdicating. But the net effect is the same. Most people see their managers starting with Style 1 and moving to Style 4.

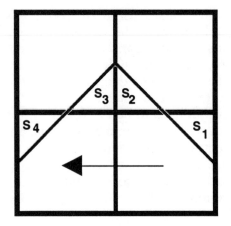

Figure 9.5   How Most Followers See Their Managers.

Is that your reality? Is that what you get from the people above you? Do they give you assignments and then let you figure out how to get them done?

And what about the people who work for you? Is that how they perceive you? There is a high probability that they do.

But that's just the first part of the picture. It's your next move that determines whether or not you will be perceived as a good leader or a bad one.

FRUSTRATION!

If people perceive you as moving from directing to delegating (or abdicating), and your tendency is to tell people what to do when they are having difficulties, you may be caught in one of the most unproductive patterns of leadership. We call it the *frustration* cycle, also known as the 1-4-1 sequence. Frustration looks like Figure 9.6.

Unfortunately, a lot of managers get caught up in the 1-4-1 cycle. They start with Style 1, they move to Style 4, and when things don't work out, they move back to Style 1. It's guaranteed that when you move back from Style 4 to Style 1, you will be perceived as dominating.

In our work with leaders throughout the world, from all kinds of organizations—public, private, manufacturing, service, big, medium, small—we ask people to talk with us about their

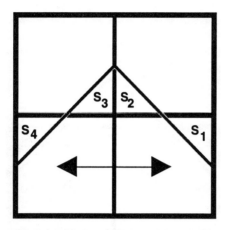

Figure 9.6 The 1-4-1 Frustration Cycle.

experiences with particularly bad leaders. One of our biggest surprises has been the consistency of the stories that we hear.

We also ask people to quantify their experiences by distributing 100 percentage points among the four leadership styles to show us how much of each style these worst leaders use. Again, we have found amazing similarities.

We will show you the similarities next, but before you read any further, take a few minutes to play with this question yourself. Think of the worst leader you have seen in your organization. It could be someone you reported to directly or it could be someone else if you were close enough to know how he/she worked with people.

Think of the leadership styles this individual used. How much directing/dominating? How much problem solving/ overinvolving? How much developing/overaccommodating? And how much delegating/abdicating?

In the spaces in Figure 9.7, distribute 100 points among the four styles to show how often this leader used each style.

Then look at Figure 9.8 so you can compare your experience with some samples from a variety of very different organizations.

In every industry, the worst leaders rely heavily on Style 1 and Style 4. They use significantly less Style 2 and Style 3. And when the people who have worked for these worst leaders talk about them, it is clear that they are guilty of dominating and abdicating.

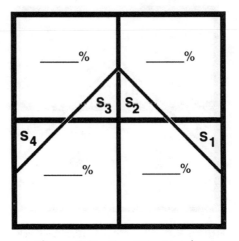

Figure 9.7 Your Worst Leader.

The war stories actually take three forms. There are some poor leaders who need to join Dominators Anonymous. They like to control everyone and want everything done their way. They get stuck in the details, they micromanage, and they don't trust anybody.

There are other ineffective leaders who should sign up for Abdicators Anonymous. You can never find them. They are very inaccessible. And if you do catch up with them, you can't get much out of them, so the next time you won't even bother. They do their jobs and leave you alone to do yours. Some truly trust

WORST LEADERS				
Accounting	43	07	04	46
Consulting	42	13	08	37
Hi Tech	45	11	10	34
Insurance	44	13	10	33
Manufacturing	43	17	07	33
Pharmaceuticals	40	12	08	40

Figure 9.8 Worst Leader Profiles.

the people below them and stay out of the way with the best intentions, but most are just too caught up in their own work or their own careers to spend time with their people.

The third type is the 1-4-1 leader. They tell you what needs to be done in fairly general terms. Then they leave you alone to handle it. Then they criticize you for not doing it the way they wanted it.

This cycle is also known as the "leave 'em alone and zap 'em" strategy.

It is also known as the "seagull technique" in which the manager swoops in from far away, flaps his wings, makes a lot of noise, leaves some droppings on everybody's windshield, and then flies off again.

Whatever you call this pattern in your organization, the result is definitely frustration for the people on the receiving end. Fortunately, there are other choices.

EMPOWERMENT

When we ask people to talk with us about the worst managers they have known, we also ask them to talk about the best ones they have worked for. Again there are striking similarities across a wide variety of industries.

We will show you the percentages in a minute, but as you did before, take a few minutes to play with this question yourself. This time, think of the best leader you have seen in your organization. In Figure 9.9, distribute 100 points among the four styles to show how often this leader used each style.

Then take a look at the data about best leaders.

As you saw with the worst leaders, there are some striking similarities with these best leaders, too. There are some variations in the percentages that different industries assign to each style, but the pattern is quite consistent and the stories that people tell are remarkably similar.

In every type of organization, people tell us that the best leaders mainly use Styles 3 and 4. They give employees lots of responsibility and are available to support them when they need some assistance.

The best leaders also use Style 2 as a backup style. They are willing to listen to recommendations and step up to the plate to make tough decisions when people need them to.

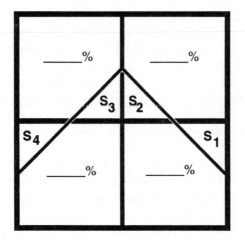

Figure 9.9 Your Best Leader.

When we ask people to describe their best leaders in words, the stories have some clear themes. One fascinating lesson for us is that the best leaders start out just like the worst leaders do. They begin with Style 1, then they move to Style 4. That's why we told you earlier that there is a high probability that the people who work for you perceive you to be using the 1-4 pattern.

That's where the similarity ends. Instead of going back to Style 1 when problems arise, the best leaders move to Style 3. They listen and ask questions to probe for a full understanding of the situation. They want to know their followers' thinking

BEST LEADERS			
Accounting	06	16	36	42
Consulting	14	24	27	35
Hi Tech	14	23	34	29
Insurance	10	20	35	35
Manufacturing	14	21	35	30
Pharmaceuticals	10	23	37	30

Figure 9.10 Best Leader Profiles.

about how to fix the problem, and they help them make up their mind about the best actions to take. When they offer support, it is to help team members with their responsibilities, not to take over and undermine their sense of accountability.

These best leaders are also willing to roll up their sleeves and get their hands dirty. If problems require them to make the decisions, they will shift to Style 2 by taking input from the key people who are involved and making timely decisions that enable their team's work to move forward.

Figure 9.11 shows you how best leaders use the four styles.

The sequence is 1-4-3-2. We call it the *empowerment* cycle because people who experience this sequence of styles consistently report that they feel truly empowered. And if any window is not opened, they don't feel empowered.

To do their best work, people want you to give them complete information, including directions, advice, explanations, and consequences. That's Style 1.

Then, they want you to trust them, delegate meaningful responsibilities to them, give them the authority they need to do what you hired them to do. That's Style 4.

When they get stuck, as everyone does sooner or later, they want your support to help them think through their own decisions without undercutting their sense of responsibility. This is where Style 3 comes in.

And finally, if they are still stuck, and need you to step up to the plate, they want you to listen to their ideas and make timely

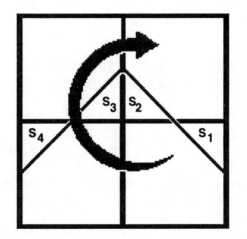

Figure 9.11 The 1-4-3-2 Empowerment Cycle.

decisions based on their recommendations. The last step is
Style 2.

When you use this 1-4-3-2 empowerment cycle, Style 3 is a
key pivot point.

By listening to people at critical check points, you do two
things simultaneously. You help them develop their own problem-solving capabilities while diagnosing problems which you
may need to resolve if they cannot.

From the Style 3 window, you give yourself maximum flexibility. You can shift back to Style 4 by simply giving people
feedback that they're on the right track, positive recognition to
encourage them to continue assuming responsibility. Or you can
stay in Style 3 by listening and giving them support with their
decision making. Or you can make a smooth transition to Style
2 in case you need to make a tough decision. The Style 3 window
helps you keep your leadership options open.

Remember, your followers already see you moving from
Style 1 to Style 4. The critical move comes next. If you go back
to Style 1, you are taking over. And even if you do it in a matter-
of-fact way, you will be perceived as dominating. The game is
over. But if you keep moving clockwise to Style 3, you are still in
the game of motivating top performance.

We need to be very clear. We are not saying that Style 3 is the
best style. That would be counter to everything we have said before.

All four styles are critical. All the time. Regardless of the
main style you are using.

And if you want to empower your people, this 1-4-3-2 cycle
can make your life and the lives of your employees a lot easier
and a lot more productive.

DON'T YOU HAVE TO USE DIFFERENT STYLES
IN DIFFERENT SITUATIONS?

Sure. But it's not enough to select the best main style for each
situation. Actually, you have to use a different mix of all four
styles in every situation. And regardless of which window is
open the most, if you open them in the 1-4-3-2 sequence, you are
going to be a lot more effective. Consider these two cases.

Joe just started working for you. He's bright and energetic
but definitely a rookie. He has limited experience with your
technology and no background in your industry, but he is enthu-

siastic about learning everything.

So what are you going to do? Developmentally, you know that Joe needs a lot of Style 1 and Style 2 from you. But do you hold his hand all day?

Of course not. You give him an assignment, tell him what he needs to know to get started. That's Style 1.

Then you leave him alone to give it a try. That's Style 4.

After awhile, you return, ask him how he's doing, listen to what he says, and look at what he's produced. That's Style 3.

Then you give him feedback and then redirect him so he learns the right ways to get the work done. That's Style 2.

You start with a lot of directing, use a little delegating, follow that with some developing, then move on to a lot of problem solving. Mostly 1 and 2 with a little 4 and 3 in between.

Elizabeth's situation is totally different. She's been working for you for a long time. She's very experienced, knows what she is doing, and is very much in sync with your thoughts about what is important. In all honesty, she knows her job responsibilities a lot better than you do.

So what mix of styles do you use with Elizabeth?

When you think of her developmentally, you know that she can operate very independently, so Style 4 is the main style you will use with her. But when you think of your full range of interactions with her, all four styles come into play.

You take time with her on a regular basis to clarify departmental goals and her individual objectives. And if a new initiative is required in her area, you give her all the information you can so that she understands what needs to be accomplished. That's Style 1.

Most of the time you stay out of her way and let her do her work. You trust her to handle it as well as, if not better than, you could. That's Style 4.

Occasionally, you check in with her to see how she's doing and find out if she needs anything from you. And once in a while she seeks you out to ask for some advice or assistance. That's Style 3.

Finally, there are a few times when Elizabeth wants you to get more involved in a sticky situation. She gives you a full briefing but relies on you to get some resolution as quickly as you can. That's Style 2.

With her, you are using a little Style 1, mostly Style 4, periodic Style 3, and occasional Style 2. The amount of each style is very different from the amounts you use with Joe. But the sequence is the same.

You have two very different people in two very different situations and you work with them in very different ways. But the 1-4-3-2 empowerment cycle enables each one of them to perform to the best of his/her potential.

With each of them, and with each of the people who work for you, 1-4-3-2 guides you to delegate as much as possible while surrounding the delegation with the right amounts of directing on the front end and the necessary amounts of developing and problem solving on the rear end. Delegating only results in empowerment if all four windows are opened. The challenge is learning what each person needs in each situation, and it is so easy to find out when you let 1-4-3-2 be your guide.

WINDOW WISDOM

Now your view of the world of leading individuals is complete. You know how to use a follower's Window of Potential to identify the best main style to use with him/her in each situation. And you also know about leadership by anticipation.

Leadership isn't the style-of-the-month club that some organizations inadvertently promote. And it isn't even the style-per-person-per-situation club that many older leadership models have suggested.

Leadership is more than that.

You have to develop people by gradually opening the windows, 1-2-3-4, to change your general approach in ways that give followers increased responsibilities.

When people are struggling due to personal or organizational reasons, you also have to intervene, 4-3-2-1, to gradually change your general approach in ways that provide increasing amounts of assistance.

And regardless of the main style that is appropriate, you will be most effective if you empower people by following the 1-4-3-2 sequence. Flexibility is the name of the game, and this last piece of Window Wisdom will help you be an outstanding leader as you guide your team to play hardball in the big leagues.

REFERENCES

Hersey, Paul, and Blanchard, Kenneth. *Management of Organizational Behavior*. Fourth Edition, New York: Prentice Hall Press, 1982.

Chapter 10

Creating Windows of Opportunity with Your People

As you have been reading the last two chapters, you have probably been thinking about how these concepts apply to you and your real-world problems. By now, you should have a good understanding of the basic concept of matching your Window of Leadership to a follower's Window of Potential. You should also have a good idea of how to adjust your main style as conditions change for the better or for worse. And you should have a solid appreciation for the value of using all four styles in the 1-4-3-2 sequence in order to empower the people who work with you.

In this chapter, you can really sink your teeth into these ideas by trying out two simple structures that make it easy to apply The L4 System to any individual on your team. The first structure is called *situational analysis*. The second is *performance contracting*.

SITUATIONAL ANALYSIS: A TOOL FOR CORRECTING PERFORMANCE PROBLEMS

Before starting the situational analysis process, you need to be sure that you really have a performance problem on your hands. Sometimes you may be uncomfortable with a person who is, in actuality, performing quite well. In that type of situation, you should talk to a friend, talk to your boss, talk to your spouse, talk to whomever you want to, but do not start messing up a good situation.

On the other hand, if there is a performance problem, then you should go ahead with a complete analysis of the situation.

Before you read any further, take a minute to think of someone who works for you whose performance does not meet your standards. As you read about the four steps, try applying the process to your own situation. You will see just how easy it is to make these concepts work for you.

Step 1

The first step is to to be specific about the goal and the tasks where the performance is not acceptable. Then, you need to focus in on those tasks where there is a difference between the actual performance and the ideal results that you expect.

1a. What goal is not being accomplished? ————————————

————————————————————————————————

————————————————————————————————

1b. What tasks or responsibilites are not being achieved satisfactorily?

Task 1 ——————————————————————————————

Task 2 ——————————————————————————————

Task 3 ——————————————————————————————

Task 4 ——————————————————————————————

Step 2

Once you are clear about the problem tasks, in Step 2 you need to identify the ideal style for dealing with this situation by diagnosing the team member's task-specific performance potential. To do that, assess ability and motivation as high (2 points), moderate (1 point), or low (0 points). Write the numbers down next to the A____ and the M____. Then just add them together to calculate the potential.

For example, if ability is high, write down A2. If motivation is moderate, write down M1. When you add them together, you get P3.

The potential tells you which style is theoretically correct. If it's a P1 situation, S1 is usually the best response; P2, S2; P3, S3; P4, S4.

---

2. For each task, identify the main style you need to use by diagnosing this person's performance potential.

T1 A_____ + M_____ = P_____ = S_____

T2 A_____ + M_____ = P_____ = S_____

T3 A_____ + M_____ = P_____ = S_____

T4 A_____ + M_____ = P_____ = S_____

The performance potential checklist, which is below, will help you make this diagnosis. Remember, if you think all four factors are okay, assign 2 points. If you have questions about any factor, assign 1 point. If you are concerned about many factors, assign 0 points.

ABILITY

- Technical Skills
- Interpersonal Skills
- Job Knowledge
- Organizational Power

MOTIVATION

- Interest in the Task
- Confidence
- Willingness to Accept Responsibility
- Alignment with Organizational Goals

Step 3

This step focuses on your role in this situation. Before taking any action, you need to determine the main style you are currently using. This is important because you may be part of the problem.

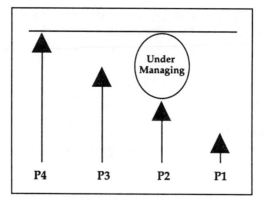

Figure 10.1   Undermanaging: Failing to Close the Gap.

You might be undermanaging, as shown in Figure 10.1, or overmanaging, as shown in Figure 10.2, and actually making the situation worse than it has to be. Remember that your job is to provide the right amount of direction and support to help team members hit the performance line. If you are not doing that, you may be contributing to the performance problem.

Or it is possible that you are doing more leading than the situation calls for. In that type of situation, you may be reducing the team member's motivation and actually making performance worse than if you had been less involved.

You can do Step 3 on your own by just thinking about what you typically do with this person, or you may want to talk with someone who can help you be objective about how you are coming across, or in some cases, you may want to ask for

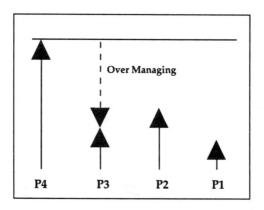

Figure 10.2   Overmanaging: Widening the Gap by Overleading.

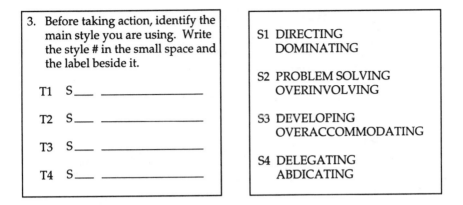

3. Before taking action, identify the main style you are using. Write the style # in the small space and the label beside it.

T1 S___ _____

T2 S___ _____

T3 S___ _____

T4 S___ _____

S1 DIRECTING
    DOMINATING

S2 PROBLEM SOLVING
    OVERINVOLVING

S3 DEVELOPING
    OVERACCOMMODATING

S4 DELEGATING
    ABDICATING

feedback from the person who's having the problem. That person really knows how you come across.

However you decide to look at your piece of the action, Step 3 is important.

Step 4

Finally, Step 4 is to take corrective action. In Step 2, you identified the main style to use for each task. That tells you the general approach to use with this individual. Remembering the development and intervention patterns, if your current style is more than one style away, be sure to go up or down one step at a time. Changing styles too abruptly can make problems worse instead of better.

More importantly, as you change your general approach, you also need to rethink the situation in terms of the 1-4-3-2 empowerment pattern. Did you give this person adequate information up front? Were you clear about the authority that you were delegating and the ways that you wanted to be kept informed? Have you really listened to understand the other person's perspective, his/her analysis of the situation and ideas for turning it around? If problem solving was necessary, have you made timely decisions when it was clear that you needed to?

Without considering the full 1-4-3-2 cycle, you may not succeed with your action plan. It won't do you much good to shift from Style 4, Abdicating, to Style 3, Developing, if you were never clear in the first place about what the performance expectations were. Likewise, it would be fruitless to shift from Style 1,

Dominating, to Style 2, Problem Solving, without giving the person some opportunity to follow your directions. And having used some Style 4 to do that, you need to spend some time using some Style 3 by asking questions and listening before you consider a shift to Style 2, Problem Solving. And who knows? A little Style 3 may be all that was really needed. Often when you let go, people surprise you with how much they can do.

---

4. To change from your current style to the correct main style, use the 1-4-3-2 cycle to identify all of the actions you need to do more of or less of to help this person perform to the best of his/her potential.

> S1 = Give Information, Clarify Expectations
> S4 = Confirm Authority, Reward taking Responsibility
> S3 = Listen, Provide Support in any area of Ability or Motivation
> S2 = Make Decisions based on Recommendations

	MORE OF	LESS OF
T1	_____	_____
T2	_____	_____
T3	_____	_____
T4	_____	_____

A CASE WHERE SITUATIONAL ANALYSIS PAID OFF

Roberta McLaughlin, another Charter Oak director, tells the story of Sandy, a young supervisor in an accounting firm. Sandy had been with the firm for five years, had been promoted to supervisor after three years, and was hoping to be promoted to manager within the next year. She had supervised many engagement teams on a wide variety of different audits.

Sandy was having a problem with another woman named Jennifer who was one of the staff on her current engagement. An important meeting with a client was coming up and the manager wanted to meet with Sandy and Jennifer prior to that meeting. The only time they could meet was early in the morning, so Sandy told Jennifer to meet her and the manager at the office at 7:30 A.M. (Meetings of this sort are not unusual in the accounting industry.)

The night before the meeting, Sandy got a phone call at home. It was Jennifer. "Does the meeting have to be at 7:30?"

"Yes. That's the only time the manager can meet with us."

"Well, I have a problem. I get up at 5:30 every morning so that I can run for half an hour, take a shower, make my lunch, and have enough time to drive to the office. If I have to be there at 7:30 I won't have time. What should I do?"

"Why don't you just get up earlier?"

"Well, I already get up at 5:30. I wouldn't want to get up any earlier than that."

"Could you skip the running or run for less time?"

"I can't do that. I have to run half an hour every morning or I'll be worthless all day."

"Okay. Could you make your lunch tonight and put it in the refrigerator?"

"I can't do that. My sandwich would be soggy and leak all over the place."

This went on for some time. Eventually, Sandy had listened long enough and said to Jennifer, "I understand your problem but you will just have to decide for yourself. The meeting cannot be changed from 7:30. I'm sure you'll figure something out."

Of course, the next morning Jennifer got there 20 minutes late. The manager was furious and Sandy was embarrassed as well as frustrated. But Sandy and Jennifer and the manager didn't address the problem. They just talked very fast for the 10 minutes they had left before the meeting with the client.

After that, Sandy still didn't say anything to Jennifer because she was afraid of being drawn into another lengthy conversation and losing more precious time.

Then, for the rest of the audit, day after day, Jennifer was late for everything.

Some months later, Sandy found out that Jennifer had decided to leave the firm and was clearly not motivated in the way that most staff are in this type of situation. That made the problem more understandable, but Sandy still wanted to know what she could have done differently.

So she used situational analysis.

Step 1

The goal was clear. Jennifer needed to be on time for meetings, work assignments, and deadlines. The critical task was for her to get up in time to take care of her own needs and be prompt for work.

Step 2

Thinking about Jennifer's overall Window of Potential, on the ability side of the equation, she had good technical skills as an accountant, was usually good at communicating with people, understood the requirements of her job very clearly, and did not need much power to complete her areas of the audit. On the motivation side, her interest was waning, she still had confidence in her abilities, she had lost her willingness to take on responsibility, and she was more aligned with her own career changes than accomplishing firm goals. So the general assessment of Jennifer's performance potential was high ability and low motivation, A2M0.

That means that Sandy should have been using Style 2 as the main style with Jennifer.

Jennifer, knowing that she was planning to leave the firm, realized that she had lost her motivation and, in her own way, tried to let Sandy know what she was dealing with. When she called and asked her supervisor to decide for her, Jennifer was inviting Sandy to use Style 2 with her.

Step 3

What was Sandy's piece of the action? She spent a lot of time listening and trying to help Jennifer figure out a way to do everything. She gave Jennifer several options hoping that one of the ideas would help Jennifer decide. Sandy really wanted to help.

What style was this? Style 3, Overaccommodating.

At the end of the telephone conversation, Sandy actually moved to Style 4, Abdicating, when she left Jennifer on her own to make the final decision. After the meeting with the Manager, Sandy was clearly using Style 4, Abdicating, when she failed to confront the late arrival. And she continued in this mode throughout the engagement.

Step 4

What should Sandy have done differently? The main style she needed to use was Style 2, Problem Solving. Her general approach should have been to anticipate that Jennifer would be able to identify problems and suggest possible solutions but not make good decisions on her own or with support. Sandy needed to call the shots. That would have included being clear about the actions that Jennifer needed to take and also enforcing consequences, like staying late or coming in even earlier the next day, if Jennifer did not take the necessary actions.

Thinking about a complete action plan, Sandy needed to consider all four windows of the 1-4-3-2 pattern. She needed some Style 1 to be crystal clear about expectations, including a specific reprimand about what happened at that first meeting. She needed to use less Style 4 which had her leaving Jennifer alone and hoping that things would get better. She needed more frequent use of Style 3 focused on Jennifer's work. This would provide more critical checkpoints to ensure that the work was getting done in a timely manner, and also give Sandy an opportunity to offer praise for doing the right things. Finally, she needed to be more willing to cross over from Style 3 to Style 2 whenever there was any chance of Jennifer's missing a deadline. At these times, Sandy needed to listen to the alternatives, be very decisive and clear about what had to be done and when it was due, and be prepared to enforce consequences if that did not happen.

Now Sandy knew what she should have done. Initially, when she was confronted with this situation, her reaction was that she was faced with an impossible situation, she had tried everything she could think of, had already spent as much time as she could with Jennifer, and was giving up. After the situational analysis, Sandy realized that she was part of the problem, that her actions actually were making a bad situation worse, and that she was not helpless. There were very specific actions she could have taken to turn that problem around.

The next time she had that kind of problem she would know what to do.

ANOTHER SUCCESS STORY

Phillippe was a manager in the Canadian operation of an international company that manufactures, installs, and maintains elevators. He had been with the company for 10 years and had worked his way up from worker to supervisor to manager.

Phillippe's problem was very different from Sandy's. In fact, when he first talked about it, he said, "Here's a situation that doesn't fit into your system. I have a problem that no one can solve."

His problem was with a woman named Marie who worked for him. Marie was extremely capable but kept asking Phillippe to make decisions for her that he wanted her to make on her own. Phillippe was sure that Marie could do more on her own because whenever he was out of the office for a few days, she handled everything perfectly. Whenever he would call in, she had everything under control and his peers told him how well Marie did in his absence.

The problem was that the minute he would come back to the office, there was Marie with a list of problems for Phillippe to deal with.

Phillippe really wanted to know how to deal with this situation, and even though he was sure that situational analysis would not help, he agreed to try out the process.

Step 1

What was the goal? Phillippe wanted Marie to handle her responsibilities independently. What were the critical tasks? Marie needed to be able to identify problems, consider the alternatives for solving those problems, weigh the pros and cons of each alternative, and make a good decision.

Step 2

What style was most appropriate for each of these tasks? Diagnosing Marie's performance potential for each task, she had high ability and high motivation, A2 M2, for the first two tasks, identifying problems and thinking of various ways to solve them. So for those tasks, she was P4, and Style 4, Delegating, was the best general approach to take.

For tasks 3 and 4, evaluating the options and making the ultimate decision, even though Marie had the ability to do that, she lacked something on the motivation side of the equation. Maybe she lacked full confidence or maybe she wanted to be sure her thinking was in alignment with Phillippe's, but for one reason or another, she appeared to be happier if she did not have to handle critical decisions alone. So Marie's potential for these tasks was A2 M1 and Phillippe's response to this P3 situation should have been Style 3, Developing.

Step 3

What was Phillippe's current leadership style? This is what he would typically do. After a trip, he would come into the office and ask Marie what problems she had for him to deal with. She would explain the problems and he would make the decisions.

In addition, if Marie would come across a problem when he was in the office, she would come to him with the information and ask him what he wanted her to do. What do you think Phillippe would do? Of course, he would make the decision and tell Marie what to do.

What type of leadership was he providing? Style 2, Overinvolving. He was inserting himself into these situations more than he wanted to and more than she really needed. Phillippe was making decisions in many instances when a little bit of support would have helped her develop her confidence and be increasingly sure that she and Phillippe were aligned in their thinking.

Step 4

Phillippe needed to shift from Style 2, Overinvolving, to Style 3, Developing. Instead of listening to the problems and telling Marie how to solve them, he needed to stay in the listening mode. To do that, he needed to ask more questions like, "How do you think that should be handled?" or "What do you think would happen if we took that course of action?" or "What would you do if I were not here and you had to decide on your own?" These questions would help Marie think out loud, get feedback from Phillippe that she is on the right track, and become more confident in handling many of these problems on her own.

There will always be some situations where she wants a supportive ear to help her think through a decision. And there may be occasional problems where Phillippe really does need to make a tough decision. But most of the time, Marie will learn that it is all right to decide on her own.

Thinking beyond this general approach, Phillippe also used 1-4-3-2 to make a complete action plan for working out this new relationship with Marie.

Rather than just start asking Marie questions and changing the conversational pattern they had developed over the years, he needed to use some Style 1 to give her feedback about his confidence in her abilities and explain that his goal was for her to make most decisions on her own. He also needed to explain that he was willing to support her whenever she felt the need. He might even want to point out some of the positive consequences that might result from this shift, like increased responsibility, good performance reviews, or promotions if those were reasonable expectations.

Then he needed to use more Style 4 to demonstrate his confidence in her. In this case, that meant not walking into the office and asking her what problems she had for him. Unintentionally, Phillippe had been sending Marie a message that he wanted her to bring him problems to solve. His new line needed to be something like, "It is so good having someone like you here who can handle everything when I have to be out of the office."

Next, he needed to be very conscious of using Style 3 when Marie would approach him with problems. He had to resist the temptation to just give her his answer. By asking questions and reflecting back her ideas, he would be investing a few minutes with her on each problem in order to gain tremendous amounts of time later on as Marie increased her willingness to handle responsibilities.

Finally, he needed to stop asking her to bring problems to his attention and he had to be less willing to put the monkey on his own back when she brought problems to him. It would be better for him and for her if she retained the decision-making responsibility.

PERFORMANCE CONTRACTING: AN EVEN MORE POWERFUL TOOL

If you liked situational analysis, you will love *performance contracting*. This structure gives you a simple way to empower the people on your team to tell you what they need. It is also a very useful tool for leading upward so that you can tell your manager when you need support and what kinds of support you need. It is an easy way to put the 1-4-3-2 empowerment pattern into practice with your people while getting for yourself the empowerment you want from your boss.

Unlike situational analysis, which you do on your own by assessing a team member's potential and then changing your styles to match that assessment, performance contracting is not done on your own. This process gets other people 100 percent involved.

Step 1

The first step is to identify goals. Do you ever take it for granted that people know what you want? Have you ever given an assignment only to find out later that what seemed perfectly clear to you was actually ambiguous to the other person?

If you have had these experiences, then you understand why it is important to do Step 1 and even more important to do it with the person who will be responsible for completing the assignment. Step 1 of the performance contracting process is nothing more than a little bit of common sense that often gets overlooked. Just sit down with each member of your team and clarify expectations. What needs to get done and when is it due?

Step 2

Have you ever discovered at the last minute that an important step in the process was left out? Have you ever been shocked that a procedure which is second nature to you was totally ignored? Have you ever been amazed that the entire approach to a problem was ill-advised? If clarifying goals is sometimes taken for granted, understanding how the work will get done is overlooked even more frequently. And if you don't know how the work will be done, there is a high probability that you and your staff will be out of sync with each other.

So, after you have explained what needs to be done and when it is due, the next step is to be sure that you know how the team member plans to achieve the goal. If the plan is all right, you can sign off on it. If it isn't, you can offer feedback.

In Step 2, you should let the team member take the lead so that you can learn how he/she is going to approach the assignment. Most often this is done in conversation, simply by asking how the follower plans to get the job done. Sometimes it may be better to have the person write down the major tasks that are needed to achieve the goal. Whether you discuss the plan or write it down, the important thing is for the person who owns the contract to tell you the actions he/she plans to take to deliver the desired results in the necessary time frame.

Step 3

Once you understand and approve of the way the work is going to get done, Step 3 is to identify the type of leadership that will guarantee follower success. It is very unlikely that you have had this type of conversation because this topic is almost never discussed up front. If it is talked about, it is usually done behind your back or after the fact when it is too late to do anything other than learn for the next time.

Step 3 should start with the team member's assessment of what he/she needs from you followed by a candid discussion with you about the leadership styles needed for each task. Should you do everything that your people ask you to do? Certainly not! But when you get a proposal, it's important to listen before you react. Then, if you don't agree with the proposal, speak up. If you want more input to certain tasks or want to make a key decision, it's important to say so. Or, conversely, if you want the team member to handle some tasks with less involvement from you, it's all right to say that. The important thing is to reconcile any discrepancies so that you are in sync before the assignment begins.

To determine which leadership style is most appropriate for each task, the first question is, "Is support needed?" If the answer is no, the team member can do that task alone, which means he/she needs Style 4 from you.

If the answer is yes, the team member should tell you the type of support that is needed. Remember, when people ask for support, it can mean anything from the ability and motivation checklists. Support can mean technical advice, interpersonal coaching about a difficult employee or a tough customer, clarifying management expectations or customer requirements, or using organizational contacts or power. Support can also mean prioritizing interests, encouraging confidence, providing incentives (carrots or sticks) to stimulate willingness to take on responsibility, or simply listening and signing off to confirm alignment.

In Step 3, whenever support is needed, it is also important to clarify who is responsible for making critical decisions. Ambiguity about this question is one of the biggest sources of organizational conflicts. So you have to go on to the second question, "Who is responsible for decision making?" If the team member can make the decision, then Style 3 is needed to provide whatever support is necessary. If you need to make the decision or simply want to make the decision, then Style 2 is needed so that you can make a well-informed decision.

Step 4

This final step is to set critical checkpoints so that you are both clear about when you need to communicate to guarantee adequate support and timely decision making. Perhaps the most important step, this helps the team member and you set milestones and plan your time efficiently. It also helps you avoid last-minute mad dashes to the goal line or being hit with unexpected problems at the eleventh hour.

Paperwork Reduction

Some people have expressed a fear that performance contracts would lead to lots of extra paperwork. We always emphasize to them that *it's not necessary to write a written contract for every organizational goal*. In fact, it's not even desirable. If you did, you would probably drive yourself and everyone around you crazy.

Most of the time the questions should just be used as a guide for short conversations about the work that needs to be done. Ten minutes here, 15 minutes there, to keep you and your team members focused and well-coordinated.

Occasionally, if you have a new employee, someone with a performance problem, have had some conflicts with one of your people, or you need to coordinate a large project, you might want to use the process more formally. But these are the exceptions, not the rule. Most performance contracts are short discussions at the beginning of an assignment or project. The two people cover the key points, understand who is going to do what, and establish ways to stay in touch with each other as the contract unfolds. It is that simple!

TRY OUT PERFORMANCE CONTRACTING FOR YOURSELF

The best way for you to understand the performance contracting process is from a team member's perspective. If you try it out as a follower, it will help you show members of your team how to use the process.

Think about yourself in relation to your manager. Focus on one goal for which you are accountable. The process is most useful if you pick a goal that requires you to get some degree of support from your manager. If you don't need any involvement from him/her, you won't learn much about how the performance contract process works.

In the spaces below, make some notes about the deliverables and time frames for this area of responsibility.

1. GOAL What goal needs to be achieved? By when?	
DELIVERABLES	**TIMEFRAMES**
_____	_____
_____	_____
_____	_____
_____	_____

Then identify the major tasks you have to accomplish to produce the expected results. Try to list them in chronological order so it will help you view the sequence of events that will enable you to complete the project.

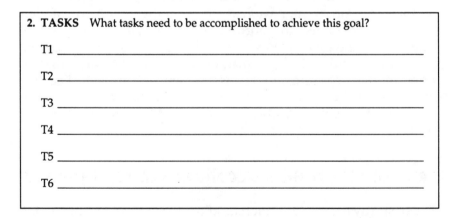

2. TASKS   What tasks need to be accomplished to achieve this goal?

T1 _____

T2 _____

T3 _____

T4 _____

T5 _____

T6 _____

In Step 3, think about the leadership styles that you need from your manager by asking yourself the two questions below. First, is support needed? If not, just check Style 4 and stop.

If support is needed, write down the type of support that you need. The most frequently requested types of support in terms of ability are technical advice, interpersonal coaching, clarifying expectations, or organizational power. In terms of motivation, people most often need prioritizing interests, encouraging confidence, incentives to stimulate willingness, or listening to signoff on alignment. But don't feel limited to these lists. In your own words, note any support that you think you need.

Whenever you need some involvement from your manager, go on to the the second question to be clear about who should make the key decisions. If it is you with your manager's input, check Style 3. If it is your manager with input from you, check Style 2.

---

3. LEADERSHIP STYLES If the answer to the support question is NO, check Style 4. If the answer to the support question is YES, write in the type of support that is needed, then answer the responsibility question and check Style 3 or Style 2.

	Is Support Needed ?		Who Is Responsible for Decisions?	
	NO = STYLE 4	**YES** = WHAT TYPE?	**Team Member** = STYLE 3	**Team Leader** = STYLE 2
T1	—	_____	—	—
T2	—	_____	—	—
T3	—	_____	—	—
T4	—	_____	—	—
T5	—	_____	—	—
T6	—	_____	—	—

Finally, in Step 4, identify the critical checkpoints for meeting with your manager to make this contract work.

---

4. CRITICAL CHECKPOINTS What are the key dates for communicating support, making timely decisions, and/or providing recognition for performance?

KEY DATES	**ACTIONS**
_____	_____
_____	_____

WHAT TYPES OF SUPPORT DO YOU NEED?

As you did this exercise, what types of support did you need? Now think about the rest of your work, the other goals for which you're accountable. What types of support do you need to achieve those goals? Technical advice? Interpersonal coaching? Clarifying expectations? Organizational contacts or power? Prioritizing interests? Encouraging confidence? A carrot or stick to take on responsibility? Listening/signoffs?

When we ask this question to groups of managers, everyone from firstline supervisors to CEOs says they need support. Almost everyone says that they need advice, expectations, power, prioritizing, and signoffs. And many people say they need every type of support at one time or another.

This point is important to remember. Most people say they need support, and when they focus on their needs, they are probably not much different from yours.

If your people were reading this chapter, what do you think they would say they need? Even though they might have stronger needs in certain areas, there is a high probability that would want essentially the same things that you do. Remember that the next time you talk with them. If you have these needs, chances are they do, too.

And if your managers were reading this chapter, they would probably say the same thing. So the next time you hesitate to ask your boss for what you need, remember that he/she is just as human as you are. If your manager needs support from time to time, why shouldn't you? And isn't it better to ask for what you need than to pretend that you don't need anything and then fail when you try to do it all yourself?

Sometimes, we mistakenly assume that the goal is for everyone to be able to function on their own. We fantasize about hiring a workforce of all P4's so that we can just turn them loose and have everything done to perfection. Reality is that if people could do everything on their own without any support, they would probably be bored. More important, if your organization is doing cutting-edge work and people are being asked to stretch, to take risks, and go the extra mile, you have to assume that everyone will need some types of support.

Performance contracting simply acknowledges this reality and makes it legitimate for people at all levels to ask for what they need. It also makes it easy for leaders like you to respond appropriately.

DO MANAGERS REALLY USE PERFORMANCE CONTRACTS?

Sure they do. Many managers tell us that this structure has helped them learn how to clarify goals and roles with those who report to them directly. Others say that even though they have been setting goals for years, performance contracts have enabled them to integrate leadership discussions into the existing planning process.

Here is one example of a manager who has gotten great results from the performance contracting process.

Bob is the director of an Organization Development department in a Fortune 500 manufacturing company. One of his primary responsibilities is starting and supporting self-directed work teams throughout North America. To achieve his goals, he has to work with lots of people from all over the organization. Most of them report to other people, so when Bob needs their involvement in his projects, he has to be as clear as possible about what he wants and be prepared to help these people see the work through to completion.

Recently, Bob asked Dave to help him start a newsletter to keep the teams from different sites around the country up-to-date on new developments. Dave reports to Bob 50 percent of his time and works for two other managers for the rest of the time. Needless to say, Dave is in demand and has to do a lot of juggling to keep up with all of his assignments.

Initially, when Bob asked Dave to handle the newsletter project, he just told him that he wanted a newsletter developed and wanted Dave to spearhead the effort. Shortly after that, L4 was introduced to all of the managers who were implementing work teams, and Bob and Dave decided to try out performance contracting to see how it worked.

Step 1 helped both Bob and Dave clarify their understanding of the goal. Initially, Bob had been somewhat vague about what he envisioned the newsletter would look like and when he was hoping to have it distributed. That vagueness had left Dave with the impression that he could develop the concept in whatever way he wanted and that time was not essential on this project. This Step 1 discussion enabled Bob to be much clearer about his expectations and Dave left the meeting knowing what Bob had in mind in terms of content, format, and timing.

Step 2 was even more illuminating for both of them. Bob had not realized how complex the assignment was until he and Dave listed all of the tasks. Dave had not known exactly how to get started until he thought through the steps with Bob. This discussion actually transformed the assignment for both the leader and follower. For Bob, the newsletter changed from a simple request to a complex endeavor. For Dave, it changed from a big and amorphous weight to a sequence of manageable tasks.

Step 3 was also enlightening for them. Bob's original tossing of the ball to Dave was based on the assumption that Style 4 was fine for someone with Dave's level of experience in the company. But when they talked, it became clear that both of them were more comfortable with Bob's using Style 2. In truth, Bob really felt the need to control this first edition. He certainly wanted major input from Dave, but since his whole project was on political thin ice, he needed to protect himself and the project's future. Dave felt the same way. He was happier with Style 2 as the general approach.

After that discussion about who had the final word, they started looking at the specific tasks. Here they found that Bob really only wanted to use Style 2 in the beginning to outline the format and at the end to have final approval of the copy. Other than that, he was willing to use Style 4 and let Dave handle the other steps on his own. Dave was all right with that for most of the tasks but there was one where he needed Bob's organizational knowledge about who was involved in successful teams and who might be good contributors to the newsletter.

So after Step 3, instead of using Style 4, abdicating on the whole project, Bob knew that he had to use Style 2 in the beginning and the end, and he knew what support he had to give Dave so he could take responsibility for the other tasks.

Step 4, setting critical checkpoints, also turned out to be important for this particular project. First, it gave Bob and Dave some clear milestones to shoot for. That helped Dave organize his time so that he could manage this project as well as the requests from his other managers. It also enabled Dave to renegotiate the timing on one part of the project when a death in the family slowed him down unexpectedly. Since he and Bob had prescheduled checkpoints, it needed only a routine conversation for them to make an adjustment.

In this entire process, all Bob and Dave wrote down were meeting times in their calendars. The initial meeting took about 30 minutes and subsequent meetings varied depending on how the project was moving forward.

Since then, Bob has used performance contracts with several other people. His rule of thumb is not to use the structure for short-term assignments or routine requests. If he has a project that will span a longer time period, especially if he is working with someone new, these up-front meetings have set the stage for clear expectations and open communications throughout the implementation.

A SYSTEMS APPROACH TO PERFORMANCE CONTRACTS

While Bob preferred using the performance contract as an informal conversation guide, some organizations have integrated this process into their formal planning and development structures.

One such organization is the Management Information Services (MIS) department of a large insurance company. This entire department, from senior vice president to first-line supervisors, participated in a teambuilding session with L4 as the foundation for the team's development. During the session, each participant formulated at least one performance contract with his/her manager. They also identified other initiatives that required more complete discussions back at the office.

After that, every employee in the department attended an L4 workshop with their supervisors so that they would understand the performance contract process and learn the value of leading upward with their supervisors.

This is not uncommon. But what this department did next was remarkable. One of their functions in the company was reducing paperwork by putting procedures and forms onto their computer systems. So they created a personal computer format for performance contracts, the PC version of PCs. Every level of manager then was instructed to clarify goals with each of his/her direct reports or immediate subordinates and enter the performance contracts into the system by a certain date so that the department could track who was doing what and systematically provide the support and timely decision making that each contract required.

For the record, that insurance company is one of the most profitable in the world. And the MIS department has played a significant role in keeping that company close to its customers and on the cutting edge of its niche in the industry.

A PC ULTIMATUM

In another Fortune 500 company, this time in the financial services industry, the firm was going through major organizational changes. Some products were no longer competitive, others weren't being marketed as well as they could have been, and the old guard of the company had grown up in a very conservative and risk-averse culture.

Organizational change efforts usually come down to changing some fundamental behaviors on the part of managers. And often that means changing the reward system that has fostered some out-of-date ways of thinking and acting.

In this instance, the executive vice president of a major division had been doing everything he could to get his management team to change. Finally, at one meeting, he said to them, "You know what the problem is? You guys have been getting rewarded for other people's work for too long now. If they perform, your departments meet their goals and you get your bonuses. But no one is stretching and you guys are doing nothing to challenge your people or develop them."

The managers had heard this speech before, so they were just taking it in stride until the EVP added, "So from now on, each of you is required to make performance contracts with every one of your direct reports. The PCs need to set forth challenging goals for every individual, and if your people can handle their objectives without your help, the goals are too easy."

This started to catch their attention. The next line was the kicker. "And from now on, you will be evaluated on the goals you set with your people and how well you support your people's efforts to achieve them. Their input to me will determine your next year's bonuses."

That was the beginning of serious change management.

THE ONE-SECOND PERFORMANCE CONTRACT

This technique for negotiating leadership styles has been perfected by Dick, who is a national director of a large department, and Paul, one of the directors who works for him. Dick and Paul have only worked together for a couple of years but have developed a good rapport and usually see eye-to-eye on most critical issues. Even though they have a close working relationship, they work in a very hierarchical organization which requires the checking and double-checking of most decisions. So Paul needs to get signoffs from Dick on many issues.

Their performance contracting technique is very simple. Paul walks into Dick's office with a problem that he wants to explain so that Dick can make a well-informed decision. As he reviews the situation and makes his recommendation, he holds up two fingers to indicate that he is just giving input and understands that this is Dick's domain for making decisions.

If Dick is okay with that, as the explanation unfolds, he also holds up two fingers. But more often than not, the more Paul talks, Dick switches to three fingers to let Paul know that he will offer Paul his input but really prefers that Paul make the decision.

Sometimes, Dick holds up four fingers and Paul just stops explaining the problem because he knows Dick doesn't want to hear any more about it and Paul has clearance to decide as he sees fit.

And on occasion, Dick holds up one finger. That means that they should both save their breath. It is a done deal from above and there isn't a thing either one of them can do about it.

Then Paul holds up five fingers and they both go out for a drink.

TRY IT, YOU'LL LIKE IT

With the written structure or without ever writing a single word, the performance contract process can help you be a more effective leader. Just remember the four steps:

First, you always need to be clear about *what* needs to get done.

Second, you need to know *how* other people are planning to do it.

Third, you need to know *who* is going to do what to make sure the plan is completed.

Fourth and last, you need to be clear about *when* you need to communicate to ensure performance.

Answering these questions will help you put The L4 System into practice.

These questions will also help you implement the 1-4-3-2 empowerment cycle. First, you clarify expectations (Style 1). Then you determine what people can do on their own (Style 4). Then you create a game plan for providing support (Style 3) when it is needed and for making those decisions that you need (or want) to make (Style 2).

To put it simply, performance contracting takes the guess-work out of working with individuals.

REFERENCES

Dumaine, Brian. "Who Needs a Boss." *Fortune*, 7 May 1990, 52–60.

Chapter 11

Making Teams Work: An Underused Window of Opportunity

Many leaders find that developing one-on-one relationships with others is relatively easy once they understand the four cycles of leadership by anticipation. Viewing followers through their Window of Potential, changing main styles to facilitate development or intervention, avoiding frustration, and using all four styles to facilitate empowerment are powerful tools for working with individuals. However, for most leaders, transforming a group of individuals, even a group of talented and motivated individuals, into a high-performing team is a still a formidable task.

THE TEAMWORK IMPERATIVE

Ask anyone in the Western world who's been part of a failed effort to transform their organization from a traditional hierarchical model to a high performing teamwork model why the effort failed (and many of them have) and you're likely to get a response similar to this: "We're just not cut out for that Japanese style stuff," or "That sort of approach just won't work outside of Japan." What these voices are saying in reality is that superficial attempts to layer Japanese techniques onto workers in other cultures fail miserably because only the Japanese have the ability or motivation to work that way.

You can see where this is headed. It is true that most

workers, Americans in particular, are not likely to mimic their Japanese counterparts by beginning their workday singing the company song. And they are not likely to spend countless off time hours building their team at the local sushi bar. And they are even less likely to defer to the boss, which is something that is almost taken for granted in Japanese companies.

But the essence of what makes teams work in the Japanese workplace *is* transferable to other organizations if the people working in those organizations have the skills to effectively manage teams and are willing to use them.

This point is not meant to minimize the cultural differences that do indeed present obstacles to teamwork throughout the world. For example, it's true that Americans are decidedly individualistic and that any approach that calls for collaboration over competition is going to be met with a great deal of suspicion. At the same time, anyone who looks at Japan's prominence in many of today's world markets would be hard-pressed to suggest that the Japanese have given up competition for the sake of collaboration. What they have done is chosen to collaborate in order to compete—and they're winning big time.

WHY TEAMS FAIL

One reason for the difficulty with teamwork found in many cultures is the fierce individualism present in that culture. For example, getting ahead in America has always meant competing with others. In fact, this rugged individualism is considered by many to be a hallmark of the "American Way." And all too often, that means beating your peers to the next promotion instead of collaborating with them to beat the real competition. Getting these individuals to function as a high-performing team has proved to be a challenge that produced far more failure than success in the 1980s and 1990s, both in the states and in other Western cultures.

Another reason for this is that most efforts at building teams have come under the aegis of some special companywide initiative which is not integrated with the day-to-day workplace. Most companies have some experience with quality circles, employee-involvement groups, or continuous-improvement programs. The problem is that most of these initiatives simply inject isolated techniques that some would call gimmicks into current organizational structures that don't support teamwork. People go off to a quality meeting, sit around a table and try to get total agreement on something (anything!), and then return to business as usual in the office or on the shop floor where there is no way that they are going to "waste their time" like that.

In response to this problem, some organizations have even experimented with what Brian Dumaine calls ". . . the breakthrough of the 1990's . . . self-managed teams, cross-functional teams, high-performance teams, or, to coin a phrase, superteams." (*Fortune*, May 7, 1990) These attempts at self-direction create structures that support teamwork, and many of these initiatives are succeeding where previous paste-on efforts had failed. But many of these projects also fail, and the number-one reason is some misunderstandings about the leadership that is needed to get a group of people to work together efficiently.

HOW TEAMS CAN SUCCEED

If the teamwork revolution that has taken the corporate world by storm is to succeed—and many believe that economic prosperity depends on it—then what needs to happen is that those charged with leading teams (in the case of self-directed work teams that means everyone) need to learn the skills necessary for making those teams work. This is not an impossible task. Quite simply, it involves giving them a road map of what happens in the course of a group's journey and a compass for navigating that course.

In this chapter, that's exactly what you will get. In chapter 12, you will then see how to integrate these group skills with the individual skills you have already learned.

WHAT IS A HIGH-PERFORMING TEAM?

Have you ever been on a high-energy, high-performing team? Take a minute to think about your experience. What were the circumstances that produced this situation? Who was involved? What was the team doing? And what role did the leader play in making this a high-energy experience?

This is a question that we have asked managers from all sorts of organizations—private, public, manufacturing, service, big, medium, and small. As we discovered with some of our other questions, there are striking similarities across people's experiences. For most of them, the team's mission had a potential for high impact with customers, or it was highly visible in their organization, or both. In many cases the pressure from impact and visibility was compounded by time pressure—a small window of opportunity.

Beyond these external factors over which the people had little or no control, there were internal factors over which they or the team's leaders had significant influence. First, the assignment could not be done by one or two people, so a team was needed. Second, everyone was working together, often in one office or job site, so that the team members had a high amount of interaction with each and were not spread out working as separate individuals. There was high involvement by the leader who was physically present with the team members most of the time. The leader set high expectations, presented the assignment as a challenge, a "Mission Impossible" situation, and an opportunity for each team member to stretch, learn, and take risks. The leader and the team members adopted a can-do attitude, but this aggressive stance was balanced by availability and support from the leader and from other teammates. People were focused on the team's mission and their roles in achieving it. The communication channels were wide open with everyone talking to whomever they needed to. As a result, people got information quickly, problems surfaced rapidly, and there was lots of problem solving when the effort hit a snag. One last factor was typical of most of these teams: They found ways to develop a team spirit and often had a lot of fun. They also found ways to celebrate their successes.

A GROUP IS NOT THE SAME AS A TEAM

When we talk about leading a high-performing team, it is important to be clear that a group is not the same as a team. Working together in the same department or having the same reporting relationship automatically makes you a member of an organizational group but it does not necessarily make you a member of a team.

A bus is a good analogy for thinking about the difference between teams and groups. If you think of 10 people riding on a city bus, they meet the technical definition of a group. They're all in one place, heading in the same direction, at the same time, at the same speed, under the direction of one leader.

   However, in reality, each of them is a distinct individual with his or her own purpose. They get on and off the bus at their own stops and while they're on the bus, they usually go out of their way to avoid contact with the others. Occasionally, a couple of people will develop a camaraderie of the trenches and establish a passing friendship.

   In contrast, if you think about a team bus, all the players get on and off at the same time. They have a clear mission, inter-related goals, clear roles and responsibilities, and strategies with contingency plans. They have practiced and developed systems and learned how to coordinate their individual efforts. On the way into the game, they get each other pumped up and moti-vated. After the game, if they won, they talk about who made the extra effort or the exceptional play that led to victory. If they lost, the conversation focuses on the extra effort that would have made the difference between winning and losing. In either case they are looking back at what helped them achieve success or hindered them.

TEAM = INDIVIDUALS + GROUP

A team is different from a group. It is also more than the sum of the individual parts. We think of it as the individuals plus the group dynamics that bond those people together. Figure 11.1 below illustrates this concept by depicting four individual con-tributors plus the circle that is created when they come together as a group.

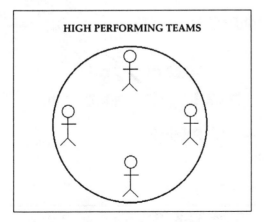

Figure 11.1 A Team = Individuals + the Group.

Think of a team this way. When you lead a team of four individuals, you also have to manage a fifth entity, the group. The group has a life of its own and needs which must be understood very differently from the way you understand individual needs. To lead a team, then, you need to know how to diagnose group needs, you need to know how to use the leadership styles with groups, and you need to understand how to use the power of groups to enhance the performance of individuals.

THE ROAD MAP—STAGES OF GROUP DEVELOPMENT

Figure 11.2 depicts what we call the *group development cycle*. It illustrates the fact that groups progress through very predictable stages of development.

When people come together in groups, the group needs will usually progress from forming to focusing, then to performing, and finally to leveling unless some actions are taken at the key intervention point which prevent leveling from occurring.

In Stage 1, Forming, the visible symptoms are individuality and cautious, polite communication. People are guarded about the demands that the group may place upon them and are more focused on the goals they are already trying to accomplish. There is dependency on the leader as people passively wait to be told what needs to get done. In essence, the group is looking for a clear definition of the boundaries.

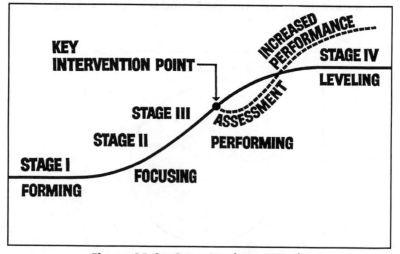

Figure 11.2 Group Development Cycle.

In the forming stage, the underlying needs are for a complete orientation, acceptance into the group, and inclusion as a needed and respected member. Most important, people want to know the group's mission and their individual roles in accomplishing that mission. Basically, they want to know why are we here and what's my piece of the action?

No matter how thoroughly you orient the group, Stage 2, Focusing, will begin with questioning. It is important to anticipate this and accept it as a part of the process which enables team members to buy into and gain ownership of the group's mission. In Stage 2, there will also be some experimentation, which is healthy but can also lead to false starts. You may also experience conflicts which can develop into power struggles. In essence, as soon as you establish the boundaries in Stage 1, the group will question and test them.

The underlying needs in Stage 2 center on buy-in and ownership. In addition, people want to know how they are expected to coordinate their efforts and what the operating structures will be. Decision-making procedures also need to be clarified. Will individuals have the authority to make their own decisions, or will they have to make recommendations to the group or the group leader? Will the group have authority to make decisions, or will it have to make recommendations to senior management? As these questions are answered, functional norms will be established, like how people will communicate and how the group will solve problems.

Some leaders try to bypass Stage 2 in the hope of avoiding conflicts and not wasting time with needless discussions. They want to go directly from Stage 1, telling the group what needs to get done, to Stage 3, just having the team members go off and do it.

The irony is that leaders who bypass the critical discussions of Stage 2 actually create the conditions that foster performance problems later on.

When the Stage 2 questions are truly answered, the group is ready to move into Stage 3, Performing, which is typified by productivity, shared responsibility, and a clear sense of purpose. Group members are confident in themselves and trust each other. There is open communication, interdependence, and members' commitment to the group's mission leads to mutual support. In Stage 1, the group needs boundaries. In Stage 2, they challenge the boundaries. In Stage 3, they accept the boundaries and work to do the most they can within those constraints.

The underlying needs at this stage are achievement, responsibility, and an opportunity to use knowledge and skills. People want spontaneous feedback and the flexibility to take quick responsive actions. And, as always, they want recognition for their efforts and their accomplishments.

Stage 4, Leveling, is next. One result of all the achievement in Stage 3 is a sense of satisfaction, relaxation, and eventually, complacency. Some people will burn out or become lethargic. Others will try to preserve the status quo and get protective or defensive in the face of any changes. And some group members will eventually feel frustrated and angry. In essence, the group starts ignoring the boundaries.

The underlying needs are to get refocused on new goals, or new procedures, or new norms for utilizing the group's resources. If that is not enough, the group needs to re-form, which means adding or subtracting members, or restructuring a large group into small groups or several small groups into one large group. Something needs to be done as a catalyst for change.

WHERE IS YOUR GROUP?

If you are leading a group of people at work or in your personal life, you will find the next section more interesting if you stop here for a minute and think about your group's stage of development. If you are not leading a group right now, you might want to think of a group that you are a member of. Just think of the visible symptoms you are aware of and consider what the underlying needs are most likely to be. Then you should be able to diagnose your group's development.

Where is your group? Forming? Focusing? Performing? Leveling?

Don't feel like your group should be in any one stage of development. It is very normal to find groups at all four stages. Typically, if we ask this question in any group of managers, about equal numbers will say that they have groups at each stage.

NOW THAT YOU KNOW WHERE YOUR GROUP IS, WHAT SHOULD YOU DO?

Once you recognize that groups of people go through predictable stages, and you understand where your team is, the question that usually comes to mind is, How do you lead groups when they are in different stages of development?

That's where the leadership styles come in. It's as easy as 1-2-3!

If your group is in Stage 1, Forming, you need to use Style 1. You need to provide the group information using clear directions, complete explanations, and pointing out consequences. You need to reduce people's ambiguity by clarifying the group's mission and identifying individual roles and responsibilities. In addition, you also need to make people feel wanted, needed and welcomed into your group.

You can see in Figure 11.3 that the communication is mostly downward in Stage 1. That doesn't mean that the leader is the only one who gets to talk. In fact, a healthy dialogue is often the best way to ensure proper flow of information. More important, in order to manage the inclusion process and make sure that everyone feels welcome, you need to encourage considerable communication among the team members as well as between them and you. The downward arrows simply indicate that after all is said and done, the bottom line in Stage 1 is for the team to understand your expectations.

If the group is in Stage 2, Focusing, you need to use Style 2. You can help people buy in by encouraging their questions and their ideas and responding openly. You should also invite their input as you establish structures and guidelines for production. And since experimentation is natural and valuable, you should

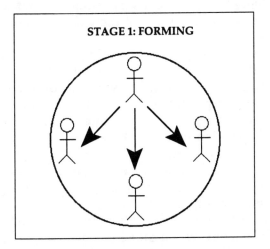

Figure 11.3 Forming Requires Giving Information to the Team.

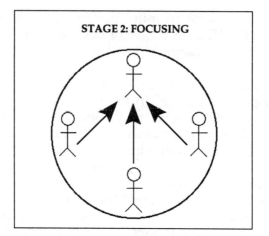

Figure 11.4 Focusing Requires Inviting Input from the Team.

anticipate providing lots of feedback to channel the groups in the right direction.

In Figure 11.4, you can see that the arrows are directed upward from the team members toward the leader. Again, this does not mean that communication is one-way from the bottom up. In Stage 2, in order to guarantee adequate problem solving about the best ways to organize and operate the team, you need to facilitate an open discussion to be sure that team members' ideas are listened to and the concerns are heard. The arrows point upward to remind you that in Stage 2, the most important issue is involving the team in determining the best ways to work together. If you are doing most of the talking, you will never get beyond Stage 2.

If the group is in Stage 3, Performing, you can assign responsibilities to individuals or subgroups so that many activities can be going on simultaneously. Often we think of it as a distributed S2 to emphasize the point that someone is always empowered to make decisions with team input. Your role then is to support other people's problem solving. You need to do a lot of active listening, act like a bee in the clover patch, and facilitate periodic team meetings for updates and mutual support. You also need to remember to give people plenty of recognition and praise for their accomplishments.

In Figure 11.5, you can see that the arrows are directed to members of the team. When Stage 3 is handled well, each member of the team is empowered to make decisions on the basis of

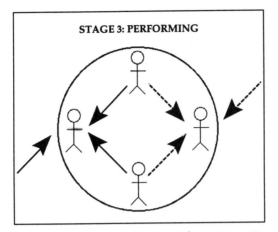

Figure 11.5   Performing Requires Steering Information to Team Members.

input from others. They may get input from other team members, or from you, or from key people outside the team. The important thing for you to remember is that, from their perspective, this looks like Style 2 since they are deciding with input. In your role as the leader, you need to use Style 3 as a facilitator who steers communication in the right directions and supports your team members with their decision making.

This picture is very different from saying that it is the group's responsibility to decide. If it is the group's decision, then it is no one's decision. Asking the group to decide is one of the biggest traps of leaders who try to make teams work. It usually results in endless discussions, pointless debates, frustration, and wasted time. True, there are some examples of teams who work through the frustration and perform very well. But the vast majority of teams that strive for group consensus end up with groupthink or worse. And that is one of the main reasons why so many companies keep talking about teams but do business as usual.

Remember this picture. Distributed Style 2. Shared responsibility. Clearly empowered team members. Clarity about who else will be involved in the decisions. And a leader who actively facilitates communication to build the trust that will make this work.

While the group is in the performing stage, you also need to legitimize activities that will keep the group's spirits high and help the team identify strategies for continuous improvement. Encourage some socializing by visiting over meals, having drinks together on occasion, bringing in pizza if you all have to work late, or just taking a few minutes to show that you care about each other as people. Celebrate from time to time, especially if you have reached a milestone. And most important, call timeouts on a regular basis to get the team to share developments in their respective assignments, to identify current or anticipated problems, and to bring up ideas for improving the way the work gets done.

If you don't make these key interventions while the team is rolling, you will begin to see some of the Stage 4 symptoms emerging. Burnout takes over if people never get a chance to renew the team spirit.

If your group is already in Stage 4, Leveling, you should not use Style 4. In fact, a leader's use of Style 4 is one of the most common causes for leveling. If you never bring your group together, you are part of the problem. If you delegate to the group, you are inviting competition and power struggles as the group tries to get refocused without the help of a leader. Besides, not much is likely to get done. You've probably heard the maxim, "If it's the group's responsibility, it's no one's responsibility."

If you want to delegate, delegate to an individual team member and empower him/her to lead the group. Or, if you want to be more egalitarian, you can delegate to several team members by empowering them to lead specific areas of responsibility. But be careful, because if you do that and still disappear for too long, the group will see you as abdicating.

Groups like to have someone in charge. If no one is, a new leader will emerge or competing leaders will get into conflicts, or the group will start to come apart out of apathy. If you are not leading the group, then an informal leader will take over, and most likely steer the group in a different direction. So the recommendation for Stage 4 is not Style 4, it is the intervention cycle.

To intervene with a group, first you need to use Style 3 to diagnose the situation by asking individuals and subgroups questions to find out their perceptions and to enlist them as contributors to the solution. Next, you should use Style 2 by bringing the group together to share your diagnosis and help you with problem solving. This refocusing should get team members involved in managing and implementing necessary changes. If that is not enough, you then need to move to Style 1 to re-form the group. The simplest move is to bring a new person in. You may also want to move someone out.

Whatever moves you make, it is important to recognize that you now have a new group, and this is an opportunity to go back to Stage 1 to clarify the mission, the individual roles and responsibilities, and to make people feel like they're part of the team. If you don't manage this transition, new people will learn the norms by the water fountain or in the cafeteria. Everyone, except you, will be determining the future of your group and you will lose the benefit of bringing in a new person. You have to manage the change.

LEADING THE GROUP + THE INDIVIDUALS

The main point of this entire discussion is that when you lead a team, you have to lead each individual with the right mix of leadership styles for his or her potential. Usually, that means using the 1-4-3-2 cycle, and from all of our data about best leaders and ideal leaders, we know that means using mostly S3 and S4 with individuals.

Simultaneously, you have to lead the group, which means that even if you were using mostly Style 4 with every individual in the group, you would still need to form the group with S1 and get the group focused with S2 before you can move to S3 to facilitate a high-performing, distributed S2, shared responsibility team effort. When you're using S3, someone is always empowered to use S2 with the group's input, so it is mostly S1 and S2 with the group.

WHAT LEADERSHIP STYLES DO YOU USE WITH GROUPS?

Remember the cases you read in Chapter 1? You already know what leadership styles you used with the eight individual cases. Now you can see what responses you chose in the last two cases, which focused on group situations.

Put your answers in the spaces on the next page to see how much of each style you used in these cases. After adding each column, multiply your totals by 10 to find out what percentage of each style you used in these situations.

These group cases presented you with two very different situations. Case 9 had to do with a new team made up of people from different departments meeting for the first time. Case 10 dealt with an existing team that had performed well over time but was starting to show signs of burnout.

	S1	S2	S3	S4
CASE 9	C ____	D ____	A ____	B ____
CASE 10	B ____	C ____	D ____	A ____
TOTALS	____	____	____	____
PERCENTAGES x totals by	____ 10	____ 10	____ 10	____ 10

Even so, cases 9 and 10 have some things in common. Both cases have to do with groups of people trying to work together as a team. Neither case calls for the use of Style 4 which would come across as abdicating since any effective group requires some degree of involvement from its leader. Both cases also require the use of multiple leadership styles, which reflects the fact that groups tend to be quite complex with stages of development shifting on an ongoing basis.

Case 9 involves a new cross-functional team organized for the purpose of improving quality in your department. Since this is a new group made up of people who know each other professionally but may not have worked together on a focused team effort, this group would start at Stage 1, Forming, and require some Style 1, Directing, to get it started.

As the leader, you would want to thank everyone for committing their time and effort, let everyone know how critical their involvement will be to the success of this group, and explain to them your perception of this team's mission, its goals and the time frames, and the roles you envision for yourself and the other members of the team.

If that is all you do at the beginning however, it will not be enough. To get the team properly focused, you then would need to use some Style 2, Problem Solving, to solicit their input, their points of view, their analysis of the current situation and their ideas about goals, time frames, everybody's roles and responsibilities, and, most important, what it will take to make this team achieve results and work smoothly together.

In Case 9, if you selected a balance of Style 1 and Style 2, you would be effective. Your use of Style 1 would insure that the team gets the complete information it needs, and your use of Style 2 would orchestrate the buy-in process which is necessary to give the team a shared mission and an open climate in which every member of the team can contribute to the team's success.

If you only used Style 1, however, you would come across as dominating. The group would have a clear understanding of your expectations, but without the opportunity to buy into a shared mission and a common set of objectives, they will see the team as yours instead of theirs. If they agree with your assessment and recommendations, you may succeed. However, since it is unlikely that everyone will agree, to use only Style 1 could put you in the position of leading with nobody following.

If you only selected Style 2 in this case, you might be all right in the long run because Style 2 leaves you in charge while being open to questions and suggestions from the team. Over time, the key members will ask all the questions that are needed in order to get clarity about the team's mission, goals, time frames, roles, etc. However, in terms of efficiency, you may be slowing down the forming process as well as delaying the focusing process by failing to give people as much information as possible at the outset.

Furthermore, if you start with Style 2, you may not come across as strongly as you need to at the outset. The other leaders who have been asked to attend this meeting want to know, "Why am I here? What's the purpose? What is this team all about? What do you expect of me?" If you start with good answers to those questions, they will see you as credible and the use of their time as being valuable. If they have to drag it out of you, they are less likely to see that their time is being well spent.

If you selected Style 3 for this case, you would be coming across as overaccommodating. Later on with this group, after specific goals have been identified, areas of responsibility have been assigned, and members of the team have been empowered to take the lead on particular tasks, Style 3 would be quite appropriate for orchestrating the group's productivity. In fact, it is the ideal way to help team members keep each other up to date, stay in close communication with each other, and get emerging problems out on the table. However at this point, when the group is new and just trying to get its feet on the ground, you would come across as the kind of leader who could waste a lot of precious time with limited chance of obtaining results.

Particularly since this group is composed of other leaders, it is important to be strong at the outset. Often leaders of this type of team make the mistake of assuming that since all the members are high-powered leaders in their own right, they won't allow anybody to lead the team very forcefully. As a result the leaders do come across as overaccommodating and lose the respect of the other members of the team. Then these high-powered leaders are quite likely to take the group over. They will get impatient and impose their own structure, which will then lead to more confusion, chaos, power struggles, etc.

If you selected Style 4 for this situation you would be abdicating. Your efforts to get other members of the team to take the lead in defining the team's mission and identifying what the team needs to do would produce one of two results. If they think the group has value, team members will compete with each other and with you in their attempts to take control of the group. If they don't think the group is important, they will simply check out. You will find them missing meetings, coming late, leaving early, withdrawing and going off to do something else which they consider a more productive use of their time.

Case 10 presents a very different kind of group situation. The group in this case is a functional work group which has been together for a number of years and has been a very productive team. Individuals on the team have performed well and have worked smoothly in collaboration with each other. One of the ways that organizations reward successful teamwork is by piling more work on those teams that succeed. The result after a while is burnout, which is what's happening right now in this case.

The best response to use in this type of situation is the intervention cycle, starting first with Style 3, which can be done with one-on-one interviews or by bringing the group together for an open discussion. In either format, your role is to ask questions, listen, and try to fully understand the different team members' point of view on what's going on in the department, what's working well, what's not working well, and what kinds of changes can be made to improve the situation.

Sometimes that kind of a meeting is sufficient to clear the air, get the team refocused and recharge people's energy. Often, however, if burnout has settled in, you will need to take the next step to use some Style 2, Problem Solving . With this approach, you would direct the group's attention to the most critical issues that surfaced in the prior discussions, and then engage in some very focused problem solving in which members of the team give you input about the causes of the problem and potential solutions. Together you think through the alternatives, consider the costs and benefits of each, and ultimately you, as the leader, must decide what action plans will be pursued as a result of these meetings. So, if you selected a balance of Style 3 and Style 2, you would be leading this group through the intervention cycle in an effective way.

If you only selected Style 3 you could come across as overaccommodating by listening to everybody's point of view and then going nowhere as a result of those discussions. In fact, you could make the problem worse by bringing it to the surface and then taking no action.

If you only used Style 2, you run the risk of overinvolving yourself too quickly. Often leaders who do this are guilty of pursuing quick-fix solutions without fully understanding the underlying causes and without getting the entire team's buy-in to the actions required for fixing the problems. Consequently these leaders often come across as going through the motions of having a meeting, getting the input, getting a quick solution, and saying that's that. Unfortunately, nothing really changes as a result.

If you selected Style 1 in this situation, you were overreacting by putting the responsibility entirely on your own shoulders for solving a problem that is better dealt with by the group. If the solutions you impose are good ones, you may get away with it and may even earn some short-term respect from your colleagues, but you are probably sowing the seeds of future resistance as well as setting yourself up to be blind-sided by future problems. No leader is good enough to anticipate all the issues that will surface in a group, and therefore you need to establish norms that encourage team members to bring problems to your attention and to always be thinking about ways of working together, smarter and better. Furthermore if the solutions you impose are not well received or don't work, then you will definitely be perceived as dominating.

If you selected Style 4 in this situation, you would come across as abdicating. Occasionally problems will go away all by themselves, but most often problems on the surface are indicators of underlying issues that need to get addressed. If you don't ask for team members' thoughts and don't encourage open dialogue about the problems and potential solutions, the group will quickly lose faith in you as a leader. Losing faith does not mean they will stop talking about the problems and what needs to be done to fix them. It simply means that they won't talk to you about them anymore. Instead they will bitch and moan to each other. In time, the focus of that complaining will usually redirect itself toward you. Instead of talking about the issues and how to fix them, you become equated with the problems, and they talk about you and your lack of effectiveness as a leader.

Now that you have thought about your responses to these hypothetical cases, here are two real cases that make these points even more dramatically!

A CONSENSUS FOR CHAOS

Denise was the new general manager for a fast-growing microelectronics firm. She was hired by the founder and CEO of the firm, Joe, to manage his growing company. A technically talented, ambitious entrepreneur, Joe decided as he watched his company grow from a start-up of 6 employees to what had become a staff of 60, that he no longer had the ability (or inclination) to manage the day-to-day operations of his shop. He knew he was too hands-on to be effective in what had become an increasingly diversified organization, and that he didn't have the skills to manage such a diverse operation.

In hiring Denise he chose someone who he believed had the skills to run a multi-faceted company that required far more coordination of disparate functions than his limited high-control style allowed for.

While just out of graduate school, Denise was an expert in *high-performance systems*, an approach to management designed to enhance a company's performance through the use of teamwork. She had expertise, Joe was led to believe, in transforming organizations from traditional hierarchical organizations to more streamlined, horizontal, participatory models. In making his decision to hire Denise, Joe was particularly impressed with her insight into the problems entrepreneurs have when their companies grow beyond the point of one person's hands-on control.

"I want you to turn us into a high-class teamwork operation," was his charge to her. "And I don't care what it takes to do it. The ball is in your hands."

Denise, exhilarated at the possiblility of applying all her hard-learned theory, set out to do the job she was hired to do. She immediately called a "community meeting" at which she announced that Joe, the CEO, had hired her to change the way things are done around here.

The decision-making process in the company, she announced, was about to change dramatically. She instituted a model she had studied in school called PPBS, which stood for Planning, Programming, and Budgeting System. The central focus of the system was on consensual decision making. This new approach meant that all the decisions made from now on would be made in an open forum. There would be frequent scheduled meetings of the entire employee group at which anyone could have a say about anything. Furthermore, she proclaimed that any member could call an additional unscheduled meeting of the entire community to address unanticipated issues as they emerged. Since the group was so large (about 60) she also added a structure within which the large group would work.

At the first full employee meeting she instructed people to form six teams of 10. Each team, she instructed, should be made up of as diverse a group of employees as possible, meaning that people should avoid clustering in teams who were in the same department or performed the same function. These teams, Denise explained, would help in managing the size of the overall group. When an issue was brought up at the meeting, each team would spend some time talking about it among themselves for a brief period to give everyone a chance to have input. Then the group would reconvene as a whole, each team would report on their conversation and after the reports, the overall group would attempt to gain consensus on whatever the issue happened to be.

While Joe was a little disconcerted over the thought of giving over so much power to so many people, Denise had come highly recommended and he decided, for the moment, to give her the benefit of the doubt.

As time went on, however, Joe's doubts grew and the possibility of any benefit coming from Denise's approach diminished rapidly. From the outset there was a great deal of confusion. People were excited about the possibility of having some say in how the organization was run, but doubted whether Joe was really going to give up control. They also had a lot of fears, most of which went unspoken except for private conversations in the washroom, about what kinds of negative repercussions would follow if anyone took a position that differed from Joe's point of view. In the past Joe, like many entrepreneurial founders of organizations, had shown little tolerance for any ideas that were divergent from his. While people had heard from Denise that decision making was now in their hands, no one really believed that was true.

During the first few community meetings people asked Denise many questions about how she intended to manage the day-to-day operations and any changes she would make. Her response to them was, "My philosophy is that we will make all important decisions in this forum." When asked more probing questions, she would most often turn the tables on the questioner and ask, "What do you think about that?"

Within a month of taking charge, things began to unravel. Some people started showing up late to the meetings, reading newspapers during the meetings, and avoiding any real substantive conversation, while others kept bringing up issues for discussion that had little or no real consequence, like whether to use powder or liquid soap in the washrooms. Joe noticed that there was a lot of conversation buzzing in the hallways, most of it negative, about the new scenario. When he asked Denise what she thought was going on, she replied that "It takes time to build a high-performing organization and people need time to get acclimated to operating in new ways." Within two weeks of that conversation Joe asked Denise for her resignation.

What happened in this scenario is being played out in corporations of all sizes all over the world. In an effort to reinvent themselves by restructuring and reshaping the way they operate, shifting from traditional pyramidlike organizations to more streamlined, horizontal, participatory approaches, organizational leaders and would-be organizational leaders are making the same mistakes Denise made.

One of her biggest mistakes was not paying attention to the stages of group development as she was trying to craft her new organization into a team-driven system. By trying to force a consensus approach out of the starting gate, she virtually ignored the first two stages of group development and tried to tap into the kind of shared responsibility that can occur only in a situation where the team has genuinely built itself up into the performing stage.

What Denise should have done was realized that her new organization and its respective teams were in the forming stage, and that they needed a lot of direction from her. She should have formed a strategic alliance with Joe, and together they should have crafted a new vision for the organization and clearly articulated what that vision was to the troops.

Next she should have orchestrated and encouraged discussion of what the new way of doing things would mean, allow people to express their concerns, and figure out how they could best succeed in the new organization. She also should have been more careful helping each of the teams determine the best use of their time and efforts and help them to develop operating systems that would work for them. All the while she should have been focusing on how to build in rewards for team performance and really send the message that what mattered was producing team results, not whether or not Joe liked what you had to say. These efforts would have helped her move the teams through the focusing stage.

Had she carefully moved her teams through these first two stages she would have had a much better chance of creating the kind of collaborative organization she had hoped to create and avoided creating the kind of chaotic one she was forced to leave.

MAKING A GOOD TEAM EVEN BETTER

Now that you've seen how to not manage teams, we'd like to tell you about a situation in which team management was handled extraordinarily well.

The team involved Karen, who was the head of a strategic planning department at a large manufacturer of building supplies. Karen and her team of six managers and four support staff were known by everyone in the organization as a high-performing team. Her bosses often used her group as an example of a model team, her department was designated as an important rotational assignment for new recruits with leadership potential, and other fast trackers were often assigned to her team to learn about teamwork. The team had a reputation for working extraordinarily hard, often putting in long hours, working evenings and weekends, and achieving extraordinary results. They were all committed to quality and to making sure that the work they did was the best it could possibly be.

Karen had done a good initial job of building her team. They had a clear mission, and all the members had bought into the goals of the group. Stages 1 and 2 of the Group Development Cycle, Forming and Focusing, had been managed very well, and high performance was now the norm. These people really cranked out the work and it was always top quality.

When we first met Karen, her team was beginning a transition process that would significantly affect their work. Some rumblings were beginning to surface that some people were growing tired of the relentless pace that their high performance had wrought. For example, one member had expressed, "I don't mind putting in long hours once in a while but it never ends."

Others complained about the fact that there seemed to be nothing but peaks in the way they worked, while others complained that they never seemed to take time to celebrate their successes. Conflicts began to emerge and it became increasingly clear that the team was heading toward serious burnout.

Without thinking per se about the stages of group development, Karen knew intuitively that her team was approaching the leveling stage and needed some refocusing. She also knew that to make that shift required her to rethink what her team was all about and how it operated.

As she began talking to some of her customers, Karen began to question whether the team was really utilizing its resources to the fullest potential and meeting the needs of the customers in the best possible way. In further discussions with her boss, they agreed that the department could offer a lot more to the future of the corporation if some changes were made.

With that in mind, Karen began the process of moving some people out of the department and recruiting replacements who could add a different kind of value to the team. In addition, she decided that some formal teambuilding might help the new team get started on the right foot.

As soon as all of the new people were on board, an offsite session was held for the purpose of getting the team properly formed and properly focused. There were two agendas for that meeting. The first was to facilitate the reforming of the group by giving people an opportunity to really get to know each other. The second was to reexamine the mission and operating norms of the team to see if they could be improved upon, so that high-quality work could be sustained without burning people out.

Even though most of the team had been together for a few years, their incredible work pace had not left them much time to really know each other. And with three brand-new team members, it was critical for the group to deal with the inclusion aspect of forming. The offsite teambuilding gave them a way to do that in a relaxed and safe environment that enabled them to let their hair down and really get connected.

As soon as the people started to feel like a solid group, the conversation shifted to rethinking the team's mission and each person's role in accomplishing. That started with Karen's sharing of her perspective, which included input from her boss and the customers she had spoken to. After that, the group moved headlong into refocusing.

Initially, the discussion was about the team's mission and

people's ideas about how to add more value by providing different services to a broader customer base. In theory, there was a lot of excitement about that. The conversation got stickier as everyone started thinking through what changes they would have to make in order to achieve the new mission.

An example of the type of issue that got addressed was the way Karen parceled out the work. Her style in the past had been to look at an assignment, determine who would be best for that assignment, sometimes based on their expertise in that area, and just as often based on her judgment that the project would stretch them developmentally. Then she would assign responsibilities on a one-to-one basis.

As the refocusing stage proceeded, one of the changes that was made was to have Karen present projects to the group before giving them to anyone and get more input from the team as to the best way to proceed. This shift would enable her to solicit their thoughts on who might be interested or skilled for a particular assignment, who might work well together, what might be a developmental opportunity for someone, etc.

As the team began to work in this new way they got energized and began to express the belief that, if this were truly the way they would now work together, they could accomplish even more than they had in the past and be assured that they were adding the most value to the organization as well. And as they talked they created for themselves what we've been calling the distributed leadership approach.

Talk about buy-in! People started saying things like, "I want to be the lead person on that project," or "I think I can make a contribution as a support person on this project," or "I'm willing to do that but only if she agrees to help me with this."

People started taking responsibility for all sorts of things that had previously been considered part of someone else's domain, including Karen's. She still retained her leadership position and her power in the group, but once she realized that utilizing everyone on the team to refocus the way they operated would not only get their buy-in, but would bring them to a new level of performance that would be even more effective than they had been in the past, she strongly embraced this new way of operating.

Perhaps the most important lesson in this case is the fact that even high-performing teams can get into trouble. The first thing a team leader needs to do is to make sure they take care to move the team through the forming and focusing stages in a way that positions the team for high performance. Karen did that very well. The next thing a team leader needs to keep in mind is that the stages of team development are not static, but rather dynamic and ongoing.

Karen could have made the mistake of assuming, as many team leaders do, that her high-performing team was at its best and was destined to stay in high performance forever. She didn't. She understood that unless a leader intervenes, a high-performing team is destined to fall into leveling. Karen responded to the leveling signals her team was sending her and did the right thing. She got input from her customers, brought in new talent, and got assistance with reforming and refocusing the group. The result was that she, with the team's help, transformed her department into an even higher-performing team than they had been.

Chapter 12

The Secrets of The Leader's Window

As we emphasized in the last chapter, in our experience the main reason why teams don't work is an inadequate understanding of what leaders have to do to make them work. Without the leadership skills required for building and maintaining group synergy, all the programs, projects, and structures in the world won't make teams successful. But as you saw in the case of Denise, bringing the whole group together for decision making can also lead to disaster. The challenge is combining what you know about group development with what you know about leading individuals. That's the power of The Leader's Window and that's what this chapter is all about.

Jack Orsburn, the lead author of *Self-Directed Work Teams* (1991, Business One/Irwin) a book that is regarded by most people as the definitive work on the self-management phenomenon, is a strong proponent of the need for integrating leadership training and coaching into any team development process. In Jack's work with his clients, whenever a team starts down the path toward higher levels of employee involvement, one of the first things he does is teach them The L4 System. He used to teach situational leadership primarily as a way to get the team members and their supervisors to start thinking about a range of leadership options. But when Jack discovered The L4 System, he realized that the behavioral descriptions of the styles made it much easier for leaders to learn how to implement each style. He also thought that the 1-4-3-2 cycle would be very helpful to supervisors as they handed off responsibilities to the team.

Most significantly, when Jack saw the four secrets of The Leader's Window, he looked at them, sat back, thought for a few minutes, then said, "Yeah, that's it. On this one piece of paper, I can tell you what went right with every team that succeeded. And I can pinpoint what went wrong with every team that failed."

This chapter ties together all of the ideas of the earlier chapters and gives you a framework for leading individuals and groups guaranteed to result in high-performing teams. You will view The Leader's Window as an integrated multidimensional structure that enables you to see the relationship among the four leadership styles, understand how to move from style to style, and learn what to do to make sure that you provide team members and the group with precisely what's needed every time all the time.

As you move through this chapter you will learn the four secrets of The Leader's Window. Secret 1 focuses on using Styles 1 and 2 with the group to provide the team with the information they need for getting started and, most important, to get the group's buy-in to achieving the team's mission. Secret 2 focuses on using Styles 1 and 4 with the individuals to give them the directions they need so that you can delegate meaningful responsibilities to them. Secret 3 focuses on using Styles 3 and 4 to give individuals the authority they need to feel empowered and the support they need to guarantee results. Finally, Secret 4 focuses on using Styles 2 and 3 to provide the group with a way to maintain communication, to share responsibility, and focus on continuous improvements.

As the secrets unfold, and you learn to open and close the windows of The Leader's Window, you will gain a clear view of how to manage a team and its members simultaneously in a way that leads to clarity of focus and crystallization of what's needed to unlock the mysteries of high performance leadership.

THE LEADER'S BOX

In chapter 8, we brought up the subject of reality to help you understand why 1-4-3-2 empowerment works with individuals. Now that we have explained the difference between individuals and groups, and have showed you how to be an effective leader of a team's group dynamics, we need to return to the subject of reality.

We never said that organizations make it easy for you to be a successful leader. In fact, since most hierarchies only have room at the top for a few people, the ones who get there often make it as hard as possible for their successors to dethrone them. Not that they do it intentionally. It's just that they become the newest senders of pressure-packed messages that make it difficult for people at the next levels to fully succeed.

With that in mind, try this question on for size. Have you ever felt like you were caught in the middle between conflicting pressures from above and below?

We certainly have, and from what we've heard all over corporate America, it happens to almost everyone who tries to lead in a complex organization. We call this dilemma The Leader's Box since the competing pressures usually make you feel boxed in.

We also think that looking at The Leader's Box in Figure 12.1 can help you understand this dilemma. Then, if you can accept the truths that are imbedded in both sides of the conflict, you will be ready to take a fresh look at organizational life through The Leader's Window.

When you think about the messages that typically come from above, they usually boil down to wanting production up and

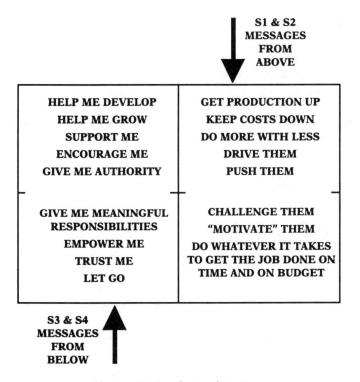

Figure 12.1 The Leader's Box.

costs down, expecting you to do more with less, telling you to challenge your people, drive them, push them, motivate them, and do whatever it takes to get results—on time and on budget. Basically, those are Style 1 or Style 2 messages.

From below, the messages you get from team members are to empower me, trust me, let me take risks, encourage me, support me, help me grow and develop. These are basically Style 3 and Style 4 messages.

WHO IS RIGHT?

Now, here's a tough question for you. Who is right? Which messages do you listen to? The ones from above or from below?

When we ask this question to groups of managers, some will agree with each point of view. Those who agree with the messages from above say things like, "Who signs your paycheck?" or "They're the bosses." Those who agree with the messages from below make comments like, "The only way you can get the results that management wants is to follow the advice from below."

Usually, someone will try to end the debate by saying that you have to pay attention to both messages. They say that you should be a buffer by paying lip service to the messages from above while really acting on the messages from below. Their coping strategy is to try to keep both sides happy.

Eventually, someone will argue that they are both right and the situation determines which one you listen to. Often they say that you should pay attention to the messages from below as long as you have the time to do it and it is working. But if you get caught in a crunch, you have to follow the advice from above.

We are convinced that you can't win if you pick one side or the other. We are also skeptical that you can please everyone. And we are equally reluctant to endorse a strategy of being suportive when you can, but sticking it to people when you have to.

In contrast, we are strongly convinced that there is truth in both sets of messages. We also believe that if you get these two messages in the right places, you can be a very effective leader. To do that, all you need to do is remember what we talked about in the last chapter.

To lead a high-perfoming team, you have to lead the group as well as the individuals. And they have different needs which require different combinations of leadership styles.

When managers say drive them, push them, challenge them,

the key word is *them*. They are talking about the group and may not even recognize them as indivduals. And they are right, groups work best when a leader is clearly in charge.

When followers say trust me, empower me, help me grow, help me develop, the key word is *me*. They're talking about themselves as individuals, and they are also right. Individuals work best with a lot of Style 4 and Style 3.

HOW DO YOU GET OUT OF THE BOX?

As shown in Figure 12.2, best leaders, instinctively or through learning, get these messages in the right places. They are good at *taking charge of the groups* they lead, challenging the team, pushing the members to give their best, encouraging everyone to take risks and stretch themselves. Simultaneously, they *empower each team member* with significant responsibilities, let them know that they are counting on them to deliver top quality results, and are available to offer support as it is needed.

Worst leaders usually get these messages backwards. They use Styles 4 or 3 with their groups, and when their groups flounder, they use Styles 1 or 2 with the individuals. They abdicate with the group by never bringing the members together and by treating them as separate individuals. Or they over-accommodate the group by sitting around trying to get complete

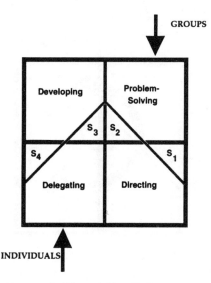

Figure 12.2 Use mostly S1 and S2 with Groups, mostly S3 and S4 with Individuals.

agreement about everything the group needs to do. Then when things go wrong, they dominate the individuals by criticizing their efforts, barking orders, and undercutting any attempts at taking responsibility. Or they overinvolve themselves by listening a little before they take over.

The way to avoid getting trapped by The Leader's Box is to use mostly directing and problem solving with groups and mostly delegating and developing with individuals.

WORKING SMARTER

Now that you understand how to get out of The Leader's Box, you are ready to hear all of the secrets of The Leader's Window. If you add the 1-4-3-2 Cycle to the last diagram, you see a guide for working smarter instead of harder, as shown in Figure 12.3.

Basically, you take advantage of the power of the group in the beginning and at the end of the empowerment cycle. Instead of having separate meetings with each individual to review their responsibilities, the idea is to meet with them as a group. This saves you time while ensuring that each team member not only knows his/her responsibilities, but is also aware of what everyone else is doing. Reviewing assignments as a group can also help you build commitment to the team and establish some peer pressure for individual performance.

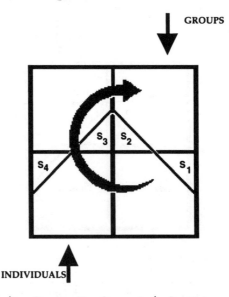

Figure 12.3 Working Smarter: Use Groups in the Beginning and End of 1-4-3-2.

After getting the group started, you use mostly delegating and developing with the individuals. This allows them the freedom to work as trusted and respected employees while providing them the support they need whenever they get stuck.

Finally, instead of doing problem solving with each individual in separate one-on-one meetings, you can again save yourself time by meeting with the entire group. This also helps keep the team members updated about progress toward team objectives as well as informed about problems that are surfacing in other people's areas of responsibility.

Often, the team members can also make your job easier and your team's efforts more productive by sharing their experiences with each other. When problem solving is needed, your brain is not the only one engaged in the process. More important, when everyone is stumped or your team is confronting cutting-edge territory, the synergy that emerges from group interaction can lead to quantum leaps in everyone's thinking and breakthrough strategies for the team.

DON'T FORGET THE GROUP DYNAMICS

In order to make this strategy work with a new group, you have to do one more thing. To get the group properly launched, you start with Style 1 to clarify the team's mission and individuals' responsibilities. Then you have to anticipate the need to move up to Style 2 with the group to get their buy-in and commitment. Then you can come back through S1 to intersect with the individual 1-4-3-2 Cycle, as shown in Figure 12.4.

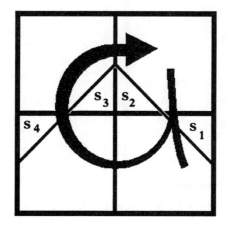

Figure 12.4 The Leader's Window.

Now the picture is complete. This is *The Leader's Window*.

Within this picture, there are four distinct phases of team-work, each requiring the use of two leadership styles to lead the team through that phase. There is a secret for each of these phases. If you know these secrets, you will be halfway to your goal of being a fantastic leader. The other half is remembering to make the right moves at the right times.

SECRET 1

Phase 1 is the team orientation phase. In this phase, the team needs to go through the forming and focusing stages of group development. This is especially important when you are creating a new team. It is also important when you are adding people to an existing team or losing some experienced team members. Even if the team is staying intact but is taking on new responsi-bilities or being given a new mission, this team orientation phase, depicted in Figure 12.5, cannot be overlooked.

Remembering what you know about group development, you know that the entire group needs to understand the team's mission, clarify their roles in accomplishing that mission, and believe that they are absolutely essential to the team's success. You also know that no matter how well you could explain those things, in order for the team members to buy in to the mission

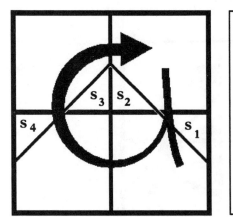

Start with S1 to orient the group by explaining the team's mission and the members' roles on the team.

Then use S2 to get the group's buy in by involving them in identifying the best ways to work together.

Figure 12.5 Phase 1: Team Orientation.

and share your commitment to the team's goals, they need a chance to ask questions, voice their concerns, raise issues that may not have been considered, and share their ideas about the best ways to make the team work effectively.

The secret to leading this team orientation phase is to use a balance of Styles 1 and 2. You need the directing style to take charge of the group, light a fire under everyone, and give them the information they need. Then, you need to use the problem solving style to get the team involved in identifying the scope of the project, the timing of critical events, the roles that each team member will play, and the ways that you will interact together. This also establishes a team norm for problem solving that will be needed later when the team is rolling at full steam.

SECRET 2

Phase 2 focuses on individual assignments. Once the group is focused in Phase 1 and everyone is clear about the overall team mission, the team's objectives, and the responsibilities of each team member, the main question on each individual's mind is, "What do I need to do to deliver results in my areas of responsibility?"

This is where the performance contracting process comes in. The individuals need to know what they are expected to accomplish and in what time frame. What are the deliverables and when are they due?

They need to have a clear action plan that will accomplish these goals, and you need to be aware of their plan so that you don't end up second guessing them later on.

They also need to be clear about the authority they have. What can I decide on my own? What can I just go ahead with? When do I need some input from you, the leader, or other key people? What decisions do you, as the leader, want to sign off on or make yourself?

And you both need to be clear about critical checkpoints in the plan. Usually, there are a few key moments when timely communication is important. If these can be anticipated, it will be easier for you and your team members to manage your time efficiently.

The secret to being an effective leader in this individual orientation phase is finding the right balance between Styles 1 and 4, as shown in Figure 12.6. You need to do enough directing to clarify expectations so that there is no ambiguity about what

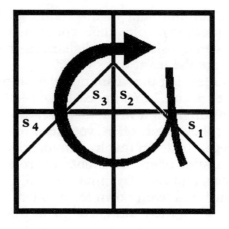

Use S1 with individual team members to clarify roles and responsibilities and to start the Performance Contract process.

Then use S4 to empower each individual by delegating authority for the tasks they can handle on their own.

Figure 12.6 Phase 2: Individual Assignments.

the outcomes look like. And you also need to do enough delegating to empower people to handle their responsibilities. That begins with the performance contracting process as you make your team members accountable for developing their own action plans, for asking for what they need in the way of support and decision making from you, and for anticipating critical points in the project plan.

In some cases, you may need to use some Style 3 to listen to the plan, understand needs, or identify critical checkpoints. And in some instances, after you have listened, you may even need to move to Style 2 to revise the proposal that you have just heard. But in most situations, if you have the right people on the team, this Phase 2 is a quick check-in with each individual to clarify the directions and be clear about the authority they have to handle their responsibilities.

SECRET 3

Phase 3, shown in Figure 12.7, is when the work actually gets done. More time is spent in Phase 3 than in any other phase. We call it the *work + support* phase to emphasize that people usually need some type of support in handling their responsibilities.

After Phase 1 in which you got the group focused, and Phase 2 in which you clarified individual assignments, now the prevailing need is to get out of the way and let your team members do what they are best at doing. They are the ones who have to get the job done on the playing field. They are being paid to handle significant tasks. You have to trust them and show them the respect you would want if you were in their position.

You also need to be available if and when they get stuck and need some input from you or some guidance about their work.

The secret to leading your team through Phase 3 is finding an appropriate balance of Styles 4 and 3. You have to do enough delegating to let people do their work and sufficient developing so that you stay informed and they get the support they require. This balance will vary from person to person and from assignmeent to assignment. Some individuals work best on their own. Others need frequent checkins to be sure they are on the right track. Some tasks present rather routine, familiar types of work. Others are new, unfamiliar, and very challenging.

Finding the right balance is an art. But knowing when to make your moves always comes down to two critical actions. First, you have to give people the space to do their work with

Use S4 to delegate to the individual team members so they can apply their knowledge and skills to their responsibilities.

Use S3 to develop individual team members when they need support to help them achieve the team's goals.

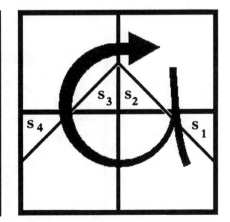

Figure 12.7   Phase 3: Work + Support

your trust in them. Second, you need to be available to listen to your team so they can use you as a sounding board and take advantage of your experience and your broader vision of the team's mission.

SECRET 4

Phase 4, depicted in Figure 12.8, is probably the most over-looked aspect of building and sustaining high performance team-work. Once the individuals start to crank out the work in Phase 3, their focus is on their respective assignments and they tend to lose their connection to the other people on the team. Even if they work closely with one or two other individuals, they pay attention to their own goals and deadlines and forget about the overall team mission.

If the individual initiatives are going to result in a solid team effort, the whole group needs to come together periodically for

Use S3 (distributed S2) with the group to facilitate updates and coordinate team members' areas of responsibility.

Also use S2 to focus the group on continuous improvement by identifying problems and giving input to solutions.

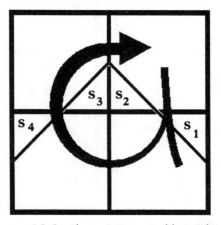

Figure 12.8 Phase 4: Team Problem Solving.

team problem solving. The team needs to take time out to keep each other informed about their progress and make each other aware of problems that are coming up. They need to work together to resolve problems, share resources, and think continuously about alternatives to improve the way they are approaching their work. Most important, they can capitalize on the synergy that often results from group interactions.

The secret to being successful with this team problem solving phase is using the right balance of Styles 2 and 3 (distributed 2). You should use Style 2 to structure the meetings, use time efficiently, and keep the meetings productive. In your areas of responsibility, you should also use the problem solving style to give team members information about new developments and seek their input about any problems that you may be wrestling with.

Where team members have been empowered to handle various responsibilities, you need to use Style 3 to facilitate the discussion. With listening skills, you can structure the conversation by asking questions, encouraging openness, reflecting people's concerns, and summarizing key points. The goal is to have an open discussion in which those who need input get to hear other people's ideas and can test the waters to see if a consensus exists.

If there is a consensus, the next step is making an action plan to implement it. If there is no consensus, the team member who is leading in that area of responsibility should be empowered to make the decision. That's why your use of Style 3 with the group is really a distributed Style 2. The group doesn't sit around forever trying to get everyone's agreement. Someone is always authorized to make key decisions.

In many organizations, Phase 4 gets addressed through quality circles, total quality management, or continuous improvement teams. Many other buzzwords are used to rationalize the bringing together of groups of people to think about better ways of doing business. Unfortunately, too many of these initiatives are not fully integrated into the day-to-day interactions of intact work teams. Often, they take place outside the normal course of work activities, or they include a cross-section of people from different units who do not work together on a regular basis. Frequently, participants report that they had trouble gettting focused and could not bring about meaningful changes.

For Phase 4 to work, team problem solving needs to be integrated into the normal flow of work and become a regular event that adds value to the team members' ability to accomplish their individual and collective goals.

Self-directed work teams always build Phase 4 into their group norms. These teams create structures for sharing responsibility and can only be successful if the people who own the responsibilities have mechanisms for coordinating their efforts.

Core teams provide a similar structure for cross-functional teams that are expected to use the strengths of their functional processes to accomplish a common mission. Again, Phase 4 is critical so these people, all of whom come from different parts of the organization and who report to different managers, can maintain their focus and coordinate their efforts.

Whether you have a group of direct reports in a functional department, a special task force, a committee, a quality team, or a cross-functional team, you need to bring the whole group together periodically. And to do that successfully, you need to use a balance of Styles 2 and 3 to make team problem solving work.

HOW WELL DOES YOUR ORGANIZATION USE THE LEADER'S WINDOW?

All four phases of The Leader's Window are shown in Figure 12.9. This picture enables you to use the 1-2-3 group development cycle with the group while simultaneously using the 1-4-3-2 empowerment cycle with individual team members. The Leader's Window is your guide for opening windows of opportunity at work. It is a road map for building high-performing teams. Most important, it shows you which windows need to be opened at what times so that you can become a highly effective leader.

With this picture in mind, stop for minute to think about how it applies to you and your place of work. How do you see The Leader's Window being used in your organization? Unless your company has learned The L4 System, it is unlikely that The Leader's Window itself is being used, but most organizations do cover some of these four phases. Which phases are encouraged by your organization's culture? Which ones are done poorly or not done at all?

When we put this question to groups of business leaders, there is usually a lively discussion about the missing pieces in their organizations.

Most often, these leaders identify problems with Phase 1, Team Orientation. They discuss teams with unclear missions and lack of direction from above. Team objectives are not as

PHASE 3 WORK + SUPPORT	PHASE 4 TEAM PROBLEM SOLVING
Use S4 to delegate to the individual team members so they can apply their knowledge and skills to their responsibilities. Use S3 to develop individual team members when they need support to help them achieve the team's goals.	Use S3 (distributed S2) with the group to facilitate updates and coordinate team members' areas of responsibility. Also use S2 to focus the group on continuous improvement by identifying problems and giving input to solutions.

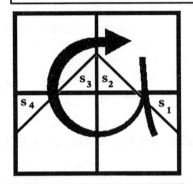

PHASE 1 TEAM ORIENTATION

Start with S1 to orient the group by explaining the team's mission and the members' roles on the team.

Then use S2 to get the group's buy-in by involving them in identifying the best ways to work together.

PHASE 2 INDIVIDUAL ASSIGNMENTS

Use S1 with individual team members to clarify roles and responsibilities and to start the Performance Contract process.

Then use S4 to empower each individual by delegating authority for the tasks they can handle on their own.

Figure 12.9 The Four Phases of The Leader's Window.

clear as they could be. As a result, everyone focuses on his/her own assignments with little or no concern for the overall team.

Phase 2, Performance Contracting, usually gets mixed reviews. In most organizations, the leaders say that they do a good job of giving out individual assignments. However, their followers often complain that the assignments they receive could be a lot clearer. The biggest concern about Phase 2 is not feeling truly empowered. Work is parceled out but a true commitment of authority is often withheld.

Phase 3, Work + Support, gets the best marks from most organizations. This is where the individual work gets accomplished, and most companies are pretty good at keeping people busy. Where this phase breaks down is in providing support to followers. Most organizational cultures are strong advocates of the individual work ethic, but it is only the best leaders within those cultures who are also available to create developmental opportunities for their people.

Like Phase 1, Phase 4, Team Problem-Solving, gets overlooked in most settings. Even though leaders will talk about institutional initiatives to use teams and to focus on quality, they still say that little or no time is spent on continuous improvement in day-to-day operations.

Is your organization like these? Which phases do you do well? Which ones get overlooked?

DOES ANYONE DO IT RIGHT?

Barry Carden, a Charter Oak director, tells the story of a highly successful executive, Ed, who at the time was a senior vice president at a high tech Fortune 500 company. Since then, he has advanced to other positions of greater responsibility. As you read this case, you will understand why. In his own way, without knowing about The Leader's Window, Ed successfully led his team through the four phases of The Leader's Window as he took over a major operating division that needed to implement broad-based changes.

Phase 1

According to Carden, Ed started out by calling together his direct reports for an initial team meeting. In essence, what he said at the start of that meeting was, "Here's who I am, this is how I like to operate, and here's what you need to know about my style in order to have a good working relationship with me."

He then went on to say, "Here's my value system and my vision. I need to change this culture. For this business to win, we've got to start doing business a very different way."

In the context of that organization, it was clear to everyone in the room that Ed was saying that, in order to turn the business around, he was going to have to be very directive in the early stages of the changes.

Once he made it clear where he stood with the group and what his expectations were, he began scanning the group for their input. He was orchestrating the focusing stage of group development by making himself an expert in what they knew and getting their buy-in at the same time. To both motivate his team and get their involvement he would say things like, "This is where we need to go, there is no doubt about it. And what I need is for you guys to help set the strategies in place that will get us there."

Phase 2

As soon as he felt that his team was "on board," Ed shifted his focus to clarifying goals for individual performance. He started saying to people, "These are the goals you will be accountable for and the behaviors that you need to exhibit. I'm going to measure your success based on those behaviors—and I'm going to give you ongoing performance feedback on how you're doing."

He went on to say, "In fact, I'm going to tie 51 percent of your salary at the end of the year to your ability to accomplish these objectives."

Following this meeting, Ed worked with each individual member of the team to establish what the specific measures of success would be. He didn't want to leave any room for guesswork or confusion about what he needed each person to accomplish. In these one-on-one discussions, not only was he able to make his expectations concrete, he also found out more about his new reports, what they were confident they could handle on their own and when they anticipated needing some input from him. In essence, without ever calling it performance contracting, Ed applied the PC process perfectly.

Phase 3

As soon as he saw that individuals on his team were clear about their roles and were ready to run with the ball, Ed was very good at getting out of the way.

Knowing that everyone was clear about the team's mission and his/her role in accomplishing that mission, he was comfortable delegating full authority to his team.

Once everyone was off and running, he continued to delegate to individuals but always modeled the type of leadership style he wanted them to use with their people by offering ongoing feedback and support when they needed it. Says Carden, "He was constantly communicating with his people on an informal basis saying things like, 'Here's what you're doing that's helping the business and here's what you're doing that's hindering it.' And once a month he would sit down with each of them to review their goals. He gave people a strong sense that they belonged and always let them know where they stood."

Phase 4

As time passed and individual members were fulfilling their respective roles, the work of the team as a whole became increasingly complex. It was at this critical point that Ed managed to harness the power of the group—and the individuals—without giving up control. Remember, he had oriented the team in Phase 1 by empowering each member with different team responsibilities, thus creating distributed leadership within the team. Now, in Phase 4, he brought everyone back together to coordinate their efforts.

Speaking about this phase, Carden said, "He was able to maintain control and a sense of accountability with the team while allowing individuals to run as freely as they were able within the context of the team.

"He was also able to manage the size of the team as it grew to 20 members. Through team problem solving, he decided (with lots of input) to charge 3 subgroups with the authority to make decisions on behalf of the total team. To expedite this, the entire team met until they signed off on each subgroup's authority. Then each subgroup would go off with its designated leader, make its decisions, and bring them back to the team to keep the other subgroups updated and identify new problems that were surfacing."

By paying attention to both the needs of the group and the capabilities of the individuals on his team, Ed was able to maximize his individual and collective resources. As Carden put it, "He was truly remarkable at getting people to really feel empowered and get beyond the bureacracy that previously hindered the organization."

What you've just read in the above case illustrates the secrets of The Leader's Window perfectly. This leader started out with a clear articulation of his vision and operating style. Then by soliciting input from his team regarding strategy, he gained their buy-in which turned his personal vision into a collectively owned team mission. That was Phase 1, Team Orientation.

Next the leader focused on individual roles and responsibilities, set parameters for individual success and gave followers room to operate. That was Phase 2, Individual Assignments.

Then he monitored their individual performance and gave them ongoing feedback as to how they were doing. He also gave them guidance whenever they needed it. That was Phase 3, Work + Support.

Finally, he capitalized on the collective resources of the group by employing a distributed approach to shared team leadership through the use of subgroups charged with authority over various aspects of the team's work. That was the ultimate Phase 4. Not only did he bring the group together for Team Problem Solving, he also shifted meaningful responsibilities to the team at the same time.

A BROKEN WINDOW STORY

Here is another case study. This one shows you what can happen if you don't apply the secrets to all four phases. A few years ago, we were working with a major insurance company, a multiline carrier with operations in every state. We started out in a training mode, teaching The L4 system to managers, assistant directors, directors, and second vice presidents in the life department. Over time, as these leaders got enthusisatic about the system, they began pushing for the leaders above them to get involved as well.

About that time, a major reorganization took place which resulted in a merging of the life department with the personal lines department (mostly automobile and homeowners insurance for individuals and families) and the commercial lines department (property–casualty insurance for medium to large organizations). The idea behind the merger was to leverage the commercial lines customers to increase sales in the other two departments. It also was designed to achieve some savings in office space and administrative costs.

Shortly after the reorganization, we began working with the regional vice presidents and the leaders of their field organizations to help them launch their newly formed organizations. Using Charter Oak's Organization Alignment model, we helped them identify what was most important to their customers, how they stacked up against their customers' expectations, and what was helping and/or hindering their organization from meeting customers' needs. We also used The L4 System to teach them how to get their teams properly focused (Secret 1), clarify individual roles and responsibilities (Secret 2), contract to provide whatever support employees needed to achieve their goals (Secret 3), and bring the team together to focus on ongoing continuous improvements (Secret 4).

This work with the field organizations enabled us to discover that people were not clear about the overall mission of the division or the goals of their particular operations. The structures and systems created obstacles instead of eliminating barriers and creating opportunities. And the culture of the division created a lot of ambiguity for everyone. The 1-4-1 frustration cycle was alive and well and killing people's motivation. Expectations, goals, and roles were vague and contradictory (underuse of Style 1 up front). Abdicating was rampant as everyone scrambled on their own to appear productive (overuse of Style 4). And mistakes were treated as career-threatening failures instead of opportunities to learn (real and feared overuse of Style 1 after the fact).

These findings led us back to the home office where we began to help the senior vice presidents of each department and the executive vice president of the entire division understand what to do to turn these problems around.

As part of that work, the EVP, David, completed the L4 Self Assessment, a longer version of the questionnaire you took in chapter 1. Then all of the SVPs who reported to David filled out an L4 Other about him. This questionnaire provides a counterbalance to the L4 Self by giving feedback about the leadership styles that a leader actually uses and the styles that he/she needs to use to help followers perform to the best of their potential. The results of this study were striking.

David saw himself using mostly Styles 3 and 4. He knew that he gave his SVPs a lot of responsibility and considered himself available for support whenever they needed him. The feedback from his team was that he used Style 4 almost exclusively. This didn't totally surprise him since they were spread out among eight different buildings and he left them on their own practically all of the time.

What did surprise him was that every single one of the SVPs needed significantly more Style 3—some even said they needed more Style 1 and Style 2. The differences between actual and ideal were huge and it was a unanimous opinion. David was quite perplexed by this. In his words, "I find this very hard to believe. These are the best people in the business. They are totally independent. I wouldn't presume to tell any of them how to do their jobs. In fact, they are so capable that any one of these guys could do my job as well as I can."

He was convinced that the questionnaires were flawed. So we went to each of the SVPs, showed them the general results of the study, and told them that their boss genuinely wanted to know if the data was accurate and, if so, what they wanted him to do differently.

We got an earful about what they needed and, interestingly, it had little to do with "telling them how to do their jobs." They needed to work on all four phases of The Leader's Window so that the senior management team could replicate the process down the line in their departments.

The follow-up to these interviews was a team meeting to address the problems. Quite predictably, the overriding concern was Phase 1, Team Orientation. They knew the general vision that had precipitated the reorganization, but there was a wide range of different opinions about what that meant. But they said they needed to revisit David's vision of why the organization was created and what his expectations were regarding their mission as a team. They also wanted to have a better understanding of their goals and roles as well as those of the other team members. They also felt the need to spend some very focused time listening to each other, participating in candid discussions which would have led to their collective buy-in and commitment to their objectives.

In addition, they also suggested that they needed to create an ongoing format for future team meetings to keep each other more up to date and keep their collective hand on the pulse of the organization. This was a Phase 4, Team Problem Solving, recommendation which was intended to overcome the physical and structural barriers that kept them operating as totally separate divisions.

Beyond that, some of the SVPs, but not all of them, wanted to feel more comfortable approaching their boss. The ones who had worked with him over the years had no hesitation about coming to him with problems, and when they did, he was as supportive as he claimed to be. The ones who were not as familiar with him had gotten the message that he valued them for being independent. So they only met with him if he summoned him. As a result, their discussions were always his agenda and never theirs. Clearly, Phase 3, Work + Support, needed some attention as well.

The one phase that they didn't say much about was Phase 2, Individual Assignments. As individuals, they thought they had a good understanding of what they needed to do in their respective departments. From where we sat, it was painfully clear to us that Phase 2 was being done entirely by the numbers, essentially focusing on sales and profit goals for the next quarter. The lack of a more focused contracting process was one of the reasons that Phase 3 was not happening for most of the SVPs. It also kept David in the dark about some of the Phase 1 and Phase 4 problems that we found out about so easily when we sat down with each SVP for a one-on-one discussion.

When we said that Phase 1, Team Orientation, would have focused the team, you may have guessed that there was not a happy ending to this story. Unfortunately, the Phase 1 work never happened. Neither did Phases 2, 3, or 4. Instead, they went back to business as usual. Their conclusion was that these issues were important but not as pressing as the day-to-day fires they were trying to put out. So, they chose to be caught up in the brushfires and emergencies and refused to spend time on the nonurgent, important issues.

There was an informal attempt to circumvent David's unwillingness to move ahead with Phase 1 or Phase 4. One of the SVPs started a "breakfast club" and invited the other SVPs to join him once a week to keep each other aware of developments in their operations and to find ways to support each other's efforts. That lasted for a few weeks but some of the SVPs never bought into the process, and it fell by the wayside.

The result was as you would predict. They plodded along for a couple of years, continued to hear frustrations percolating up from the field people, and progressively lost market share in some core products. Eventually, the organization was dismantled. David retired and so did some of the SVPs. Some people moved on to different positions in the company. Others went to work for competitors or for themselves as consultants.

The field organization never did get the answers they were looking for but they were prepared for the changes when they came. They had known for a long tme that the organization had gotten off to a rough start. As one vice president put it, "When we started, it was like declaring a war without any tanks or ships or planes or even hand weapons. Some of the guys weren't even in the right uniforms. The boys upstairs just said, 'Go do it,' and hoped we'd get it done like we always have."

Maybe they will try The Leader's Window the next time. Organizational change is much easier if you start with Phase 1 and pay careful attention to Phases 2, 3, and 4.

Stories like this one don't have to happen.

A WINDOW ON COMMUNICATIONS

Tony Daloisio, another Charter Oak director, tells a success story in which all the right things happened. A major telecommunications company had identified the need to shift its new product development group to create a faster, more efficient process in an area that was growing too fast to tolerate a traditional organizational hierarchy.

"Bill, the senior vice president in charge of network services" says Daloisio, "realized that, over time, the company had created a functional organization with very strong fiefdoms within the various segments of the division. As more products were being developed and customers realized the potential for even more possibilities, marketing requests surged to the point where the organization could no longer respond as swiftly and effectively as it needed to in order to retain its market share.

"When you think about this problem in terms of organizaton alignment, the environment was putting competitive pressure on this department. New developments by competitors and extremely tight time frames for getting products to market had made their functional structure outmoded. The change required some sort of restructuring. The challenge was to reorganize in a way that would work. And that meant focusing on the culture of the overall organization as well as the departmental norms which could be impacted by Bill's's leadership."

The process began with helping Bill realize that his use of leadership styles, which was in line with the culture of the organization, fell into a 1-4 profile. He would direct his instructions to each of his respective charges and then delegate responsibility for implementation to each of them. When that assignment was completed, he would give them new directions. Essentially, the whole flow of work was centered around his position.

While this seemed to work well for him as a one-to-one

leader, he realized that each of the people he was giving duties to was not communicating cross-functionally with the other people on his team. The result was that this led to a much slower and less efficient product development cycle than was needed. Somehow they needed to know more about what everyone else was doing, and the work needed to be better coordinated.

The culture of the division and the structure both had to be addressed. Unless this leadership pattern changed, there was not much point in reorganizing the the team. So, to help Bill manage this change successfully, Daloisio worked with him to implement the four phases of The Leader's Window.

Phase 1

Bill's first step was to call a meeting of his executive team. He pointed out that the product development cycle with its six stages of design, piloting, redesign, test marketing, redesign, and marketing, needed to be streamlined and tightened in order to more effectively meet market demands. He invited input from his team, asking for their suggestions on how they thought the process could be improved.

In addition to receiving a great deal of input, the meeting generated a lot of excitement over the prospect of creating new ways of operating. Everyone was excited about being listened to by people in other areas, some perhaps for the first time. They were even more enthusiastic about the possibility of having input into each other's areas.

And most important, since everyone participated in redesigning the product development cycle, they felt ownership over the cross-functional teams that were created to improve the work flow.

This was Phase 1, Team Orientation. In this case, it was not enough for the leader to set the group off on a new mission and get their ideas about how to make it happen. It required giving people a chance to understand each other's perspective. This gave everyone an idea of what the problem looked like from Bill's vantage point. It also enabled people to start feeling like one big team instead of several small units.

Phase 2

Next, Bill met with each of the individual members of his executive team and focused on how the new configuration would affect each of their roles and responsibilites. Once everyone was clear about expectations, Bill directed each executive to go off on his own to do what needed to be done.

This was Phase 2, Individual Assignments, and it didn't take them long. They were already good at Phase 2.

Phase 3

Since he knew that he was asking his executives to operate in a different way, Bill did not leave them alone as was his usual habit. "He knew he was asking his people to think and operate differently," says Daloisio, "so he was careful not to create conditions in which they felt overwhelmed. He knew he had to make some fundamental changes in his leadership approach if he expected his people to make changes with the people below them. Instead of riding herd over every aspect of every product's development, he downloaded responsibility and authority for overall development and his job became more of a counselor or coach."

In Phase 3, Work + Support, the biggest change was on the part of the leader. He let his team have more control that he had ever before but, instead of just disappearing as many leaders do when they first let go, he still met with his team members on a regular basis. The difference was that now he was helping them figure out their challenges instead of parcelling out assignments and directing their work.

Phase 4

Group meetings, which prior to the change rarely occurred, and were at the worst one-way communications from Bill and at the best report-and-update sessions by various executives, took on quite a different form. Cross-functional project teams were designed in order to break down the functional barriers that had previously proliferated throughout the organization, and coordinators were assigned for each of the project teams. Meetings consisted of brief presentations by various project team coordinators and often lengthy problem-solving sessions where Bill and other executives offered support and guidance to the project teams.

Phase 4, Team Problem Solving, was absolutely critical to making these structural changes really work. While the new cross-functional teams would have had a short-term positive impact, if the leaders of these teams did not build communication links these new teams would have become as isolated as the old functional ones.

The overall result of the process was a dramatic increase in cross-functional communication, and dramatic improvements in the product development and delivery cycles.

The short-term, quick-fix solution would have been to have some cross-functional meetings or maybe even put together a couple of cross-functional teams. The long-term benefit came from involving people in a structured and organized way that led to shared responsibility for the process and the ultimate outcomes. Using The Leader's Window is what made that happen.

NOW IT'S YOUR TURN

So that's it. Now you know the four secrets and The Leader's Window is yours to put into action. If it sounds easy, it's not. It really takes a lot of practice to get it all to work the way it's supposed to. But remember, practice makes perfect.

If we have learned anything about high-performing teams, it is that experimentation is a hallmark of the very best. So give yourself permission to experiment and learn from your mistakes. We all make them.

And if you get stuck, don't forget to lead upward or outward or in any direction that you can so that you can get whatever support you need to keep yourself on the cutting edge.

REFERENCES

Orsburn, Jack, Moran, Linda, Musselwhite, Ed, and Zenger, John. *Self-Directed Work Teams*, New York: Business One/Irwin, 1991.

Epilogue

We've covered a lot of territory in the last twelve chapters to help clarify your view of The Leader's Window. We'd like to leave you with a short summary of the most important points about working with individuals and groups in ways that lead to high-performing teams. These are the keys for putting it all together to make The Leader's Window work for you.

TEAM = INDIVIDUALS + GROUP

Teamwork doesn't mean sending each individual team member onto the playing field to do his/her own thing. Neither does it mean bringing everyone together for endless discussions to try to achieve total consensus on every decision. Instead, it requires working with each individual in unique ways that are right for that person relative to the tasks he/she has to accomplish. It also requires orchestrating the group dynamics that develop when those individuals come together as a team.

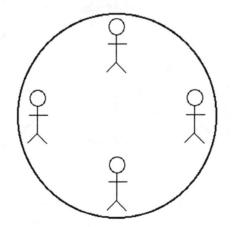

Figure E.1 Team = Individuals + Group.

THE FOUR KEYS TO WORKING WITH INDIVIDUALS

1. Use all four leadership styles on a regular basis and when you use each one integrate your actions so that your communication and recognition strategies are consistent with the decision-making methods you need to use.

2. Match your main style to each team member's performance potential (ability + motivation) on a task-specific basis.

3. Remember Leadership by Anticipation:
   - Use the 1-2-3-4 Development cycle to give followers increasing amounts of responsibility without feeling overwhelmed.
   - Use the 4-3-2-1 Intervention cycle to gradually reinvolve yourself as performance drops or pressures mount.
   - Try to avoid the 1-4-1 Frustration cycle.
   - Use the 1-4-3-2 Empowerment cycle to surround your delegating with the upfront directing, ongoing developing, and timely problem solving that leads to true Empowerment.

4. Use the performance contracting process to implement 1-4-3-2 with each team member.

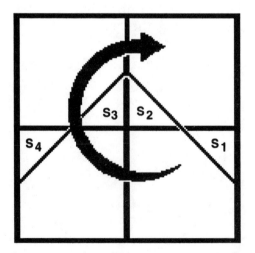

Figure E.2 The 1-4-3-2 Empowerment Cycle.

THE FOUR KEYS TO WORKING WITH GROUPS

1. Since groups have needs that are beyond the needs of the individual, it is necessary to lead the group dynamics that occur when your team members come together.
2. Stay focused on the group development cycle to help members move through the stages in a way that leads to the greatest level of productivity.
3. Remember to shift your style of leadership to match the stage of group development the team is in by using:
   - Style 1, Directing when the team is in Stage 1, Forming.
   - Style 2, Problem Solving when the team is in Stage 2, Focusing.
   - Style 3, Developing when the team is in Stage 3, Performing.
   - The Intervention Cycle, moving from Developing to Problem Solving to Directing as required, to overcome the Leveling Stage.
4. If it's everyone's responsibility, it's no one's responsibility. So don't use Style 4, Delegating with the group. Instead, delegate to an individual and ask him/her to lead the whole group or a subgroup.

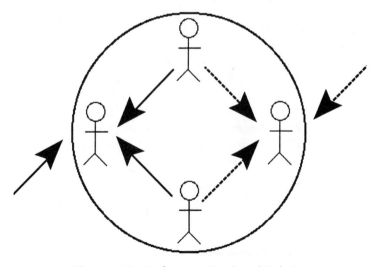

Figure E.3   Performing: Distributed Style 2.

THE FOUR PHASES OF THE LEADER'S WINDOW

Move through the four phases of The Leader's Window to simultaneously lead the individual and the group dynamics:

1. Phase 1—Team Orientation. Use Style 1, Directing to orient the group by explaining the team's mission and members' roles. Use Style 2, Problem Solving to get the group's buy-in and identify best ways of working.
2. Phase 2—Individual Assignments. Use Style 1, Directing with individuals to clarify roles and begin performance contracting. Empower individuals with Style 4, Delegating to assign authority for tasks they can handle on their own.
3. Phase 3—Work + Support. Continue Style 4, Delegating by allowing team members to apply their knowledge and skills. Use Style 3, Developing to support individuals whenever they need help achieving team goals.
4. Phase 4—Team Problem Solving. Use Style 3, Developing to facilitate a distributed responsibility approach by supporting team members with their leadership responsibilities. Use Style 2, Problem Solving to focus the group on continuous improvement by identifying problems and getting input to your decisions.

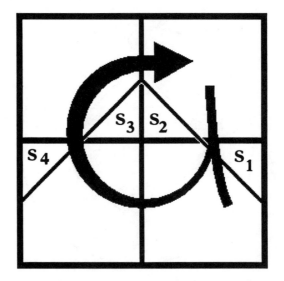

Figure E.4 The Leader's Window.

We wish you good luck with your leadership efforts, and may all your windows be open with the right people in the right places at the right times!

Our firm, the Charter Oak Consulting Group, specializes in Leadership Development, Team Building, Organization Development, and Managing Change. Please let us know if we can help you put The Leader's Window into action:

Charter Oak Consulting Group, Inc.
Mill Crossing Office Park
1224 Mill Street
East Berlin, Connecticut 06023
(203) 828-2092

Index